stolen

Editing: Deborah Young
Cover and Text Design: Eddie & Jan Thornton; RedJet Media Design
All artwork: Eddie Thornton

RedJet Website: RedJetMedia.com
Stolen Website: JEddieThornton.com

© Copyright 2006. J. Eddie Thornton III
All rights reserved. No part of this book may be reproduced by any mechanical, photographic, or electronic process, or in the process of phonographic recording without the express written consent of the author. Nor may it be stored in a retrieval system, transmitted, or otherwise copied or reproduced for public or private use without permission from the author.

Published 2007
Printed in the United States of America.

ISBN 1-59975-852-0

Library of Congress Catalogue in Publication Data.
TXu1-285-153

biography

Eddie Thornton is the typical American artist-as-outsider, ranging from Truman Capote to Norman Mailer, who sees what insiders don't. Born half white, half African America on Chicago's Southside, his father murdered when Eddie was only three years old and replaced by an abusive drug addicted con-man step-father who today would be labeled a sociopath. Through beatings he tried to turn Eddie into the animal he himself was. His lessons to Eddie - steal, cheat and hate.

Living in neighborhoods where violence was the only means of communication, a communication echoed in his home and one that he carried with him to school Eddie was forced, as he says in his story "Jumped!" to survive "through creativity and independence." And that, he notes, "makes it so hard to fit in with the rest of the world."

However, a moment of clarity happened when he looked in the mirror one day and saw his step-father, Thornton got it: The anger, the hate and the street was going to take him to his grave. He became serious about his education and embraced the help and caring of others - he went on to earn first an associate degree in fine arts along with an associate degree in illustration and a BA with a focus on Computer Graphics at the American Academy of Art. Another moment of clarity came during a writing course taught by Dr. Immaculate Kizza at the University of Tennessee, "Tell your story, your journey, your struggle" she said. The result is "Stolen" containing over a hundred personal stories recounting Thornton's adaptation to his neighborhood and family clash of rage, sadism and glimmers of affection.

Eddie still fights against all those negative teachings but has learned how to become a man, not just a broken animal. He has fought his childhood, embraced the few morsels of good and has discovered what he is truly made of. He is truly unique.

Thornton works as a graphic designer in L.A. is an actor and lives in domestic tranquility with his wife Jan and their two dogs Sammie and Chance.

stolen
Stories from a Violent Childhood

J. Eddie Thornton III

acknowledgements

God for giving me a Heart of Flesh

My wife Jan - that she married me, and I her, says everything.

My Mother for being my mom who gave all she had.

My sister Pamela, my hero.

Sal Romeo, my friend and acting coach who gave freely his time, energy, space, knowledge, experience…a big brother.

Stacy Martino, my friend, acting teacher, and actor extraordinaire for helping me to love and forgive… myself.

Dr. Immaculate Kizza, wonderful teacher at the University of Tennessee at Chattanooga, for encouraging us all to, "Tell your story, your journey."

And to all my teachers who believed in me and went the extra mile.

Robert Espeseth, my rowing coach at University of Tennessee at Chattanooga and four-time Olympian for teaching the true spirit of the word "Team".

Cindy Dorsey for enjoying my tale and helping us get this story into presentable shape.

Tom Dorsey for his support, enthusiasm, and encouragement.

And that cop at the Foster Avenue police station for believing me, and his words of wisdom about the dog shit.

For Mom
Who did the best she could with what she had.

And for Pamela
Who broke the cycle and survived.

introduction

Hope.

Hope is the reason I wrote this. Actually, several hopes: mine, and those of others. Many, many hopes.

My first and foremost hope is that this story can help someone. Help by offering hope. Hope for change. Hope for improvement. Hope for healing. Hope for the future. Hope for something better. If nothing else, I hope you find this an interesting journey.

If you have no hope, you'd better go get some quick, because the "good book" says: "Where hope faileth, the people perish."

You can't get there from here. The things you want, you don't have. First, you must be open to accept them. You must be prepared to use them once you have them. What's the use of wanting, hoping, dreaming, and praying for a Lamborghini if you don't know how to drive?

First we must prepare, practice and strengthen the skills we need in life, in relationships (to ourselves and others). Sharpen the talents we have; improve the faults that lie within us.

Sound like a lot of work? It is.

I've been on the road to recovery for over two decades and I'm nowhere near where I want to be. But I'm a hell of a lot closer than I was before.

Okay, so here you are. We are us. Each one. Where do you want to go? Why? How ya gonna get there? Do you have a map or are you just going to follow your nose until you are somewhere else? Will that somewhere else be where you want to be? If not, wha 'cha gonna do then? Keep trying the same old thing? Good luck.

There is a saying they use in the military. I'm going to give it to you here. Right now. Free.

"Proper previous preparation prevents piss-poor performance."

Like it? Keep it. It's yours.
Believe it or not the simplest task in life requires:
1) a goal; and
2) a plan to accomplish it.
It's just one stop on your journey. And that's all life is: a series of stops and starts in the great adventure.

Enough people from all walks of life have asked me, over the years, to tell them this story. Did ya hear the one about the angry kid who cursed every third word, who carried a pistol and a blackjack, and a knife (for those stubborn, hard to reach places), and few other goodies as well? Who fought all the time, who hated everybody and everything around him, including God and himself? Who tried his best to self-destruct before the age of 13…?

How did he become this man who… suffers from ADD, PTSD, has antisocial tendencies with a lean toward sociopath behavior…? Well, uh… let me put it this way. A friend of mine summed it up when, not long after we met and I told her just a little bit about my history, she told me, "You're kidding me! I always thought you grew up this spoiled little rich kid with not a hair out of place." Well… she meant it to be a compliment. But you get the picture. Looks can be deceiving. I'm not the same man now that I was when I first became a man. Thank God!

If, deep down, you want to change something about yourself, whether one HUGE thing, or a lot of little things, it doesn't really matter. In all my years of living, I've never ever met a person who could not change, only those who would not. It ain't gonna be easy, but I guarantee you it can… be.

I've spoken with so many people who have said to me, "I couldn't change if I wanted to." Well, I can't tell you how many times I thought that of myself. The only difference was that I had Hope. I didn't think I could change the many things I wanted to about myself, but I Hoped, desperately HOPED, that I could, because I couldn't stand the thought of living with myself and all the things wrong about me for the rest of my natural life. So I went forward. I moved ahead and got on with it. I put my head down and charged. And, like you do when you are running through a blinding storm, I didn't look up until I thought I had arrived. If I hadn't, I just put my head down and kept going. MOVE!

Now to be honest, some people have been honest enough with themselves to tell me, "I just don't want to work that hard." Or that long. And that's okay, as long as you are being absolutely honest. Because when some people say that, what we really hear is, "I can't change, so I'll just pretend and tell myself, and everyone else, that I'm happy with the way I am." I know you've all heard it: "I'm proud of the way I am!" Suuure you are. I always say you can bullshit yourself, but don't try to bullshit me. It just don't fly. I'm not buying it, no matter how much you try to sell it.

NEWSFLASH: Mamma can't do it for you. Daddy can't do it. Husbands, wives, lovers, brothers, sisters, sons, daughters; none of them can change you. Not even God. They can show you things you can choose to see or not see. They can tell you things you can choose to hear or not to hear. But upon seeing, or hearing, or knowing, YOU are the only one who can change you. Think about it: Jesus lived on this earth for 32 years, suffered, bled, and died, and went back to heaven just to give you, YOU, the opportunity to change. He didn't change anybody. And you think you can? I know damned well that I can't change you. My ego ain't that big. Wouldn't if I could, because then you would be missing out on all that He came to show us.

So here it is before you: Hope.

The choice is left up to you.

- Eddie

P.S. If you come across a story that is too much to delve into just now or one that gets you hung up, just skip it for now. Keep moving. Come back to it later when you are up for it. It'll still be there, I promise.

stories

family

Blood	1	Mom	6
The Father	3	Pamela	8
Larry	5		

descent

Tricycle	13	Math	51
Sparky and Boots	15	Shotgun	53
Clock	18	An Unexpected Visitor	54
Killer Instinct	21	Height	56
Playtime	23	Fire	58
Chittlins	27	Jumper	60
Jalapeño	28	Jumped	61
Wild Irish Rose	32	Elevator	75
Almost Suicide	32	Bully	78
Christmas Eve Night	34	Boys' Club	81
A Mother's Blood	36	Curtis Dies…	
Chicago	38	in a Vacant Lot	83
Let it Snow	39	Lakeside Gang-fight	84
920 Lakeside Place	42	Gar	86
He Returns	50	Herbert	88

glenwood

Finding Home	95	High	112
Again	101	My First Pistol	113
Gregg and Mr. Leiss	105		

georgia

Georgia Summers	117	Chicken Chokin'	127
Papa	122	Wayne's World	129
Granny	125		

normalcy

The Aranus Family	141	The Forrester's	144

the yard

Joan F. Arai	153	E.J.	163
Sears	156		

northside boogie

"Kill the Niggers!"	171	Lawrence Avenue	
Friday Nights	174	Assassins	201
The Wooden Nickel	177	Meeting with God	
Help	180	On the train tracks	206
Niggers Shot Curt	185	George + Knife =	213
Gokes	190	Laying in Wait	220
Jerry	191	Kill 'im	221
Jim	195		

escape

Me and John's Last Fight	227	Remedial	271
Colors	231	"Teacher"	279
Reflection	235	Dad's End	284
Andrew M.	240	Truman Gang-fight	289
Guns at Ravenswood	248	Golden Waffle	292
Stalking Dad	254	Kung Fu	297
Mateen	257	Drive	304
Sink or Swim	260	Mom's Love	307

headed east

D.C	313	Quarter	342
Sam	316	Thanksgiving in	
"Freeze!"	328	Southeast D.C.	345
Rescue	334		

back to chi-town

Fuse	351	For the Boys	365
Violent Notes	364		

home

The Difference	373	The Destroyer	374

family

 family

Blood

I must have been around seven. My stepfather used to disappear into the bathroom with his friends, two and three at a time, for long periods of time. You never, ever, disturbed them. Mom would grow silent and sober, serious.

Once, in my single-minded urgency to pee, I forgot to knock and barged right in. Lou, my dad's friend, was passed out. He was sitting on the floor with his back against the wall, elbow on the tub and head on his knees. My dad was passed out sitting on the toilet in the opposite corner from Lou with his head sunken on his chest and leaning against the sink. A syringe with about a quarter an inch of blood and yellowish-clear plasma backed up into it, was dangling from the prominent vein in his left elbow.

I stared at this morbid scene before me, absorbing, frozen. I thought they were dead.

Fear and indecision had paralyzed me. I knew I was *not* supposed to be there. I *knew* a child should not see this. It was a thing I *shouldn't* understand.

I stared at Dad, searching for signs of life. I wanted to shake him, tell him to wake up... desperately. But I also knew I would be beaten for being where I wasn't supposed to be.

And deep down... I wished he were dead, and then felt guilty immediately afterward.

A dry rasp in his throat, almost a snore, confirmed both his life and patheticness. I didn't bother to check Lou. If Dad was still alive, then Lou was his problem. Before this I had always liked Lou. He was kind of like an uncle to me. Unlike Dad, he never hit me, and he had never said a bad word to me. But now, seeing him this way, placed him on the same plane of existence as my dad, representing the same evil, the same animal, the same monster... the same beast.

I remained standing in the doorway just inside the threshold and there at my feet were drops of scarlet. I stared transfixed at the perfectly round bubbles on the octagonal patterned white tiles with black grouting in between. Those three tiny crimson drops fascinated me. Squatting down, I examined them further. The red had separated to form a clear liquid. It had a watery, slightly oily, consistency, but not the potent coppery smell that had always accompanied the taste of my own blood.

Then I remembered a movie with Bill Cosby and Robert Culp, *Hickey and Boggs*. Dad and I saw it in the theater not long before. In the movie there was a scene where they approached an apartment where blood was pooling out from under the door. Cosby knelt down, touched his fingers to it, and touched them to his tongue to find that it was blood. I always associate that movie with my ill-fated trip to the bathroom that summer afternoon.

I now imagine my stepfather coming out of his nod groggily, dreamily, opening his eyes and abstractly focusing on those three crimson drops. Zooming in to an extreme close-up, he sees the larger of the spots has the imprint of a child's fingerprint. Realizing what has happened, he stares... frozen.

The Father

I've only seen two pictures of my real father. It's all I know of him. Well, that and the stories people tell. My mom, my sister and Jimmy are the only ones who spoke of him. Not even my mother's parents have ever talked about him, like he didn't exist at all.

The first photograph I came across of him was lost in a boxful of old photos. They ranged from the '60's to the 70's, and they were like some kind of lost and found, a place where old photos go to die, a hodgepodge of just about everyone from family to complete strangers.

I loved those old pictures. The box was at my mother's family's house in the North Georgia Mountains, so the faces in the photos were all poor white Southerners. Some of them were beautiful. Lyrical. Almost Faulknerian in their statements about "being" in the South of my ancestors.

One photo is of an old woman. Dried out and shrunken, but still straight as a rod. Like an Andrew Wyeth painting, it haunts me. The stories she could have told me, if, that is, she would have spoken to someone of my complexion.

The photo of my father and mother together was taken in a bar in Chicago. Looks to be about 1960. They're both seated at a table for two surrounded by smiling friends, mostly black. Filled with the music of the times, they're all *alive. Happening.* It's a full house and activity is everywhere. Sheer energy.

There he is looking sharp and a little devilish, wide-brimmed hat with a wide band around it, pressed suit, greatcoat, and a smile ear-to-ear.

Across the table is Mom. She's looking at the camera smiling, but this was some other "mom", not the one I knew. Not the timid, reclusive, nervous, extremely reserved lady that passed quietly through my life. No, this is "the woman in red". Red, red, red. Red everywhere. Bright red lips, hair done back and styled. A red choker. And that red dress: cut from a bolt of scarlet, sewn with stitches of crimson. Spaghetti strapped, mid-thigh.

Hot... or hooker? I can't honestly tell which, because as a man, I saw hot. As a son, I saw hooker. But just as startling as the red was the *life*. My mother, the woman I knew, never went anywhere, never did anything. No friends. No men. Nothing. Just work, home and television. Silence. Solitude. Nothing. But here she's LIVING. She's SMILING! Open! Living! I could see the energy radiating from her face. She's poised as though she's just pausing to sit briefly between dances. Wow.

The only other photo of my father I ever saw was the one on the cover of his funeral program. The paper was yellow and the photo black and white – now black and yellow. It was his military picture. He had a calm smile, head to the side, uniform pressed and buttons polished.

My father died in 1968 when I was three. He was murdered, killed by a couple of white guys in their own place of business, a saloon that never even closed after the murder. When the coroner took the body away and the police left, there were still people swilling booze at the oaken bar. I wonder if they even bothered to clean up the blood or was it just left there for people to step around or walk in. A white judge determined my father's murder was a suicide. How many suicides occur in a crowded bar? And how many of those are by folks shooting themselves in the back at an upward angle?

The fantasies of my mother about my father bordered on the fanaticism. Anytime I would ask her about him, I would get, "Oh, he was just so perfect!" Bullshit! That gave me nothing. I could never get the *man* out of the fantasy. Never once would she tell me what he was like. What were his hobbies, his strong points, and his weak points? Nothing factual. Just dreams. Who was he? What was he about? Where did he come from? Where was he going?

Larry

My "Dad", Lawrence /Larry/ Winston, was actually my stepfather. He was a tall, lean, muscular Korean War veteran and he was a street hustler, a handsome charismatic user of people, women, alcohol and drugs. Heroin to be precise.

My dad molded abuse into an art form. He was very creative and very good. He took every opportunity to fuck with our heads. He was abusive in every conceivable way. As a consequence, violence ruled my childhood. So did prostitutes, pornography, drugs, booze, lies, and deceit.

Dad also taught me how to shoplift. When we went to the local grocery store, he would make me shove cold, wet steaks and pork chops down my pants and tell me not to walk funny as we went out past the cashiers, past the manager, and past the security guards. Later, I got banned from that store when the manager caught me stealing some candy with a friend of mine. But I got better at it. For many years, thievery was my best talent. Stores, factories, offices, homes, you name it - and I could break in and be back out before anyone knew what happened. Most of the time they never even knew I'd been there. I didn't do it because I needed to eat; I did it because it's what I knew. It's what I did; it's what I always did. I did it because I could. It is what I was taught. The thrill, the risk, the adrenaline. It was exciting, it was a challenge, and it was reckless. It was self-destructive.

Lawrence tried to mold me into the living image of himself. I didn't want to be "my dad". At the age of about 20, I made the decision to change. It wasn't easy, but I decided who I wanted to be, what kind of man I would become, and set out on that road.

Survival? That's another matter entirely.

Mom

I love my mom. Today we enjoy a relationship much more appropriate of mother and son than in years previous. Today she is happy, bold, funny, and a delightfully outgoing woman. It took me years to understand the forces that made her what she was. Her parents, her environment, the times. I see now that there were plenty of factors involved in making her the type of person that allowed what happened to us to continue.

While we were with my dad, and for years afterward, my mother remained an empty shell of a woman. She remained frightened and as jumpy as a field mouse, as timid as a deer. And as closed mouthed as a bull terrier.

Now years later, she is bright, outgoing, and vivacious, a stark contrast to who she was with him. But even then there were sparks of the delightful person that was entombed beneath her surface. Rebellious, smart-allecky and cunning. This resourcefulness is what I remember most. A lot of the survival skills I use today come from her. She taught Pamela and I how to check windows for reflections to see if there were any shady characters tracking us. She taught us signs to watch out for to identify the street hustlers who were constantly on the lookout for a mark to cheat out of the paltry few dollars they had. She taught us how to pay attention to, and trust, our instincts when it came to dealing with questionable situations, people, places, and things. She would quiz us on danger signs to look out for so that we did not walk into questionable situations in the first place.

She showed us how to survive financially. In high school I was shocked that, as dumb as I was, I was one of the only ones in my class that knew how to balance a checkbook and do taxes. She made sure we knew how to get by creditors' threats and squeeze a few more days out of a past due notice to avoid having our power, water, electricity, or gas cut off. She showed us how to build lines of credit at stores so that we could finally keep clothes on our backs and shoes on our feet.

And after we left our stepfather, it became quickly apparent what a drain he had been financially, as well as physically and emotionally. Soon after we had gotten an apartment on our own, we slowly began to have some financial breathing space. We began to have money for extras like pastries, cookies, jelly, and peanut butter. Later still, we could buy new clothes when the seasons demanded them; boots and gloves in winter. Toys, comic books, kung fu classes, and when our shitty little twelve-inch black and white television with the tinfoil and coat hanger antenna busted, we actually had enough money to go buy a new shitty little twelve-inch black and white television sans the tinfoil and coat hanger. And boy, were we thankful for it. It was all possible because of Mom's astute maneuverings. Or as she called it: "Robbing Peter to pay Paul." And man was she doin' some jackin'!

When it came to my interest in art, she never said no. If she could scrape up the money, beg, borrow, or steal, I'd have whatever I needed to draw or paint. When I got to art school it was tougher, but she was still just as committed. In spite of never *feeling* loved, protected, taken care of, provided for, safe, healthy or happy, I always *knew* she loved me. And the art was the one evidence of a mother's love that I could *always* count on.

For all her shortcomings as a mother, I could never fault her heart. While I always hated what she subjected us to, I always knew she meant well and hoped for the best, even it she didn't always know what *was* for the best.

Pamela

Over the years, I've met and talked to abuse victims all across the country. I've listened, in self-help groups and twelve-step programs, to other abuse victims, and I've read autobiographies. In all those accounts and experiences, I've only met two other people who suffered worse abuse than I did.

One of them is my sister, Pamela.

As kids, Pamela and I led separate lives, there being a five year age gap, with me being the youngest. Her friends were mostly older girls and mine younger guys. But she would sometimes tell me a story or read to me from some book she liked. I remember Andre Norton's "Warlock of the Witch World" and Edgar Rice Burroughs' *Tarzan* series. I used to love to hear those tales and look at the beautifully painted covers. I would just stare at those paintings of heroes in battle and adventure, and imagine myself right there with them.

Pamela was my hero. She was smart and funny, tough and cool. She, in my eyes, has always done things right.

Often nowadays when we talk, she tells me she feels guilty for leaving me alone with our stepfather. But hell, what could she do? It would have been hard enough for her not getting raped, killed, or prostituted, or sent out by herself at such a young age to such mean streets. At best we would have become orphans in a city which proved that it did not care. Of all the times the police were called by our neighbors or ourselves, only once did they actually remove our stepfather from the premises. He would always be twice as angry and twice as vengeful after they left.

I've lost count of the times we lay in our beds staring across the room into each other's quietly crying eyes and me wishing *she* weren't there. Not her, not my mom, not me.

It was hard enough being tortured the way I was, but it was unbearable to hear the screams of the people I loved night after night and not being able to do a goddamned thing about it.

When she was not there, I had at least some peace of mind knowing that one of us had escaped the Madness.

Pamela was and still is, smart, cool, funny, kind and baaaaad when you get her angry. Sure she and I fought like... well... like brother and sister when we were young. She was in charge of me quite often and took her job seriously. I was independent, rebellious and had a problem with authority. Go figure. So she and I were always getting into fights when I wanted to sneak out or didn't want to take my cold medicine (that cherry stuff used to make me wanna puke).

But we loved each other and looked out for each other as a given. I remember when she was about ten and I was six. I came around the corner and saw a couple of big girls trying to beat her up. I charged into them like a Tasmanian devil to protect her. I heard her screaming turn to laughter as she pulled me out of their midst. She told me, "Since my birthday was yesterday, they were just giving me my birthday licks."

Then there was the time I was fighting with some neighborhood bully and she came out and broke up the fight. As we walked away, the guy yelled something about "Yo mama!" She turned right around and went back. "Don't you *ever* talk about my mama," she quietly told him. He caved in and slunk away.

Because Pamela was beautiful, I always had to squash shit whenever one of the homies would say, "Man, that's your sister? She is fine! Does she have a boyfriend?"

"She may not have a boyfriend, but if you keep talkin' you're gonna be my new bitch." That would usually end ANY talk about my sister.

I remember one Halloween at our apartment when our stepfather wasn't home we were visited by some family friends, Claudia, Jimmy and the kids... all five of them. Pamela was the oldest of us all and the big sister as well. She invented all kinds of spooky, scary games for us to play. In one she called herself "Witchie-poo", the wickedest witch of the East, and she was looking for children to boil for her dinner. We turned out all the lights and scattered like rats, screaming and hiding. For hours she hunted and captured us, and let us escape by ones and twos. It was one of the few carefree times I remember having as a kid, and it was all due to my sister Pamela.

But Pamela did the smartest thing a child could, she saved herself. She was always doing great in school. She was always studying. She even had great penmanship. All kinds of extra-curricular activities filled up her days. She was in band, orchestra and went to all-city every year. Dance, volleyball and anything else that would keep her away from home was her salvation. It kept her not just sane, but alive. She began running when she was in grammar school. It was the best thing for her to get out of our family, city, and life.

In college she was able to breathe. But she still harbored the fear that our stepfather would just show up one day and the pain would begin anew.

It took her years and years to outgrow that fear. And sometimes, in times of weakness or distress, it returns, creeping up like a malarial fever.

Today Pamela, like me, still has to battle demons. When in the Bible it says sins of the father will be visited upon the children's children unto the third and fourth generation, it wasn't a curse, it was just a fact of reality, of existence. And sometimes I still see echoes of him in Pamela's children, my nephews and nieces. We may not have asked for our stepfather, but we still had to live with him.

We still had to survive.

descent

 descent

Tricycle

Kindergarten? First grade? I dunno... I was walking down the block towards home from school when coming towards me was a kid a year or two younger than me riding a green tricycle. As he rode closer, I could see the flapping streamers in red, white, and blue. Closer still I could make out the flecks of reflective paint beneath the green, and the white-wall tires cinched the deal.

"Hey! That's my bike!" I said incredulously, jumping in front of him to grab the handlebars, stopping the startled kid in his tracks.

"No it's not," the boy cried.

"Yes it is! Get off!"

When he wouldn't, I forced him and the bike into a u-turn and set off down the street. Screaming and crying, he hung on tight. I had to give the kid credit. He was tenacious. But I was too, and it was MY BIKE! Finally exhausted in his efforts, he fell to the ground, still hanging onto the rear of the frame. I really wanted to beat this kid up for stealing my bike, but he didn't look like a bad kid, just a little confused, so I decided not to slug him. But I did drag his pathetic, crying, little thieving self down the street like some bad guy in a western who drags the good guy behind him on his horse. Eventually, the little schmuck let go. I thought he'd had enough. But no, he continued to follow me down the street, screeching like a harpy.

This made me really want to kill him. I considered giving the bike back to him just to shut him up and then in the next instant, I thought about beating him up again - just to shut him up. Geez! This kid was really getting on my nerves! Looking around nervously and a little guiltily, I noticed the curious stares we were getting from the few midday pedestrians on the block. This kept me from knocking the piss outta the annoying little squirt. I continued on my way and he continued to follow, screaming. Loudly.

Finally, I arrived at my house with the runt in tow. With him still crying and holding onto the bicycle seat, I dragged both through the gangway, entering the backyard where to my surprise, I found my folks on their hands and knees doing something I had never seen them do before or since - gardening... in the backyard of our apartment.

Dad looked up at me with a familiar expression, the one that said there was nothing going on in this world that he could possibly care about. It was the look he usually got just before he began jonesing for the needle and started destroying everything around him.

He looked from me to the now silent brat standing there behind me, then back to me again. Here his expression changed subtly. He was waiting for an explanation. One that he would not care about.

Jerking my thumb over my shoulder, I told him, "This kid stole my bike."

Bending back to his spade and soil, he said, "No he didn't. It's not yours anymore. You're too big for it."

I looked from the back of his uncaring head to my mother's concerned but silent face. Then it struck me what had happened; he had sold my bike without telling me and probably for drug money. Slowly my hands slid from the bars of my... his... tricycle, once lost, now found. The very one I had just won back. And how hatefully, gleeful, that little kid took his prize and ran. I listened to the sound of his footsteps and the accompanying squeak of the wheels. I watched the last fluttering of those red, white and blue streamers.

Even now, I can still feel his freedom as he fled from my household. He was the lucky one. At my hands he had only the tiniest hint of the quagmire of injustice and unfairness that I lived in constantly. Einstein said that for every action there is an equal and opposite reaction. Even then, I knew it to be true. For every action I took, he, Dad, had a response, a way to fuck it up, to turn it against you. So you learn to do, to be... nothing.

Sparky and Boots

My first pet was a little, pure black kitten I named Sparky. Dad and I were at a friend's house and his cat had just borne a litter. They let me take my pick from several. I chose the one that seemed to be at peace. The others were mewling, crawling across each other, chasing or running from one another, but Sparky was the calm in the center of the storm. Since they didn't allow pets in our apartment complex, I had to sneak him inside under my shirt. We had Sparky two or three years when Dad brought home another raggedy looking stray. He just walked in the house with it and plopped her down in the hallway and went into the bedroom. I guess we got a new pet. She was white with black colorations and each of her little feet seemed to be wearing a different, white, boot. Pamela got to name this one and she called her Boots.

Boots had been with us for less than a year or so when in the middle of the night Pamela and I were awakened by the sounds of shouting and screaming. We lay in bed silently wishing it would stop, but then Dad came storming into our room in another one if his usual rages, fits, tantrums, cursing everyone and God. "Get in here rightgoddamnednow!"

Jumping up, we hurried into the living room where Mom already was. He explained that one of the cats had urinated on one of his shirts, which he had left laying in the middle of the floor. I restrained myself from asking him why the hell he left it laying on the floor if he wanted to keep it nice. I could see the same question on Mom's face. And further, how do you know which cat it was? Instead, we all remained silent. "I want that cat NOW!" We all scurried off pretending to look for Boots. I accidentally found her cowering under my bed and went on with my "searching".

Without warning, he appeared at our bedroom door. And to our eternal horror, he was holding a terrified Sparky by the scruff of his neck. "If you don't find me Boots, I'm takin' Sparky. You got five seconds! One... two... " and he headed towards the door. Until he started counting, I had been frozen with disbelief. I couldn't conceive of Dad hurting Sparky. He was there when we got him. His friend had given him to us, and... it was just a little kitten! And then the question: What do I do? How can I be expected to choose? I'm just a little kid. I looked into Pamela's eyes. She was just as frozen as I was. Then I looked at Sparky. And then I thought about Boots. She had been found on the streets, a stray. She would be able to survive back out on the streets, the same streets she came from. Sparky had been a housecat since birth and would not know how to survive. Reluctantly, I made my choice. And my young heart would bear the responsibility for that burden for the rest of my life.

I went under my bed where Boots had been cowering and I betrayed my charge. And there I sacrificed one pet under my care for another. My mind said it was logic and loyalty. My little heart cried out "COWARD!" Then with a heavy heart, I gathered her trembling, little body up in my arms and delivered her unto he who would become her executioner.

Dropping Sparky, he yanked Boots out of my arms by her neck and went storming out the front door. Only to our eternal horror instead of turning left towards the elevator banks, he turned right towards the incinerator shaft! I put my back to the wall near the open door and closed my eyes, unable to face the horrible event unfolding before me. There I heard the door of the incinerator room open. I tried to convince my ears to refuse the sound of the rusty incinerator bay opening. I denied the tortured howling of my poor pet. And I did not, could not, accept the sound of finality - that steel incinerator bay door slamming shut with cruel finality. I tried not to imagine the screaming terror of a twenty-four-floor fall in darkness. I tried to fight out the horror from the image of the flaming cauldron that awaited her at the bottom of that long lonely fall. Against all hope, I summoned up the courage to peek out the door, praying that I would see her small fragile form darting out to safety. But when he yanked the door to that small room open, she had more than enough room to escape. And then he emerged... alone.

Numb, I turned and walked slowly back into the apartment. When he came back in empty-handed, he stormed right past me still cursing and yelling. But I could scarcely hear him. I was unaware of anything. I made my way to our bedroom and lay myself down. There I lay unmoving as one dead. I remember nothing else. My consciousness faded as screams, shouts and cursing filled the air around me.

Boots wasn't the first of my pets to be murdered by that devil in human flesh, nor was she the last to be so cruelly snuffed out.

To this day I'm still working on forgiving myself for the death of my pitiful pet. I am growing to accept my true helplessness in that situation. As horrendous as my choice was, the alternative would have been far worse to my young soul.

The trail often leads to a cold, half-dead place. But hope is not gone. There is still faith. Faith that God did not lead me this far only to let me fall by the wayside.

Overall the damage that has been done cannot be estimated. There is something broken about my soul. God has helped me heal and has healed much for me, but there is still so much sadness in me. It is a yawning chasm so wide and so deep that I wonder how much can ever be repaired.

I am torn sometimes between the continual fight for my humanity and devoting my time and energy to some other venture, thinking I'm well enough just to get through this life. Not always, but it's there, lurking beneath the surface.

Waiting.

Waiting for a moment of hardship, of weakness.

Then it emerges.

It creeps out from underneath its rock and festers like a boil until I begin to doubt, to forget where I have come from, how far I've come, and where I am going.

Clock

The last time I trusted a human being was when I was seven years old. I had come home from school to our apartment on Lakeside. My Dad was home when I got there. I said hi as I went to my room to drop off my books. His voice followed me down the hall.

"Come see me when you're done," he said from the couch as he calmly read his copy of the *Chicago Tribune*. "I need to talk to you about something."

"Okay," I said. I put down my things and then returned to the living room.

As I stood there by his side, for a long minute he didn't even acknowledge me. So long, in fact, that I thought that he'd forgotten summoning me. Slowly turning the page, he glanced at it briefly before folding the paper up, putting it down and standing up.

He said, "Come in here." Leading me into the darkened kitchen it crossed my mind that maybe he was going to ask me what I wanted for dinner. A thing that was extremely unusual. Instead he stopped at the entrance and indicated for me to go on in. Once inside the kitchen, I turned to face him wondering why, if he was going to make us something to eat, he wasn't turning on the light.

"What happened?" he asked me as he leaned against the doorway.

"Huh?"

"You heard me. What happened?"

"Where?" My child-sized mind was befuddled, having no room in it for what was coming next, no way to comprehend the unfairness, the injustice that was about to occur.

"Come over here." I closed the three feet of space that separated us. He turned his head to indicate the wind-up clock that sat on the kitchen counter. Looking up to it, then over to him, my mind was busy trying to figure out what the time of day had to do anything. Did I take too long to come home from school? Was Pamela taking too long to get home? Was Mom? What? What? What!!

"What happened to the clock?" he said smoothly, fooling my little mind into thinking he was not angry.

"I dunno," I replied. He picked up the clock in his big hand and put it in front of my face saying nothing. It was a small, old, white, cheap plastic wind-up model. Made in China. $1.99.

After staring at it a moment, I noticed that it was not ticking nor was the second hand moving. When I did not reply, he said, with the first traces of anger, "What happened to the clock?" he repeated.

"Whaddayamean 'what happened to the clock?'" I thought. I just got here. And I can barely even tell time at that. Did he think that I had taken it to school to show all my friends and snuck it back in before he'd noticed?

"I don't know," I said. "I didn't touch it." When he knelt down in front of me, I could see the evil lurking just behind his eyes. I was already beginning to learn how to recognize the signs. He took the deep breath of a real parent being patient with a wayward child.

"Okay Eddie. You can tell me. And if you're honest with me, everything will be okay. Nothing will happen," he said in his most charming tone. It had never really occurred to me to lie before that day, but I soon would learn that I had absolutely nothing to win by being honest

But I relaxed. He said it would be okay. Exhaling the breath I had been holding, I looked him right in the eye, smiled up at him, and said, "I don't know what happened to the clock."

I heard two cracks in almost instantaneous succession. And the world went black.

When I opened my eyes again, my knees had already buckled and I was beginning to slide down the wall. As I tried to steady myself, I strove to chase the stars out of the shadows of my mind. I then noticed that my face and head were numb and my ears were ringing. There was a coppery, watery taste in my mouth.

He grabbed me by my collar and yanked me away from the wall. This spun me around and as he drug me from the kitchen, I noticed a round indentation with a circle drawn around it in cracked plaster and paint at the height of my head. After dragging me into the dining room, he threw me on the ground and began kicking me. I was dimly aware of him screaming and cursing me but couldn't quite make out what he was saying. It didn't matter though, I knew it wasn't important. It was just more of the same I'd heard before, and it was probably just as well I couldn't hear it. I was busy screaming and crying on my own. Desperately, I tried vainly to stop the blows.

As he grew tired, the kicking slowed down. He then reached down and grabbed a handful of my curly brown hair, yanked me clear off the ground and propelled me towards the bedroom. Then he set my feet down so hard that they were driven out from under me and I fell to the ground again, landing hard on my behind. He lifted me again and with both of my hands, I frantically sought purchase on his hand and wrist to keep my hair from being pulled out by the roots. He must've liked this arrangement, because he kept repeating it. As soon as my feet were under me, he would kick me in the anus and testicles with those hard, sharp, pointy-toed boots of his, driving the toe painfully into me again and again and again.

Three, four, five times this process was repeated with both our screams filling the tiny apartment. When we reached my bedroom, he threw me on the ground again. "Get your bedclothes on and get in bed, and I don't want to hear a sound outta this room all goddamned night!" he screamed. He slammed the door to my room. That was at 3:45 in the afternoon.

I didn't leave my room even to use the bathroom until the next morning. As usual, he acted just as if nothing had happened, alternately joking with me or ignoring me altogether.

Killer Instinct

I must have been the happiest kid in the world when Dad and I were play-fighting that day. We were in the living room boxing. Inevitably our "play" sessions would turn serious all too soon, but as a child, I was able to ignore or forget that fact. I was so happy to, even for a few moments, have a real "Dad" in a real "family" in a "normal" moment in time. Or maybe it was just denial. But at this moment, on this summer's day, I was normal - just a regular kid playing with his dad. He would tap me on the head, or face, or chest, or stomach with his opened hand and I would go for anything I could reach, my little fists tapping him about the midsection. Then all of a sudden, in the middle of it all, he stops and says "Forget it," and walks away from me. A bitter, disappointed look covered his face. "Forget it," he said.

"What?" I ask, wanting Daddy to be happy with me just a while longer. I would have done anything to have him love me, as if it would erase all the bitterness and shame. I hadn't yet learned hatred.

"You don't have it," he says.

"What?"

"Never mind. It's no good."

What? What? What! my mind cries. Just tell me how to make you be happy with me. I'll be good. I'll do better. Just tell me what you want me to do.

Oh, he was good. He was soooo good. It wasn't until after this that I knew. Knew just how calculating he was. Every thought, every word, every gesture was designed, crafted by a master craftsman for a purpose. Later I would begin to follow the clues like a roadmap to the chest of gold, the "X" that marks the spot.

"The Killer Instinct. You don't have it."

"What do I do?" I ask.

"No. You're not taking this seriously."

I thought a moment while he pretended to walk away from me, abandon me again. I didn't know what the "Killer Instinct" was, but "killer" I was familiar with. "Serious" I knew.

"Okay," I said.

"What?"

"Okay," I repeated. Looking at me, he paused for dramatic effect, as if deciding whether I was worthy of wasting his time on.

"Okay," he said, getting back up off the couch.

As we started boxing again there were no smiles, no father and son, just the demon and his little apprentice. As we began again, my tiny hands curled into fists held tight by skinny, undernourished arms. For the first time, my mind opened to the bitterness built by years of PAIN. I began to fight. And this time I fought, not to fight, but to hurt. I fought to kill the beast that I hated, that I loved. I fought HIM. I pounded his body because it was what I could reach. My little fists thumped off of his bare, washboard stomach, and his tightened ribs, all to no effect. Unnoticed.

Then out of the corner of my eye, I found I was presented with a gift. He had overextended himself reaching out and down towards my stomach. And there it was, just as I was stepping in. There! Just coming into range was his handsome, hard-lined jaw. And I went for it. Before I'd even thought about it, I was lunging forward and straining upwards. Lashing out, I connected squarely on his chin with a right cross that had all the anger of the world behind it. And it felt GREAT! The sound of flesh impacting flesh. The jarring that occurs when bone smashes into bone. It was exhilarating! More satisfying than anything in my young life. It felt so good I could taste it. Helping me was the fact that he was just about to plant his right leg as I stepped into it.

Caught off guard and off balance, my punch was just enough to make him trip sideways and backwards before he recovered.

"Motherfu...!!"

When he got upright again, there was murder in his eyes and fear in mine.

"I'm sorry!" I quickly shouted as he caught himself. This wasn't in his plan and he had no backup prepared for falling on his ass in front of his little boy. Caught by his pantywaist son who could never do anything right. "Forget it," he mumbled as he stomped off to his room in a foul mood that had him snapping at everyone for the rest of the day.

I lied. I had said that I was sorry. But that was just to head off the beating I knew would follow. But I wasn't. I was glad. My heart rejoiced that David had found a chink in Goliath's armor. I was giddy with excitement that a useless, good-for-nothing, little sissy like me could effectively land a blow for the weak and helpless of the world. It started a habit, a trend in my life that would last a lifetime: Sticking my finger in the eye of the giant.

Playtime

It was kind of sickening. Every time I got to play with my dad it always became some type of violation. Sure it always started off fun. I was just a child longing to connect with my dad, wanting desperately to please him, to have Daddy love me, or even like me.

He was always so charming. Easy laugh, rhythmic flow to his speech, joking, playful...or so it always started. Joking, playing, wrestling, tickling until my cheeks and stomach cramped up painfully and he would still not stop. Rougher, more, faster. Then the pain came. Always... always.

And you'd better not cry. Don't even dare.

There was the choke hold that made you feel like your eyes were going to pop out of your sockets. He squeezed until you begin to grey out. And sometimes the blackness came.

Or he lay across your chest or back until you could not breathe.

Sometimes the gentleness of a pillow would be put across my face, and then he would lie across that until I couldn't hear my own screams. Until they were muffled like the burning breath trapped within my lungs.

An arm, twisted behind my back, lifting my feet free of the ground. Tendons straining, stretching, screaming. All the while his laughter filled my ears.

"What's the matter with you?" he would demand when my giggles had ceased, replaced with the concentration of swallowed pain. "Why you always gotta fuck things up? Huh? Why you gotta ruin everything?! We can't even play without you cryin' and whinin' about it! I can't even have a little fun without yo' ass fuckin' it up!! God-damn!"

And that would make me want to cry even more than the physical pain. But I would hold it back. I did not want to ever fulfill that prophesy.

Then he would go stomping off, grumbling about how I always ruined everything. About how I never could do anything right, pissed off that I, a tiny child, had somehow managed to ruin his day, his week, and his life.

Yet and still, each time he would come into my room with his playful swagger and me like a puppy returning to his master, would come running. Tail wagging and ears up. Eager to make Daddy happy. Anxious to be blessed by a kind word or a smile, regardless that those smiles always brought cruelty.

Pain is pain, be it disguised as accidents or fun, passive or active.

But there came a moment, after years of enduring such abuse, where I was able to let him taste a portion of my surprise, my pain, my confusion, my frustration, my… anger. A small dose of that same "accidental" fun.

When I was about eight, Mom, Dad, and I were leaving our apartment building on Lakeside. We had just turned right on Sheridan and would soon turn left on Lawrence Avenue, headed for the El (elevated train).

He and I were roughhousing as Mom walked ahead. At one point he had spun me around, twisted my right arm behind my back with one hand, grabbed my hair with the other, tripped me with his foot, and threw me to the concrete sidewalk. I came down hard on my knees, scraping them, and fell on my elbow hard enough to hear it. He was laughing the whole time.

As I lay there on the sidewalk rubbing my new bruises, I watched him as he, still laughing that beautiful resonant laugh, turned and caught up to Mom. She was oblivious. She was always, conveniently, unconsciously, oblivious to our "playtime".

It was the laughter that did it. It told me, for the first time on a conscious level, that he did not mind my pain at all. Not a whit. It had not yet begun to sink in that the pain he provided was on purpose. It was under the guise of "toughening me up," but really meant to break me down, to destroy my spirit, my soul, as his had been.

Not until years later would I understand that the consistently, constantly painful playing around, was just an extension of all the other abuses. Just an extension of his twisted soul.

Then there began a strange, unfamiliar burning in my head, right behind my eyes. That sensation would become more and more familiar, more and more powerful over the next half of my life. It was one of the earliest internal encounters with RAGE.

But then the burning just grew, until I stood up and launched myself at him.

Building up speed, I ran faster and faster. Until then, I had never ran faster or harder for anything.

As I approached him from behind, I focused on the smallest, weakest, most vulnerable point in my sights.

Powered by pumping legs, fueled by my newfound anger, I put my entire being from the earth up into my right fist. And when I struck his arrogant, laughing form, it found its target in the small of his back, just above his pelvis and slightly to the left of his spine.

I didn't know what I'd hit, but it had an unimagined effect.

He let out an unexpected "Uhff!" Both of his legs buckled and his left knee cracked down onto the concrete before he caught himself by putting his left hand down. There was an instant, a fraction of a second, that I had never seen before and would never see again. In that brief instant with his head hanging down and his teeth clenched, I saw pain.

Now I have to tell ya, I've been in lots of fights. I've won many and lost more than a couple. But that, right there? That was the single most satisfying blow I've ever landed in my nearly forty years of living. I never liked fighting, until it starts, and then I enjoy the hell out of it. But never have I felt more pleasure in the sensation of my fist impacting someone's body. Never have I enjoyed more the sensation in the sound of my knuckles popping into skin, muscle, and bone. To me, in that moment, it felt like... LIFE.

Yes, he was beginning to turn me into the same type of beast that he was.

And then it was over. Quickly regaining his feet, he pushed himself off the ground, took three short, soft, almost woozy steps, and uttered a confused, "Goddamnit..."

I had stopped and turned to face him immediately after I struck. Waiting for the beating I knew was to come. But all he did was stand there. That and softly repeat to himself, "Goddammit."

It seemed as if he was going to say something, ask something, as we stood there facing each other. Then confused, he changed his mind. Finally he just turned, put his arm around my also confused mother, and together they just walked off, leaving me there. There with my secret triumph, secret victory, and lingering thoughts of repercussions never to come.

Chittlins

There was no surer way to be beaten half to death than to show weakness. That was the one thing above all others that he could not stand.

And his sadism was explosive. Volcanic. So much so that when I responded to an inane question: "Do you like chittlins" with a timidly offered, "Not so much," he dumped the entire contents of the pot on my plate. It covered the broccoli, the cornbread, and overflowed onto the table then down into my lap.

"Now eat that. Eat all of it. I'm gonna come back in an hour and if it ain't all finished, I'm beatin' yo ass."

And with that he left the dinner table and went into the bedroom and closed the door. I looked over at my mother. She avoided my eyes as she calmly, quietly, put away the other dishes and left the room.

I ate. I ate and I kept eating. I ate until I thought I was going to throw up. Then I waited for the nausea and bile to subside. Then I ate some more, all the while keeping an eye on that big-ass wall clock, the one that sprinted around like a runner on a track when I was playing, but now the minute hand moved around oh, so painfully slow.

I started to panic when an hour had gone by and I had only finished about two-thirds of the pot. After an hour and a half my stomach was hurting badly and the nausea and bile had gotten so bad that its taste was continually in my mouth. I decided he could beat me if he wanted to, because I wasn't eating another forkful of that shit. So I sat and waited, determined to take the ass kicking. And I waited.

After about two hours he still hadn't come out. So I went in after him just to get it over with. And there he lay, passed out on the bed. And there lay my mom next to him, watching TV. I think that was the first time in my life I dared to get angry with them. Angry at his sorry ass for making me eat all that shit for nothing, and her for either forgetting or not giving a shit enough to come out and help me by telling me he was asleep. I stood there in their doorway staring dumbly for a few more seconds, then turned and went to my room. I didn't even bother to clean up that mess. I never ate another bite of chittlins again though, I'll tell you that. He could beat me to death. I'm still mad to this day.

And I still don't eat chittlins.

Jalapeño

It was a beautiful spring day. In our bedroom the screenless window was wide open. I couldn't go outside to play, but I was just as happy as if I could. I leaned my scrawny, ten-year-old elbows on our 24th floor windowsill, feeling the warm moist breeze caress my face and hair. It smelled of soil and lake water with a hint of greenery. I was stuck inside and dreaming I was not. My mind was in the sky far above the city. Soaring. Looking down, I saw humanity below me, tiny as ants with lives in the living. While I was stuck there. But that day I didn't mind. My mind was wandering free, delving into the mysteries of the world.

Down below me, in the back of our apartment complex, past the parking lot, was a vacant lot. The lot was filled with bricks, whiskey bottles, boards, planks, broken glass, rusting cans, buckets, and nails. It and many others in our neighborhood just like it, served as our playgrounds. Some of the guys were down there now playing softball. There were about twelve of 'em. Nate, Tony, Malcomb, Steve, Godfrey, and Jeff were all down there, and some kids I didn't know, all in T-shirts, tank tops, old worn out jeans, and sneakers with holes in 'em.

From this height you couldn't hear voices, just the general sounds of play and excitement mingled with the lull of anticipation. You heard the passing of cars and busses flowing up and down Lawrence Avenue. Their exhaust fumes, bitter, acrid, mingled with the lake air, each awaiting its turn at the tip of tongue or nostril. I watched as they would swing and miss and curse, or swing and hit and run. Catch and throw or miss and curse. The cheers and curses alike rose to meet me, first rising, now falling. From up here as I watched them run their hearts out, it seemed as if they were moving through molasses. The ball that sped so fast at you as you hold the bat now seemed to take its lazy time in reaching the swinger.

Then suddenly I was marveling at a new discovery: I had actually, just for the first time, seen the speed of sound. With my eyes I saw the pitcher toss the big, worn, sixteen-inch ball in a fast, underhand arc. I saw the dirty brown-grey ball travel the distance in dreamtime. I watched the batter wind up, swing and saw the ball instantly yanked high in the air where it seemed to float for a looooong time. Then, suddenly, miraculously, I heard the pop.

Incredible! Was it my ears playing tricks on me? I paid close attention to the next pitch and it happened again. Throw... swing... hit... soar... then... POP! Wow! That was really cool! I tried to count the fractions of a second it took the sound to travel from the bat to my ears high above. I began thinking of the jets that break the sound barrier each summer over Lake Michigan during the annual Air and Water Show.

Then I stopped and threw my little mind in a quandary when I asked myself this: If the sound, traveling at the speed of sound, reached my ears a second after the light reached my eyes, how far ahead did the light, traveling at the speed of light, reach my eyes ahead of the actual swing? And what is the speed of... thought? I think I hurt myself with the next thought: What was the speed of reality?

My mind was spared a complete meltdown by something even more ominous: the smile on my Dad's face.

He had just come into my room like a mischievous kid. I noticed his hands were conspicuously hidden from view.

Playfully, he asked me, "What you doin'?"

"Nothin." From behind his back he brought out this bright, green thing I'd never seen before. I didn't know whether it was a fruit or a vegetable. It was about three inches long, tapered slightly, curved and had a stem on the large end. As if to pique my curiosity, he bit the tip off and chewed it, savoring every bite.

"Boy, boy, boy! That sho' is good," he said.

Now, I might be young, but I knew a set-up when I saw one, so when he asked me if I wanted to try it, I said, "No, thank you." At first he prodded and teased, then pushed. But when it became apparent to him that I wasn't as stupid as he always said I was, all the laughter left his eyes.

"Take it," he said, dead serious.

Reluctantly I did.

"Take a bite."

Putting the little green thing in my mouth, I toughed my tongue to the bitter end that he had bitten off, then quickly drew back after tasting fire. It was like sticking my tongue in lava. My eyes quickly watered up and even my nostrils stung. Looking up at him, I at first didn't comprehend. What was the point of this?

When I hesitated, he shouted, "BITE IT!" at me.

My mind was racing, trying to figure out the reason for his anger. What did I do or say? What did I forget to do or say? Was this punishment for something I had done before? Finding no escape, I took a bite. Fire! With agony, I chewed and swallowed as quickly as I could and a fireball consumed me. I was in flames from my cheeks, to lips, nose, gums, tongue, throat, chest and stomach.

The blinding tears were threatening to spill out over my eyelids and down onto my cheeks. Even though inside I was crying, I knew that to let it show would be my doom.

The trick to not crying, I had found, was not to blink. That would break the surface tension that kept the tears in check. Keep your head up and the air would dry them before long. Just don't blink. Just don't blink. Just don't blink.

When that arduous torture was over, when I had finished his sadistic little test, I held the remaining two-thirds of it out to him, wanting to be rid of the poisonous thing. I will never forget the look of contempt I saw in his face. The look of utter disgust.

Then the ground dropped out from under me when I heard him say, "Finish it." In a snake's whisper, he said, "Finish it or I'll knock the shit outta' you."

By now my nose, cheeks, and lips were numb and rubbery. My throat and tongue felt like I had gargled with broken glass and iodine. My eyes were burning and it hurt to breath, but I looked that bastard in the eye and I ate it. I ate that whole thing, all the while looking at him. My eyes could no longer contain the tears as they welled up and poured out. But there was no sorrow behind them, only silent, steady hatred.

When I got to the stem, I held it out in front of my mouth to see if he wanted me to eat that too. But before I could, he straightened, looked at me for a long moment and with a look of pure anger, then turned and left.

Whenever little tortures like this took place, neither he nor I ever spoke of them. Like they never happened. He never explained or excused any of these mind games of his. But I know one thing: He hated weakness, any sign of weakness. In his anger and his play, I was always the "Pantywaist," the "Nigger," the "Pussy," the things he hated most: Himself. I suppose somewhere inside the subterranean recesses of his being he was trying to "toughen me up" rather than break me. He became even more furious when I wouldn't break. But the only way he knew to toughen something up was to break it. Over and over again. Now I'm happy to say that he failed in both cases. But he came close. He came oh, so close. He tried every day and every night for over TEN long, miserable, furious years to make me just like him: a killer, a destroyer. Dead inside and out. And I learned. I learned well.

Wild Irish Rose

Dad gave me my first drink. It was Wild Irish Rose from the bottle. A fifth. "Here, drink this. It'll put hair on your chest," he said.

It was sweet and strong and heady stuff for a little tyke like me. As we shared the bottle, he told me, "If I ever catch you drinkin', I'll beat the shit out of you." He gave me my first smoke. I was around ten. It was a Camel unfiltered. "Don't ever smoke," he warned. "It'll stunt your growth." But he let me try Pall Mall, Lucky Strike, Marlboro, and Virginia Slims menthol. I liked the pipe tobacco the most. There was a wild cherry blend that was as sweet as candy.

Almost Suicide

When I wasn't but about ten years old, on a cold night just before Christmas, I looked death in the eye. I came face to face with the old specter himself. We actually got to exchange a few words. But he wasn't ready for me yet... or I wasn't ready for him.

Mom, Dad and I were in the living room stringing up the tree with Christmas lights. They were those big old ones. You know the kind, shaped like Easter eggs, all reds, greens and blues. The night had started out with Dad's yuletide excitement, but soon enough he started to lose his high and thus would begin our rapid descent into hell. Our laughter quickly fell to silence as we pretended the future did not lie before us. He would snap orders, then shout reprimands when they weren't carried out fast enough, slow enough or well enough. He would shout because we were too loud, then yell when we fell silent. He would demand that we look at him and then bellow at us because we did.

These demands were not an unusual occurrence, but a daily, nightly, constant ritual. And there came a moment, a snapshot in time, where I stopped and stared at our little family drama and our torturer, and all sound stopped. I saw him etched sharply against the backdrop of the city lights through our high window, his dark skin highlighted in red, green and blue. Anger and hatred of life as a whole was written all over his face. My mother's nervous anxiety showed in every feature, every movement, and every glance.

Slowly his words beat their way through my eardrums, through my subconscious, into my conscious mind. "Watch what the hell you're doing!" I looked down and saw the string of glowing lights in my hands. Snatching them away, he continued to berate me. "What the fuck is wrong with you? You wanna get yourself electrocuted!? Don't you see that motherfuckin' light bulb missing!?" From an eerily calm stillness I looked at the empty socket in his hand. "Do you know what would happen if you stuck your finger in that goddamned socket?!" I looked at him as if for the first time in all of my eight years of living, from the calm center of the psychic storm. I saw this raving lunatic, completely out of touch with all proportionate reality. And it was always like that. No warning. No talking. The first thing you heard was yelling. If you were lucky. If not, he would catch you from behind, sometimes with a fist, sometimes with a foot. So, with the yelling at least, you could prepare for what usually followed. Get in the zone: Numb. But this time, for me, there was clarity. Sharp, focused and present. That he extended the invitation. "Go ahead!" he yelled, "stick your finger in there and see what happens! I dare you!!" He extended the empty socked out toward me invitingly where it beckoned me with its dark, empty, coldness. He held it out even further, taunting me. Daring.

And that's when it came. Standing there, looking him in the eye with him waiting for my response. I should do it, I thought. I should stick my finger in that socket just to fuck him up, piss him off real good. That would show him. He'd look pretty stupid standing there wondering what the hell just happened, with me lying dead on the floor. Go ahead. Do it. But then, right behind that came was another less satisfying thought. *I wouldn't be around to appreciate it.* Looking over at my mother's anxious face, I thought about what it would do to her mind to see that happen. In addition, I would be leaving her alone with him. What was I thinking? Hurt myself just to get even with him? Damn. I was on for the ride. Me, the tree, the socket and my Dad.

The moment passed and I had chosen life. And I smiled. Just a little. Standing there looking from that empty socket to him. I don't know why, but it was quiet for the rest of the night.

Christmas Eve Night

I remember one wonderful Christmas Eve. It was one of the few times I saw my dad smile. Not the con man. Not the devil. Just my dad smiling at me.

I was tiny. We were living in a three flat on 107th Street on the South side. I had on a pair of white pajamas with little faint red fire trucks on them. They were clean and there were no holes in them.

Dad, Mom, and I were sitting in the living room. Talking. Just talking.

I was playing on the floor as they sat on the couch. He had his arm around her and she was snuggled up against him.

There had been talk of Santa sightings earlier in the night. It was one of those magical times in a child's life where we knew there is no Santa, or Tooth Fairy, or Easter Bunny, but yet we still got excited by the magic that came along with the myth. There was a tree. It had decorations and lights and presents under it. And not just one present either, but several. They were all carefully wrapped in the festive greens and reds and golds of the holiday. Each present had a name tag and several bore my name in my mother's circular, flowing hand.

It was around ten o'clock at night and it occurred to me that, technically, it would be Christmas in just two, short hours. My excitement grew almost beyond my control. I couldn't wait to see what Santa had brought us in those bright, beautiful, shiny, foil wrappings. Working up my courage, I asked if I could stay up until midnight and open my presents then. Dad smiled as he thought about it, looked at Mom who smiled back at us, then came to a compromise.

"Tell you what. If you can stay awake till midnight, you can open up one present."

"Can I pick which one?" I asked hopefully.

"Can you pick which one?!" he repeated, his voice rising. He gave Mom that, "can you believe this?" look and said to her, "Will you look at this?"

That was when the train almost came off the track. I waited with that hoping, fearing, sinking sensation you get on a rollercoaster as you approach that first, BIG drop. Then with a laugh he said, "Yeah, you can pick which one."

With the danger averted, I felt the joy of someone given a second chance at life and vowed not to squander it.

It was a hard fight staying awake, playing and not getting Dad mad at me but I sat up that night content. Even if I didn't get to open that one present, I was content for this night.

When finally midnight struck, I chose carefully. Based on feel, weight, size, shape, and sound, I picked the one with the white wrapping and the gold foil and white snowflakes. Carrying my treasure reverently to the center of the living room floor before them, I prepared myself by taking a moment with a deep, deep breath and then set to work. After peeling and tearing off all the paper, I had in my hands a cardboard box that seemed about as long as my arm and there through the cellophane window was a rip-cord drag-racer! And it was new! It would actually work! And it was RED! My favorite color! "Wow! Cool!" I practically shouted. If happiness had a ceiling, I had just gone through it.

As I looked up at them, profoundly grateful, I saw something in their eyes I had never seen before and would never see again; they were beaming down at me. There was a happiness on their faces that was pure as sunshine on a mountaintop. There in that moment, we were a family. I didn't know why, but it was a holy gift. A gift I've hidden in my heart for the last thirty-five years.

A Mother's Blood

Screams were a constant in my life. They haunt me to this day. My screams, Pamela's, Mom's. Sometimes we were all beaten together, sometimes separately. The beatings have all blurred in my memories, but the screams remain crystal clear. Trips to the hospital were not unusual for Mom. Her nose and foot had been broken at different times, and she had been admitted to the emergency room for internal injuries. At least once that I can remember, an ambulance had to be called.

Usually when my mother was getting beaten, she would hustle Pamela and I into our bedroom to keep us from being sucked into the middle of it. And it usually worked. Once in a while he would burst in and question us like an SS officer about what she said or he said, or someone did. Then he would threaten us and leave, or drag us back in with them. Out of sight, out of mind, she figured. It also was a way of shielding everyone from the aftermath.

One day Mom's screams had been coming through the thin walls for some time. Pamela and I could hear the sounds of flesh impacting flesh, and her body being thrown into walls would rattle the small apartment. Then, for some reason I cannot remember, I did the unthinkable. I opened the door. I had to hear what was going on. Finally I couldn't stand it. I had to do something. Maybe it was some sudden silence that worried me. We always lived in fear that one day he would go too far and there would be a funeral that the surviving members would be forced to attend with the murderer.

But just as I opened the door, my mother was walking past. "Get back inside," she whispered as she rushed to the bathroom. But I would not. I wanted to do something. Something had to be done, but I didn't know what. After a moment she returned from the bathroom with a washcloth held to her mouth. Lowering the cloth, she said, "Honey, get back inside!" What I saw froze me. Several of her front teeth were missing. They had been knocked completely out and blood streamed out of her mouth, so much so that the cloth could not contain it and she ran back to the bathroom.

Something welled up within me. My little body seemed possessed. Like a sleepwalker, I headed towards the living room. "Eddie!" Pamela whispered to me. "Come back in here!" she desperately pleaded, worried for my safety. There was a Bullworker in the hallway near the entrance to the living room. It was a piece of exercise equipment that was like a big, thick, steel tube. The two ends slid into each other and there was a spring inside for resistance. The thing was so heavy I could barely lift it, let alone swing it. Holding it by both hands, I headed for where my dad was, dragging it behind me. In my mind, I knew what I had planned was futile. But I just remember wondering if I would even get a hit in before he threw me out of the window, how long the fall would take, would I feel the impact...

Then I heard my mother whisper behind me a desperate, "Honey, stop!" Hearing the panic in her voice was nearly painful. Mom and Pamela reached me at the same time. Mom took me by the shoulders and Pamela grabbed the Bullworker, taking it from my frozen hands. Turning me around, they each took me by the arms and took me back inside the bedroom.

I knew then that he would kill me sooner or later, either by accident or by design. I knew he could not suffer threats. And in my mind it, was only a matter of time before I made my move again. I knew it would be futile, I knew I might die, but it would happen. One way or another, it would end. I would do whatever I could to ensure it.

Chicago

Nine months of bitter winter, one month of spring, and one for summer, one for fall. Then it was right back to the eternal northern iron-grey skies with perpetual coldness, deluging rains, gusting winds, and bitter chill.

In the spring the skies would open up for what seemed like weeks at a time and just pour. Within about three steps out of your front door you were soaked to the bone. There was no point in trying to stay dry. Umbrellas, overhangs, awnings, all worked to no avail. In the ten feet between them, you would be drenched all over again and again and again. The skies would darken to a slate gray and would remain so for days upon days, so that it began to feel that we had entered upon the twilight of earth's existence. If the winds were strong, the rain just came at you sideways, filling up gutters, curbs and sidewalks so that at any given moment you would be up to your ankles with wet, cold, dirty water or slush, depending upon the season.

The winds could be as deadly as the ice. Each year there were dozens of cases of broken bones and lost lives due solely to the cold, glacial winds that flowed down Lake Michigan and blasted us regularly. I have seen with my own eyes more than one person who had been blown in front of oncoming traffic and churned to pink hamburger by the braking tires.

Going downtown in the winter was taking your life into your own hands. There were streets where the skyscrapers reached up high into some jet stream and dragged it down along its length only to send it back along Adams, Jackson, Van Buren, Franklin or Clark.

I used to have to brace myself before crossing and fold down my umbrella because the crosswind would just tear it right out of your hands if you didn't hang on with a strong hand. And if you did, it would simply turn it inside out and rip it apart. If there was ice, I would pray first. I don't know how the older people did it. I know for a fact that some used to take the long way around.

But the tail end of spring and the summer months were my favorites. That's when the smells would pour forth from all the open windows. Just walking the few blocks to the train, I would travel the world by my nose. From inside those tiny little apartments, sounds of laughter and foreign tongues would come wafting out. The moist warm air would bring the smells of Indian Naan, Korean Chop Chae, Mexican Chorizo, Russian Cabbage, Native American Fried Bread, Vietnamese Pho, Filipino Afritada, Cuban Garlic and Lemon Chicken, and oh so many more exotic spices and flavors. Along with the smells and the languages came the music. You could hear the accordion that the Nortenios listened to, the high pitched singing from India, old guttural underground Russian singing, and the sexy, sensual Brazilian drums. From neighborhood to neighborhood it would go from Heavy Metal to Acid Rock, to Classic Rock, to Country. There was Bluegrass, Blues, Jazz, Hip-hop, Opera, and Classical. Salsa, Cumbia, Meringue, Mariachi, Boss nova. Reggae and Calypso. Qawwali. Bhojpuri. Many, many more.

Let It Snow!

The first few weeks of winter were always the best. And I don't mean winter in the equinoctial sense, I mean the first falling of snow. The cold hadn't yet had a chance to seep into your bones. The bitter winds had yet to become your adversary. And the rolling blanket of gray that covered the heavens hadn't yet started to sap your motivation and will.

But we kids absolutely loved those first few days of white. When the snow stuck and at least a foot of it accumulated through the night, you could smell it before you even climbed out of your bed and bolted for the window to see how much had fallen. When you first stepped out into it, the light it reflected was so bright it was blinding and it took you a few moments before your eyes could handle it. After they teared up and your pupils dialed down the volume, you were ready to rock and roll.

When that first big snow hit, the entire neighborhood got turned into a circus. There were kids everywhere. I mean, kids you hadn't seen in so long you thought they had moved away came crawling out of their holes to come out and play in that white stuff. Everywhere you turned kids were running, jumping, rolling, and romping in a wild frenzy of joy. It was as if we had all heeded the same soft, silent call.

Hats, coats, gloves, scarves, mittens, shoes, boots, and earmuffs of ALL colors dotted the streets like a scattering of gumballs from a broken machine.

As for me, I had a ritual. One I continue to follow to this day. The very first thing I do is make a snowball, because this will tell me what to look forward to for the day's adventure. It told me how to plan. If when I squeezed the snow into a ball it was dry, powdery and did not stick together well, and I had to squeeze REAL HARD to make it stick, it would be a day for SPEED. This was because the dry, super cold snow had fallen from the high, frigid jet stream and was like freeze-dried particles of translucent, crystalline dust with very little moisture. And that meant sliding!

I would make a b-line for the nearest incline looking for something to slide down it on. Any piece of wood wide enough to balance yourself on would do. Street signs worked nicely too. Cardboard was usually the easiest to find, but it got soggy pretty quickly. But linoleum was the best. It was smooth, slick, and fast! It was soft enough to flow over the cracks and bumps, and not get stuck on the uneven surfaces. Very few kids had sleds or toboggans, but the one who did was king for a day. There would be a loooooong line of us wanting to take just one run down that slope on it.

If, however, that first handful of snow clumped together and packed easily into a hard, dense ball, it was time for WAR! All-out, twenty-to-a-side, take-no-prisoners war, carried out from behind the fortified defenses of a well-constructed and reinforced ice fortress.

The groups would form by themselves and we would start digging in about as far away from the other team as we could throw. Whoever was first to finish was first to strike. Hard packed snowballs thrown over a long distance would arc high in the air and come pelting down on heads, faces, and bodies. And woe to those who didn't have at least a foxhole to hide in.

Thus the long-range bombardment would begin. It would test our arms and our aim, and would continue with the air above our heads a swarm with solidly packed snowballs until the tide of battle began to swing to one side or the other. Then, in the face of fierce enemy fire, the superior force would charge the weaker force and overwhelm them, sending them scattering, thereby seizing and occupying the enemy fort.

Occasionally the tactically inferior side, if led by a gutsy young warrior, would charge, catching the bigger force off guard, scattering them to the four winds.

After making my first snowball, I would find a pristine, undisturbed patch of snow, jump into the center of it and lay flat on my back. Then, smiling up to the heavens, I would simultaneously raise my arms high above my head and scissor my legs out to the side, then back again. After that I would get up, jump back out, and admire my masterpiece on a crystal canvas. My snow angel would be as perfect as a Christmas card.

Lastly, after we had helped push out many stuck motorists, after we had snuck onto the back bumpers of slow moving cars and surfed down the block behind them laughing gleefully but quietly, after all our wars had been fought and won or lost, I would begin my final task.

Scooping up an armful of snow and making as big a snowball as I could, I would put it down and begin rolling it around and around in ever widening circles until the snow began to stick to it and build up. Larger and larger it would grow with no end in sight. And when it got so big I could no longer move it, I would start another.

When the second was slightly smaller than the first I would stop and then try to lift it on top of the first one. Sometimes I got a little ahead of myself and made the second one so big I couldn't lift it and had to punch and kick it down to a more manageable size.

Finally, with it balanced and mortared into place with fresh snow, I would begin the third and final piece. It would be smaller still than the second one and it would be placed at the very top of the other two. The finishing touches would be either carved by hand or made up with creative use of nearby litter. Old broken mop handles, broomsticks or towel racks would be stuck into the sides. Whiskey bottle caps or pop-tops at hand would become eyes, nose or several could comprise a mouth. Often, if I had time and energy, my snowman would be taller than I was and as fat as old St. Nick himself. Afterwards I would survey my final work with the satisfaction of a hard job well done.

And if by then the streetlights had begun to turn themselves on, the streets would be comfortingly silent. The fat, fluffy snowflakes would seem to float upon the crisp, cold air like a huge urban snow globe. All the other children would be home for dinner with their families or their parents would be anxiously expecting them at any moment to come bounding in the door.

I would always savor those few moments, frozen in time. Still. Peaceful. Quiet. And... Alone.

920 Lakeside Place

We had lived on Chicago's South side, which was predominantly black. On one of the several occasions when my mother decided she'd had enough and left my stepfather, we moved to the north side, Uptown.

We moved to 920 W. Lakeside Place after we left my stepfather the next to the last time. It was a 24 floor, high-rise, government housing project, and a real piece of shit. There were about 24 units on each floor for a total of around 576 units, 576 families. And in Chicago, that's a whole lot of culture.

We moved in with a family of friends, Claudia and Jimmy and their five children. It was only a two-bedroom apartment, but we all loved each other so it was good times for us kids. We must've driven the adults nuts though. Steve and Frankie were Pamela's age, around twelve. The twins, Marcia and Michelle, were a couple of years younger. I was a tiny six or seven, and Bo was about a year younger and smaller than me. It became more like one family than two living in that hovel.

I can still smell the pop-tarts that Claudia cooked in the oven because there was no money for a toaster. There would be "sack lunches" with bologna sandwiches wrapped in wax paper and a handful of potato chips that oil-stained through the little brown paper bags. Occasionally there would be apples or bananas as well. Their apartment was on the sixth floor. Jimmy was a garbage man, strong and quiet with a great smile and a good sense of humor. Claudia was a woman to be reckoned with when angry. She was no-nonsense, but loved a good laugh as well. Steve was quiet. Frankie outgoing. Marcia and Michelle were beautiful, smart and fun. Bo was the funniest of all, a natural comedian.

After about six months with Claudia, Jimmy and the family, we finally were able to move into an apartment of our own down on the second floor It was apartment #207. Mom got the bedroom and Pamela and I slept on the floor on blankets using our clothes as pillows. Eventually we were able to get a foldout bed for Mom, but Pamela and I fought the rats and roaches for floor space in the living room. Often we were woken up by rats running, awakened in the early pre-dawn light by four-legged creatures scurrying over us. It was an even smaller one-bedroom, but it was all ours. It felt great. It felt like freedom. It was open and free, and we could breathe.

Lakeside was located in the heart of Chicago's Uptown area once in the Guinness Book of World Records as having the most ethnic variety per square block than any place in the world. Dozens of countries were represented there as well as almost every American region and dialect. There were many people that in thirty years of living around the United States, I still have not seen again.

In all senses of the word, Uptown was a ghetto and unfortunately to ALL of these races, I was a NIGGER. Occasionally, I was a SPICK. Never did anyone accuse me of being honkey, cracker or Wonderbread, even though I was predominantly raised by my white mother and looked and acted just about 50% white. My first personal pronouns became Nigger, Monkey, Jungle Bunny, Spook, Spick, Wet Back, Bastard, Punk, and Coon among others. The word "little" always seemed to precede them.

Having been born in Chicago's all black South side, it was a revelation to me when we moved there. I was around eight at the time and it was like falling into a living rainbow. Out of the dozens of kids I hung out with, I doubt there was more than three of any one ethnic group. I personally found it impossible to label any one race with *those people*. You know, like, "Those people are always…"

Being multi-racial, it's not like there are a lot of people like me sitting around complaining about any one particular group. Anytime I found something to complain about, I would quickly find another person in that group with completely opposite characteristics.

From the apartment management on down the line, they set up this, "I don't give a fuck about you" attitude that was all too apparent by the way they all addressed us, in the few instances they had contact with us.

The building was run down. In the four years we lived there, we moved three times. Three different apartments. And each one was just as shitty as the last. There were roaches everywhere along with water bugs, rats, spiders, and silverfish.

In Apartment #207, Mom slept in the bedroom on the rollaway bed while my sister Pamela and I slept on the floor in the living room. I remember waking up in the middle of the night with something tickling my face. It was a cockroach.

There were also times when I was awakened by a rat crawling over my body.

There were always holes in the hallways, graffiti, burn marks, trash, etc. In the elevators you could hardly tell which buttons were for which floors, because someone had taken a cigarette lighter and burned the plastic buttons with the numbers on them. The ceilings of the elevators had also been burned, scorched with people's names and other acts of vandalism. These elevators would get stuck on a regular basis. After the first few times I was stuck in one, I realized there was no one to help get me out. You could ring that emergency bell all day and night, if it worked, and no one would ever come. No one. The first couple of times I got trapped, I would just ring the bell. Then after an hour or so I would start yelling. Never was there a response. It was like I wasn't even there. So eventually I learned not to bother. I found that you could trigger the doors open from the elevator shaft. I learned how to coax the doors open from the inside. Then it was only a matter of triggering the doors above or below you and crawling out. If that didn't work there was an access panel in the ceiling, which I could jump to, crawl out, then trigger the doors in the shaft.

Lakeside was an ugly building, plain grey stone with pebbled balconies of similar color. It looked like the foundation planted above ground instead of below. There were three parking levels laid out across each other like Lincoln Logs. One was at ground level, one above and one below. Each level had its share of abandoned or burned out vehicles, but the one below was the worse. It was the one folks avoided unless you had friends with you. Even when all the lights were working, it was foreboding at best. With half the lights shot out or burned out, it was like a third world dungeon, some post-apocalyptic wasteland a maze of secret happenings to be avoided or passed through as quickly and silently as possible. Cats and rats and roaches were to be found in abundance on the two lower levels. They contributed to the smells of burned rubber and fabric, urine, feces, beer, and booze. This was our playground.

The "playground" that was designated for us was on an upper level. It consisted of a row of two missing and one broken see-saw, and three chain swings, one of which had the plastic seat burned through. When the building was first built, there was a light installed for the playground, but the light and its cover and socket had long since been torn apart. There was, however, still electricity leading to it. We knew this because we ten-year-olds would amuse ourselves when bored by rubbing the exposed red and black wires together in order to make the sparks fly. In all the years we lived there, never once did we see any repairs whatsoever. Not for safety. Not for kids. Not for humanity.

The neighborhood was pure low income, welfare, section eight, disabled, unemployed and underemployed. There were very few people in their middle years, in my building especially. Mostly there were elderly adults or younger kids my age. And it seemed the former were constantly at war with the latter. It's a wonder I'm not still a racist. Sure I was raised a racist by my stepfather, but it was bolstered by the fact that it seemed that not a day went by that some old white guy was giving me shit about something I did or did not do. Over stupid shit too. Once, some old man started trying to give me shit about bringing my bike in the elevator. There was more than enough room. I even stood the bike up on end so as to make even more room once I got in. But as soon as the doors opened, this asshole cut in front of me, rushed in the elevator, then started yellin', "Why don't ya take that thing up the stairs, ya little punk?"

Like I was keeping him from something important. So right back at 'im, I say, "I'm on the 24th floor. Ya wanna carry it for me?"

Holding the doors open for him, I say, "Go, I'll wait."

When the fucker had nothing else to contribute, I let the doors go and heard nothing further from him.

Another time I was riding my bike by nearby Lake Michigan when another old man walking in the middle of the path shouts, "Hey, you little fucker, watch where you're goin'!"

Screeching to a halt, I turned to him and pointing to a nearby sign, I said, "You see that sign right there?" When he looked over I told him, "It says BIKE PATH!!" Startled by my reply, he merely opened his mouth. When nothing came out, I continued on my way. I tell you, it was always something. And it was always over nothing.

Our neighborhood was the hub. It was the nexus of gang activity for miles around us. Our corner was where no less than five city-wide gangs from various territories came together to settle all kinds of scores from women, to money, to drugs. Black, Latin, Mexican, Neo-Nazi White, Hillbilly KKK White and members of several other smaller gangs of many, many other nationalities and races did battle all around our hood. Citywide one statistic states that in the '80s there were nearly a hundred and fifty gangs and almost twenty thousand gang members.

Shootings, stabbings, beatings, kidnappings, rapes, robberies and all sorts of acts of vengeance and violence filled our lives. And I'm not talking about gossip; I'm talking about firsthand knowledge. I've personally witnessed more acts of violence than I can remember. Growing up with it becomes commonplace. You think nothing of it. You just try to steer clear of the cops who were more of a threat than the crooks themselves. See, the crooks knew you; the cops couldn't give a shit. You were all crooks in their eyes. There have been times when gang-bangers threatening to kick my ass surrounded me and one would step up and say, "Naw man. He's cool. Leave him alone." And that would be that. I wouldn't have to worry about being harassed by them again. But anytime the cops would stop me, they would accuse me of all kinds of things and accuse me of anything that crossed their minds. Generally, they treated us like shit and tried their best to make us feel that way too.

According to them, I had no business leaving my house. It was always something.

I would get stopped constantly. I'm talking at ten years old! What the fuck could I possible be getting into at ten years old that those treating me like a piece of shit would keep me out of?! It's no wonder that some kids look up to the gangsters. At least they treated me with respect half the time, which is more than I could have said about the police.

Out of the hundred odd gangs in the city, each was aligned under one of two factions. And these two gangs had members and affiliates all over the city. Even though each gang was autonomous, they were all ruled by one culture. Colors. "What you ride?" was not a query as to your mode of transportation. "What you be about?" was not a way of finding out about your personal moral philosophy.

Each gang sprawled its graffiti over that of the others. It seemed that every square inch of wall space was accounted for by some gang or random artist. They covered the range from scrawled signatures to "King Killers," to huge memorial murals for some dead gang member. We never complained much. Bright colorful things in a world of dirty grays were welcomed. We couldn't understand the homeowner's complaints about their rundown, piece-of-shit, paint-peeling garages being given a little... character. Billboards, sidewalks, telephone poles, walls, cars, everything was fair game for Tagers.

The Lawrence Avenue train station was the closest station to our place. It was about three blocks away near Broadway. Chicago's CTA (Chicago Transit Authority) was another playground of sorts for us. The neighborhood kids never had the 50 cents or so it costs for a ride so we would usually wait below until we heard the train approaching in the direction we needed to go. Then we would all rush up together and vault over the turnstile, rush up the stairs, and board the train just before the doors closed on us. Once we were all on, we would just ride, ride, ride. Sometimes we would ride from one end of the line, switch trains, and then ride all the way to the other end. We could occupy the entire day riding those trains. I would watch as the trains migrated as if across the globe from neighborhood to neighborhood, color to color, country to country. Black, White, Asian, Latino, Indian...

There was an intersection just before you got to the Lawrence station. Mom called it, "The devil's hangout." On that corner there was a mailbox that all the neighborhood miscreants congregated about everyday. They would be drawn to it like filings to a magnet. All manner of street life could be found there from early afternoon until early in the morning. Usually there was an assortment of winos, pimps, hookers, and hustlers that gathered around. It was the place to be. It was like today's Internet. You could find out what was happening with whom in the hood. You could go there and find out who had been arrested, shot, stabbed, raped, robbed or killed. You could find out who had scored and who had lost. Guys would just hang out, pass a fifth of Wild Irish Rose or cheap whisky, and talk about what numbers had hit, or who the police were looking for. Anybody you wanted to find you just had to drop by. "Where Cha'ley at?"

"He's holed up with Verna. His ol' lady been after him fo' a week"

"That nigga' owe me from last Wednesday from that liquor sto' we hit. Tell that muthafucka' if he don't find me I'm a let him know who he fuckin' wit."

Once I left my apartment building and rounded the corner from Lakeside to Sheridan headed towards Lawrence. It was in the afternoon, sun shining and warm with a cool lake breeze. There on the ground lay an older gentleman, upper-lower class and seemingly of Ukrainian descent. He had short salt and pepper hair and blue-gray eyes. He lay on his side in a semi-fetal position with his elbow for a pillow and his other hand covering the side of his head. As I passed, he looked up at me through the blood that was streaming down his face. He had the frightened, frozen look on his face my dog gets when she knows she's in trouble and wants to run but dare not. I didn't even slow my pace. I was on my way to John's to play and this was so... normal that I didn't even tell him about it.

Once you get out of Uptown, the city is rather segregated. Here is the way it goes. The city is divided into co- eccentric rings. Downtown are all businesses and corporations with everyone working there. The North side is predominantly white. Moving West, that side of the city is mostly Latino.

Then, on the South side, it is pretty much black. This was the innermost ring. Going out further the colors would reverse and then reverse again, like some kind of magnetic polarization.

He Returns

Throughout our childhood, our mother had taken us and fled our stepfather's abuses several times. And each time he would come waltzing back into our lives and our home. And she would let him. Just open the door, step aside and watch him walk on in. The first few times I was too young and do not remember.

When we left my dad this time, we had about six months of peace. We did not see nor hear from him at all. At least I didn't. Then one day I was standing in the crowded lobby waiting for the elevator when I felt a big heavy hand on my shoulder. Turning, I expected it to be Jimmy or Frankie or Steve. When I turned around, I saw that same old leather jacket with the windmill patterned leather buttons that I was so familiar with. It was my stepfather. I felt electricity jolt from the tip of my skull to the toes of my feet and I was frozen. We stood there, him smiling down at me, me looking up at him unmoving. "Ain't you gonna say hi to your dad? Ain't you happy to see me?"

"NO!" my mind screamed, "I thought you were gone! I thought you were dead to us!" But I just stood silent, refusing to lie and say yes.

After the silence his smile faded and a steely, cool anger transformed his face into a neutral stone. "I'll see you upstairs." Taking his hand from my shoulder, he walked into the waiting elevator and the doors closed between us.

I wanted to scream! Leave them all behind. I wanted to find them and warn them that he had found us! I wanted to run, but there was no place to go. No one to turn to. I remember standing there in that lobby looking around at the people still waiting for the crowded elevators. I remember rows upon rows of mailboxes that represented whole, entire families: mother, father, children, brothers, sisters... families. Standing there alone in a crowd of humanity, I felt more alone than I ever had before. Somehow I just couldn't bring myself to go up there into that apartment where he was, even if Mom and Pam were there. I turned around, went back outside and wandered around until it was well past dark, far beyond my normal curfew. The stunned numbness never seemed to leave me. But eventually I had to go back home. And there he sat. At the dinner table he was reading the paper like nothing had ever happened. Violence, vengeance, anger, even death, I was prepared for it all. I was prepared for anything... anything but nothing. He didn't even look up when I came in, like he didn't know I was there. Which was just fine with me. I hoped it would stay that way forever. My hope, however, was futile. Things went back to the way they were before we escaped. My mother returned us to the life we had just escaped from. And Pamela and I were left with more false hopes and broken dreams than we left with.

A few more years crept by with its usual morbid routine of pain and torture. A funny thing about pain: it's something every living creature seeks to avoid. Until a certain point. Once you've had it long enough and in certain forms, you grow accustomed to it. Then if you are deprived of it, you begin to seek it out in different forms. You feel somehow incomplete without it. It is the only way you know how to function. So you continue...

Math

Lou was a friend of Dad's from the Army. I think it was the longest friendship he ever had. Lou wasn't around constantly, but he was always just around the corner. He was always nice to me. Short and stocky, he didn't talk much shit. Easy-going and even a little playful. Once at an outing the three of us were splashing around the waterfront. Dad made me climb on Lou's back while he swam around the tumbled remnants of the foundations of the World's Fair. I remember not knowing whether to be more afraid of being seen in public in my undies, or drowning. I was scared shitless.

Lou and his girlfriend, Susan, were the nicest to me of all the alcoholics, drug addicts, pimps, prostitutes, liars and thieves he had for friends. She was sweet and pretty, and had long, straight blond hair like my mom's. But she liked me. I mean... she liked me. She listened to my babble, she laughed at my jokes, she smiled when she saw me, and she always made sure to say goodbye to me when she left. I was in love.

Then one afternoon they were over for supper. Mom was helping me in the kitchen with my math homework using flashcards. Math was my worst subject. We got to a problem I didn't know the answer to. When Mom tried to give me a hint, Dad angrily stopped her. "Naw! Naw! Don't help him out! Make him do it!" It was that tone, that old savagery, that old venom. It got my adrenaline, my fight, freeze or flight response going. Even though I was terrified of the violence that waited, deep down I thought I was safe, because he never beat us when there were witnesses present. Today however, I learned company only stopped the physical beatings. As my mind raced from potential solution to the next, he got even angrier. "Goddamnit! You useless son of a bitch! Stupid motherfucker! You are gonna sit there until you get the answer – and if you guess again, I will beat the shit outta you!"

I could have died in that moment. I was so mortified I wanted to cease to exist. Out of the corner of my eye I can still see Lou and my first "girlfriend" looking wordlessly on. I had no hope that they would come to my rescue, as I knew Mom never would. I knew the world better than that even then. But before this moment, his abuse, our shame, had always been our secret. None had ever seen it firsthand. And now, not 10 feet away from me, three grown, living human adults stood and watched me with my face reddened, eyes watering, lip trembling – fighting the tears. I wrestled with the terrible agony of a soul-deep indescribable pain that no physical beating could even come close to... and said not a word, moved not a finger. So there I sat... alone.

"You can sit there until you turn as black as the inside of my ass, but you will get it right." And with that he turned back to his spaghetti and they all returned to their garlic bread and Kool-Aid, and resumed their small talk, their chit-chat. I sat paralyzed staring through tears, snot running down my lip, and I died.

Shotgun

We were living on the twenty-fourth floor when Dad came home with a shotgun. He had stolen it from someone or somewhere and was proud to show it off to us. Then he gave me that spiel about, "This is not a toy." And, "I don't wanna ever catch you playing with this." Then he loaded it and propped it in a corner for easy access in case he ever needed it in a hurry.

When the Fourth of July rolled around, he was nowhere to be found until shortly before midnight. He came in, flipped on the lights, and got everyone out of bed. "C'mon in here, Goddamnit'." But he was happy for a change. Happy and high. You'd have thought he'd hit the numbers of something. He had the shotgun in his hand as we rounded the corner into the dining room.

Once everyone was in the room, he slid open the window, after having a little bit of trouble he wouldn't have had were he not high. Undaunted by the screen covering the window, he proceeded to shove the barrel right through the screen at the left-hand side before ripping it down to the right. Not satisfied, he reached his hand through the hole he'd just made, grabbed it by the aluminum frame and ripped the whole thing out of the window, leaving it hanging by the lower right corner.

The rest of us wisely kept our distance from him, knowing anything was possible in spite of his deceptive smiles and jubilant behavior.

Stepping up to the open windowsill, he leaned out, pointed the barrel skyward and let loose a blast of twelve-gauge buck. BLA-DOW! BLA-DOW! BLA-DOW!

He laughed like it was the funniest thing in the world. Then went into the kitchen and fixed himself something to eat, leaving us standing there like we didn't exist.

An Unexpected Visitor

I used to think falling twenty-four floors would take forever. If you were the one falling, I imagine it would feel like eternity. But to those of us watching, it can be over in an instant.

Mom and I were in the dining room. She had just gotten out of the shower and was lying on the couch with her head towards the windowed wall. A threadbare, pink towel was wrapped around her head soaking up the moisture from her long, blonde hair, which she held in place from behind with her right hand. I stood to her left. It was one of those nowhere moments, the time between one answer and the next question. A time of stillness. A time of silence.

A movement to my right caught my eye and as I looked out on the sunny, cloudless sky to the north, I saw what for the moment was the impossible. On our narrow four-inch-wide pebbled windowsill walked a cat. Black. Sparky?!? I thought, panic rising. No. Taller, thinner and with shorter hair than our own.

"How'd he get up here?" I puzzled. Mom craned her head around from where she lay, still holding her towel in place, then returned to her original position. Then she did a double-take, puzzlement on her face.

The window was open, but the screens were fixed in place and could not be opened. The cat arched her back and rubbed herself gently against the soft, giving, barrier, mewling softly. Then she turned around and did it again as Mom watched from the corner of her eye. And there we were. Neither of us spoke. It seemed we held our breath while we watched that cat go back and forth, and watched the wind tug at her fur. Neither of us moved for fear of upsetting her delicate balance.

A thousand thoughts raced through my head. I'd imagined she had jumped from sill to sill from neighbors down the hall. Each window ledge was separated from the next by a three or four foot chasm that led to the asphalt below. As I stood frozen, I tried to will her to go back the way she'd came and return to the safety of the open, screenless window of her home.

Then it happened. On her final turn, her hind legs slipped of the edge and my heart froze painfully in my chest. Mom let out a soft cry of surprise and started to rise, startled from her reclining position. Then salvation. The front claws, splayed across the rocky surface found solid purchase and arrested her fall.

Simultaneously Mom and I both let out the breaths we had been holding in a mutual sigh of relief. And in an instant she was gone. Just as she began to pull herself up, her claws failed her and she was gone before we even realized she was falling. Mom slowly eased herself back into her prone position, resigned, as all emotion left her face.

As fast as I could, I ran into my bedroom where there was no screen to keep me from seeing her descending form. I'd imagined she would be about halfway to the ground by the time I got there. Charging the window, I stopped my momentum with my hands braced on the sill. Thrusting my head and shoulders out into space, I reached downward with my eyes only to find I was too late. Far below I could make out the tiny, black spot that made up her remains. Unmoving. Surprisingly intact in a nearly empty parking level, twenty-three stories below. I had imagined she would have shattered like a pumpkin, but I couldn't even see a spray of blood.

The next day, as soon as I was allowed outside, I made my way to that upper level of the lot and found only a dark, greasy looking stain where that gentle, playful visitor came to rest.

Height

Oh God, I am so small. Dad was high and screwing around, wrestling with Mom and me like he usually did before losing it. We were living on the top floor, the 24th floor of the project. It was summertime and our high windows were partially open to let in a cool lake breeze. Right now, adding to my fear of heights, the last psychological barrier to freefall, the window screen had been ripped free only moments earlier, leaving nothing between us inside and a 24-story freefall. At some point during his horsing around, Dad had scooped up my little body up in his arms, we were all laughter and smiles. However, my nervousness grew as we came nearer the open window. Stopping before it, he asked, "How'd you like it if I dropped you out the window?" And I laughed at Daddy's joke just before he faked in that direction, three feet away. I had become aware of my mother standing stiffly in the middle of the room. He swung me again as my laughter became more of a nervous giggle while his continued as strong as ever. This time my feet and legs had gone out the window.

Turning, he faced the window head on and held me with one arm while with his other he ripped the window open as wide as it would go. Mom took a step forward and froze. She and I both knew that the more we protested, the more it would goad him on. He walked forward until his thighs touched the lower edge of the windowsill. And as I was carried out over that open space, I thought about that cat Mom and I saw fall from the next ledge over. Looking down, I could still see the darkened stain its blood left on the top deck of the parking lot.

Outside, the always-high winds tugged at my hair and clothing like a greedy thief.

When he tossed me up into the air the first time, my eyes went wide like an animal caught in a trap. "Wait! Stop!" I shouted. A cry escaped my mother's lips and laughter came from his. At first my arms had been wrapped tightly around his neck, but as he tossed me up the second time he nearly broke their grip and it threatened to roll me out of his arms. I clung even tighter. The third toss broke Mom completely and she began to scream for him to stop. They were the screams that have been permanently seared into my mind:

"Stop!" "Winston!" "Stop!"

Those three words screamed, cried, begged, and sobbed, over and over again in my mind for nearly a decade. And then echo for eternity. If I met God today, I would ask him to erase those words from the universe.

In that instant I realized that he would only keep going until both Mom and I stopped giving him any reaction at all. You see, he lived for the torture. He loved to see us beg, scream, cry.

So I let go. Closing my mouth to my screams, I lay back and stared up at the clouds. I can still see the pale, cerulean blueness and the wispy, thin whiteness of the brush-painted clouds. Several tosses later, Mom's cries had subsided as well as his laughter, but I didn't see either of them, just the lazy slowness of those clouds.

When he pulled me in, I was almost disappointed. He seemed bothered like a drunk sobering. Mom still stood, jaw clenched, in the middle of the floor, her hands across her mouth. Setting my feet on solid ground again, he stared at me mutely for a moment. "What's the matter? You didn't think I was gonna drop you, did you?" And I gave him nothing. I just stood there looking at him, waiting for whatever was next. He stood, she stood, and I stood.

To this day I don't know which would have a more severe and lasting effect on me, what came before or what would come next. His sadism not having drunk its fill with me, he turned next to my mother. She moved stiffly forward where he pushed her to the open window. At the window again, he picked her up from the floor, held her out the window and repeated his twisted ritual. Hugging herself, she squeezed her eyes tight and endured the trial with only a brief yelp on the first toss out the high window. His laughter was more subdued and shorter lived this time, taking less pleasure in the game. Watching intently, I took secret joy in our thieving of his sport. With a few more tosses of her rag-doll form, he grew bored and pulled her back in. Setting her back on the floor, he seemed genuinely upset. Again we stood and stared. With nowhere to run, we patiently awaited his next torture while he desperately tried to think of something else to ruin us. Becoming frustrated, he finally looked at us disgustedly and muttered, "You guys don't know how to have any fun," and stomped off into the bedroom.

Fire

Several times there were fires in the building. The first time was no big deal. I mean, we were on the second floor. I jumped from greater heights just for fun. But after we moved up to the 24th floor, it was a different story. I can still clearly hear my dad's voice from that day. "Eddie, wake up." There was something unusual in the sound of those words. Something that made me awaken instantly. At first I thought it was just the sleep in my eyes, but then I became aware of the smell of smoke.

As Dad hustled Pamela, Mom and me to the window, I heard the sound of fire engines. Instantly it popped into my head that we were going to the window where the fire trucks would raise ladders and we would climb down. Cool! I was actually excited by the idea. Imagine the sinking feeling in the pit of my stomach when after reaching the window, I realized we were no longer on the 2nd floor! Looking down on those tiny red specks that were the fire trucks, my jaw must have dropped halfway to the floor. Then against all hope, I found myself praying that they had some newfangled kind of ladder that would miraculously be able to reach us as we stood there. Such was not to be the case. When all the ladders were fully extended, they only reached a few stories up. Oh-my-God. We're dead. Dad told us to get washcloths, wet them and hold them over our nose and mouth. Meanwhile, he wet a bath towel and placed it along the bottom of the bedroom door to keep the smoke out.

And then we waited.

I remember asking Mom if they were going to land helicopters on the roof to evacuate us, but she said the roof wouldn't support the weight. Hell, it can hover can't it? I can climb a rope! We watched thick smoke oozing from the windows far below. The fire eventually spread almost completely across the third and fourth floors before it could be contained. It took most of the day before the smoke had cleared enough so that we could leave our apartment.

There is nothing like the terror of going to leave your top floor apartment and seeing the halls full of dense, poisonous smoke. Once I ventured to try the stairwells on either side of our building to see which one was passable. The first one was full of black poison and heat. The second was full of fire. I can't tell you how many fires we had there over the years. I can only say that after a while you just resign yourself to your fate. Like the video of the Twin Towers or the hotel in Asia, you will eventually make your choice. And sometimes it changes: face the fire or jump.

The prospect of fire is pretty terrifying. The anticipation is a monster. The belching, billowing smoke, the acrid, cloying smell tearing through your nose, throat and chest were all too real. The foggy-headedness is indescribable, because of the mixed feelings it brings. At first you fight the panic, then you become drowsy and tired. And then you become afraid of the drowsiness. It seeks to drag you down into the well of unconsciousness. And like that it goes on for as long as you can hold out or until you surrender. You can either surrender to death... or surrender to Life.

The surrender to Life is the most wonderful thing. You cease to care about all of the pain and hardships that seemed an insurmountable wall only moments ago. They become merely speed bumps on the highway to Life. Nothing else really matters. You are aware of obstacles, but what you really see is the path around, above, below, between or through them. There you find peace. Like being in a Zen fugue state, your existence is stripped to its basic elements, the bare essentials. The eye of the hurricane.

Jumper

I rode my bike from Lakeside to John's house on Argyle. Passing under the "El" at Lawrence, I emerged at the short street behind the Uptown National Bank, which was on Broadway. This was the bank that would eventually sponsor the competition where, my senior year in high school, I would win a citywide essay contest with my essay entitled: "Big Business and the American Dream." Looking down that lonely, little side street, I saw what looked like one of the thousands of homeless men that populated back alleys all across the city. But he was lying in the street. From half a block away, something struck my nine-year-old brain as odd. Riding closer, I noted that he was wearing the brightest, whitest, cleanest pair of boxer-shorts I had ever seen anywhere, let alone on a homeless person.

As I drew closer, details begin to emerge. There were bright red, perfect polka dots on the boxers. And his pants were down around his thighs and... he had no head. He was lying on his stomach and his shoulders were butting right up against the curb. He had a curb in place of a head. Strangely there was no blood visible. A matted, dark, roundish thing covered with dark, brown hair lay on the other side of me. Stopping my bike about ten feet from the body, I looked from one to the other wondering... if...

Looking up to the top of the fifteen story, art-deco style building, I saw there were no open windows as it was a cold day. He had to have gone off the top. A story flashed through my mind. Dad once told me, as we were watching the old black-and-white Superman TV show, that the guy who played Superman thought he really could fly and killed himself by jumping off an old, art-deco style skyscraper.

I wondered if he jumped, or was he pushed. Why was he up there? Why were his pants down? The fall? The impact? I pictured George Reeves in his Superman outfit jumping off a black-and-white rooftop under a black-and-white sky.

Sitting there I accepted the insanity as part of the strange sanity that was my life. I took a moment. Looking left, right, body, and head. Not a soul around me stopped or even looked in our direction. It was like a Kafka film. Unreal... surreal. "If this isn't real, then I'm not really here either." Nope, there they were. Body, head, left, right.

Having no idea what to do, I left. Calling the police was never a consideration. I knew even then that historically the police either didn't listen to kids, or else took out their frustrations on them because they could. Cops were to be avoided. "Shut up," and "Get outta the way," or "Keep it movin' folks," were the usual messages we could expect from them. Tell my folks? Why? What would they do anyway? Heck, Dad would probably use it as just another excuse to beat me.

Arriving at John's place, I told him everything. He wanted to see, so we mounted up and headed back over. By now the area was crawling with cops, ambulances and crowds of on-lookers. The mob was so thick we couldn't even see through their legs. From desolation to mob scene. One minute nobody wanted to hear what you had to say, the next minute the whole world wanted to know. The extremes only added to the insanity. Shaking our heads, we rode on by.

Jumped!

Life in the ghetto is, to say the least, unpredictable. That is the one thing that forces further creativity and independence.

It is also the one thing that makes it so hard to fit in to the rest of the world.

We who are raised there forget that we make up only the smallest fraction of our country. That we were the minutest fragment of the world at large wasn't even a consideration. When you are struggling just for physical, mental, and emotional survival, the rest of the world pretty much ceases to exist. The surreal jungle you dwell in becomes your only reality, the only reality. Your focus becomes the one square city block where you are at that moment.

You must constantly be aware of your surroundings, you must constantly be on alert, and you can never let your guard down. For the jungle doesn't care that you are weak, young, girl, boy, rich, or poor. It only sees predators and prey.

We were about ten years old, John and I . We're walking up Lawrence Avenue. We had gotten about three blocks from my place when out of a doorway just in front of us poured five guys. Each of them was about twice our size and at least fifteen years old. Three were Black, one White and one Latino. Two of them had pistols.

"Get in there!" one shouted as they shoved us roughly into the doorway in which they had been lying in wait. Once in the small, now crowded foyer of the three-flat, the biggest one pushed a chrome semi-automatic in my face. Another shoved a gunmetal blue revolver at John.

Surrounding us, they jabbed those guns painfully into our ribs, stomach, and face. They threatened to shoot us and demanded our money. Then they threatened to take our money and just shoot us for the fun of it. Fortunately, we were two poor, broke, ten-year-olds and didn't have any money to be stolen. Unfortunately, they weren't really after the money. What they wanted was a victim. And we were it.

Just when they were getting warmed up and the real beating was about to begin, we heard a door close up above and two voices. When our assailants heard this, they quickly hid the guns behind our bodies and their leader hissed loudly down at us, "Y'all better not say nothin'!" They started chatting with each other trying not to look like the jackals they were.

Moments later a middle-aged white couple came down the stairs. When they reached the bottom, they looked up and saw us.

John and I saw this as our one chance at salvation. I remember looking into their eyes with a silent, desperate scream for help. I know they saw the petrified pleading there in my face. Taking in the scene they hesitated, almost backing up.

Then the spell was broken. Rather than save us, they chose to ignore us. The man took his woman by the elbow, put his head down and they silently hurried past us and out the door. When I watched that door close in on us after they had disappeared outside, it was like a lid closing on my coffin.

We were then told that we were going to be taking a little walk. "All right now, when I open up this door you are going to run across the street and down the alley, and if you stop or try to get away, I'm gonna put this up your nose and pull the trigger." He waved the big gleaming gun slowly under my nostrils for emphasis.

One of the others opened the door, stepped out and looked up and down the street. After a moment, he stepped back in. "Let's go!"

Suddenly John and I were both shoved out the door onto the street and were propelled quickly across it. Looking both ways, I saw no hope of rescue. Secretly I cursed the couple for not even bothering to send help for us.

Those young men were experienced professionals. They surrounded us immediately on all four sides. In the middle of Lawrence Avenue, I made a decision.

Whispering to John, I told him what I had in mind. "Just before we enter the alley, you break right and I'll go left. They'll have to split up to catch us." I was thinking maybe we could lose at least a few of them and even out the odds a bit.

"Naw man, just be cool," he shot back.

Great, I thought. He's got a plan too. Looking up the alley, I tried to think ahead and figure out what his plan was. Was there a better escape avenue ahead? Did he see someone up there he knew? I decided to wait and follow his lead.

As we went deeper into the alley, my sense of dread grew. I could see only one reason they would want such a secluded location. Now I know what one must feel like walking to the gallows or guillotine or firing squad.

We came upon a recessed loading dock of a closed business. They stopped and savagely shoved us both into a huge cavernous loading bay. "Get in there!"

My feeling of foreboding just took a big leap ahead. It was like a big, dirty mausoleum. It was dark and dirty, and secluded and scary, maybe sixty feet across, thirty deep and covered above.

John was shoved so hard that he sprawled face first on the ground. Another one grabbed him, picked him up and along with me, they threw us against the wall.

The creepiest thing about it was that three of them were in the background near our prison's entrance gleefully cavorting around. They were jumping, shoving each other, throwing bricks and breaking bottles on the ground. It was like an orgy of violence. They were clearly working themselves up into a frenzy. The two who faced us had smirks on their faces like they knew something that we didn't.

John ducked and moved as one threw random punches at his face and head. When the guy pulled his dick out, I cannot describe to you the depths of fear and apprehension that hit me like an irresistible tidal wave.

I felt panic gnawing at my guts and I prepared myself to break and run, and if John wanted to "just be cool," he could do that by his damned self. In some bizarre way, having the shit stomped out of me didn't scare me half as much as being raped did.

Even at such a young age, I'd heard stories of women I knew being raped. Kids get to hear that kind of stuff on the news, in the movies and on the streets all the time.

But before I could move, a thick stream of urine poured forth in a long, steady arc from him to John. I stared at the yellow stream dumbfounded, confused as the yellow line drew patters across John's pants, legs, and feet.

Caught between relief and wondering what the hell he was pissing on John for, I told myself to stop expecting it to make sense. He was doing it because he could. As I stepped aside, John danced and moved trying to avoid the stream while those assholes laughed at us. Eventually his legs from the knees to his feet were crisscrossed with dark wetness.

My attacker faced me and looked me up and down while he tried to think of something creative he could do to outdo his partner. Then he saw that I was wearing an almost new pair of Converse All-Stars.

Back then they were not expensive, but in demand. Also they were the only pair of maroon ones I had seen. Apparently my captor liked them also. Looking down into my eyes, he stepped menacingly closer. "Gimme those shoes," he said through a twisted smile.

At my response all action ceased. "No."

The silence was immediate. Everyone stopped what they were doing, even the guy pissing. "What?!"

Now all eyes were on him. His friends gathered around us not knowing what to do next. Waiting to see what he would do, they looked from him to me. John was temporarily forgotten beside me.

"I said take 'em off, motherfucker!!" Feeling my defiance growing within me, I stood a little taller, enjoying the confusion I had caused among them. "I'm ain't takin' off my shoes."

This pair of shoes was one of the few nice things that I had ever owned in my entire life up to that point. I'd had ten years of hand-me-down clothes, food stamps and second-hand toys. It was nice to have all those, but I was always aware that they all belonged to someone else first.

These had never been worn by anyone else but me. And they fit. And far above any of that, it was my only pair of shoes. I'd be damned if I was going to take them of and just hand them over to some asshole just because he said so. If he wanted to beat my ass and take them off me then so be it. But I wasn't going to just hand them over.

"What!?!" he stammered, his voice rising another octave. Fists balled up at his sides. I waited for him to swing. He was so mad that his whole body began to tremble. Looking at him, I almost laughed as his lip quivered, and his friends all stood around sputtering and fuming but not knowing what to do.

I knew better than to laugh at him in front of all his friends. The situation was bad enough without adding fuel to the fire. While I was fully prepared to take his punches, I wasn't prepared for what happened next.

He began to pace the dock. He roamed around so furious he did not know what to do with himself. Then he started searching. He went around looking at the bricks and broken bottles lying around on the ground. My eyes followed his searching of every brick, every item. He selected, picked up, and then rejected two of each.

Then he found it.

There lying on the ground was a wicked sharp, jagged, burned remnant of a one-by-four with twisted rusted nails sticking out of the sharpened end. His eyes lit up in triumph. Snatching it up, he stomped back over to me and in one motion jabbed it hard into my stomach.

I had tensed up my stomach in reflex and it backed me up against the cold of the brick wall behind me, and held me there hard with the sharp points digging into my stomach.

In a low whisper, he hissed at me, "I said take 'em off." Looking in his eyes I saw that whereas before he hadn't been prepared for any resistance now he was fully prepared to gut me like a fish. In order to keep his rep on the street, to keep his crew following him, I would have to be made an example of.

While I was fully prepared to take an ass-kicking by five guys just to keep my All-Stars, I was not, however, prepared to be eviscerated, killed for a pair of shoes. So with that firmly in mind I slowly and reluctantly took them off.

With my shoes now in his possession, it was time for the fat lady to sing. Pushing us into the center, they formed up in a ring around us giddy with anticipation.

Both John and I knew it was about to begin in earnest. A sob escaped his lips an instant before the first blow fell. They fell upon us like a pack of wild animals.

The terrifying thing was not the beating, but the blood-chilling frenzied delight they all took in it. It was like being caught up in a howling tornado.

Screaming and whooping like banshees, they punched, kicked and stomped us from every angle. Blows rained down on us from all sides.

Eventually in the midst of the chaos, we were knocked to the ground. Both of us dodged and rolled around trying to avoid ten stomping and kicking feet.

I can still hear the popping as my numb, tingling, ringing head rebounded off the gritty concrete again and again.

Out of the corner of my eye, I saw one of them raising a huge chunk of concrete above his head with both hands.

I screamed out just as John moved his face out of the way of falling death.

I then began to cry. A cry of rage, a scream of anguish for the unfairness of it all. Our cries mixed with theirs with that unholy chorus.

Through my tears I saw John rise, picking up his thick black glasses with the coke-bottle lenses. He stood there trying to put them on and before he could finish, a savage kick knocked him right back down. Then the grim dance would repeat itself.

Three times he got up. Three times he got knocked back down. I watched as they laughed at him like a wind-up toy that will bump into the wall only to back up and do it again repeatedly until it winds down.

Throughout all this, two things were constant in the back of my mind. One: somewhere nearby a dog was barking. Incessantly. It was a German Shepard by the sound of it and it knew what was going on. Was its owner not home? Why was no one checking to see what it was barking at? Second: Why was no one attracted to the sounds of our attack? Neither our cries nor the screams of our attackers drew any attention from the neighbors.

It was impossible that no one had heard us. The warehouse was just off two busy streets: Lawrence and Sheridan. And it was also just across the alley from homes that stretched up the street. It was a residential neighborhood.

My mind drifted around the block seeing in my mind's eye the traffic, pedestrians, and people sitting in their comfortable homes drinking coffee and watching television, and turning up the volume to drown out our screams.

Then suddenly it was over.

I don't even remember them leaving. They were just... gone. I must've lost consciousness. For how long, I don't know. I just remember becoming aware of sobbing.

It was mine.

John was lying there curled into a fetal position with his back to me, motionless. I lay there listening for the sounds of our assailants but heard none. Then I just lay there some more. Our crying echoed across the empty cavern.

Then I became aware that the dog was no longer barking. I began to wonder how much time had passed. The chill, gray daylight had not changed that I could tell.

Finally when I had rested enough, I tried to move. Slowly at first, gingerly. I hurt all over. Rolling over on my back, I looked to my right. There, not fifty feet away, was that German Shepard. And standing at the fence by his side was a gray-haired old lady in her house robe. There was silver covering her head and in her hand she held a white mug of coffee. She was just staring at us.

She had been standing there for some time, just watching us.

"What are you kids doing back here?"

"Bleeding, dumb-ass," was what I wanted to say. Instead I gave her my most withering look.

It never even crossed my mind to ask her for help. If our screams hadn't elicited it, then asking wouldn't either.

It had been at least ten minutes from the beginning of the screaming until it was over. And that bitch just hid up in her house until it was all over. She couldn't even pick up the phone. Then she came down here to stare at us, rubberneck. To fuckin' spectate.

"I heard my dog barking and I thought you kids might've been playing 'cause you know kids are always playing back here and it's dangerous and..."

Yeah, that explains why you waited for it all to be over before you came back here to check things out.

Imagine: You come out your door, down into your yard where your dog has been barking incessantly for the last quarter of an hour. You discover two ten-year-old kids lying semi-conscious in a brick and glass-strewn back alley. They are bloodied, bruised, and their clothes are torn. One boy has no shoes, only torn and dirtied once-white socks.

Now, what do you do? Run to help them? Shout for help? Call 911? Ask them if they need help? They can barely stand, so they obviously do.

No, this old biddy stands and watches us like ants under a magnifying glass. I wanted to shout at her, to scream, to wake her up: HELP US!!! But at the time all I really wanted to do was go home.

Finally, rolling over, I made my way up onto my hands and knees. I crawled slowly towards where John lay. As I got closer, I heard a faint moaning. He had begun to slowly, subtly rock himself back and forth. Shaking him gently, I got no response.

Then I began to worry.

It took me a few tries to rouse him. Calling his name and shaking him harder, I asked him if he was okay just to see if he would respond. He slowly began to stir. He was disoriented and at first and did not know what was happening. When I told him they were gone, he anxiously looked around to find out if it was true.

"My glasses!" he blurted out in a panic. It seemed surreal that after what we had just endured he would be in a panic about those ugly-assed glasses of his.

I helped him scour the loading dock looking for them. We both crawled around on our hands and knees like a couple of stray dogs until he finally found them broken.

By then I'd had enough of crawling around and was ready to attempt standing up on shaky legs. It took me a while and once on my feet I was dizzy, so I did not trust myself to walk. But after a minute my head began to steady.

I walked over to where John was sitting on the ground and asked him if he felt like he could walk, but he didn't answer. He was in pretty bad shape and I was trying to decide if I should call an ambulance, but I did not want to leave him alone in that alley. Dragging him out was about all I could manage on my own and that didn't seem like a good idea.

Just then he rose up to his knees and I helped him to his feet. He was as unsteady as I had been. Finally we both steadied ourselves by leaning on each other.

In one of the most sublime moments I have ever experienced, John looked down and saw my shoeless feet amidst all the broken glass and rock. At first, I thought he was about to fall over. As my grip around him tightened, I realized that he was not falling but bending.

Eventually he bent all the way down. Then he untied his left shoe. It was a black suede Rocker with a black sole. Once untied, he removed it... and handed it to me. "Here, put this on."

That single act of kindness touched me in a way that few things have in my long and eventful life.

I tied it on, that loose suede Rocker, black and fuzzy, and together, each supported by the other, we limped out of that alley.

At the corner, he asked, "What are you gonna do now? Do you wanna come to my house?" His house was twice as far away as my apartment.

"No, I'm gonna go home." Handing his shoe back to him, I told him thanks. Neither of us knew what to say at this point, so without even saying good-bye, we each turned to our separate points of the compass and headed home.

I wasn't surprised, but it's always kind of odd when you are walking through throngs of people bloodied and torn. They all notice you, but pretend not to. They look at your body, but not your eyes. They show concerned looks on their faces, but not enough to break that barrier that is the code of the street: mind your own business. So they just pass you by. We were like ghosts passing without touching each other's lives. Strangers trapped together.

When I entered our apartment, Pamela was sitting at the dining room table doing homework. Pamela is five years older than me and much taller. Whereas I was the loudmouth, the clown, or the troublemaker (depending on which of my teachers you spoke to), she was always considered the good one, quiet and studious.

As soon as I opened the door she looked up at me, and instantly I saw shock written across her face. I didn't even want to look in a mirror. I knew what I must look like.

"What happened to you? Who beat you up? Where are your shoes!?"

"I got jumped."

When I moved towards the bedroom to lie down, she stopped me. "Who jumped you?" I told her briefly where and what had happened and she stood silently for a moment. Then a dark look crossed her face.

"Go get your jacket," she said to me.

Damn. I just wanted go to bed. When I got back from getting my jacket, she handed me a pair of shoes. They were a pair of her brown suede sandals and could be tightened enough to fit me.

Once I had them on, she said, "Come with me," and taking my hand in hers, we headed for the door.

"W… where we goin'?"

"We're going to get your shoes back."

I stopped there in the hallway torn between two opposing thoughts: On the one hand, I was afraid to put her safety at risk with a bunch of thugs her age. Not to mention getting my own ass kicked for the second time in the same afternoon. On the other hand, she was determined. And I have to be honest with you, I was surprised. Not because I didn't think she cared, but because no one, and I mean no one, had ever stuck up for me before and to be honest, I wanted to see how it worked.

I saw them from a block away. I recognized the leader in his bright red hoodie, but the other three guys I didn't. Each was about the same age and height as my sister. They were clowning around with no fear of anyone. Fresh from their latest conquest and full of their own bravado, they pushed and shoved each other around like they owned the streets.

As we got closer he recognized me and turned his face to the brick wall as if examining the mortar, obviously trying not to be seen.

"Are these the people that beat you up?" Pamela asked me.

"Yeah, that's one of 'em," I said, pointing to the asshole. The other three guys I didn't recognize. Bold, they gathered around us to see what was happening. This time when they surrounded us, I was not afraid. One: I was determined to fight back. Earlier I had tried the "turn other cheek" thing hoping things wouldn't be as bad. That didn't go well at all. Two: I was motivated this time by the instinct to protect my sister, even though she was older than me and calling the shots. I was fully prepared to kill everyone there to protect her.

The leader had turned and started off up the street. "Hey you!" she shouted at him.

Trying his best to look innocent, he sheepishly asked, "Who, me?" His friends laughed out loud at him knowing that he was in trouble being called out by a girl.

"Don't act stupid. You know who I'm talkin' to!" At this his friends all fell silent sensing that she meant business. I became aware of someone coming up the alley. I watched as he approached to see if I recognized him. When he looked up and saw me, he immediately did an about-face.

"There's another one!" I shouted.

"Get back here!" she called out to him. He hesitated and when he did, she said with more menace than I have ever heard from her, "Don't make me chase you down."

It worked. He turned back to us and sheepishly came and stood before us with guilty, downcast eyes. Now the other boys had backed off as if fearing she would suddenly erupt and they would be caught up in her fury.

Squaring off nose to nose with the two attackers, she spoke calmly and clearly. "Now, I don't know why y'all beat up my little brother and I don't care. But I want his shoes back and I want them back now."

I was going to step in front of her in case one of them took a swing, but honestly I was afraid of her as well.

"HEY!" came a booming shout from across the street. Everyone turned to see who the voice belonged to.

Ooooh-my-God. I saw coming across the street, two of the hugest women I had ever seen in my life. Both were as tall as Pamela, who is a tall girl, and each weighed in at about two, two-fifty. Easy.

"What 'chu doin' with my brother?!"

Those five assholes twice my size with my sister by my side, I was prepared for 'em. Now add these two into the mix and I was ready to rethink the whole thing. But Pamela, however, was unfazed.

Turning to face them, she said, "Your brother and his friends jumped my little brother here, beat him up and stole his shoes."

"What?"

"Nuh-uh! No we didn't!" he shouted.

Turning to her friend, the asshole's sister said, "Didn't I see Terrel carrying a pair of shoes?"

"Yeah, those All-Stars?" The sister looked down at me and asked, "Were they maroon All-Stars?"

"Yeah, brand new," I replied.

Turning back to her brother, she said "Boy! Go get this child his shoes back!" As he opened his mouth to protest, quick as a whip, she smacked him across the side of his head. "Now!"

To us she said, "Ought to be ashamed of hisself, beatin' up a little kid. You okay baby?"

"Yeah," I said.

While I watched her brother run off down the street and disappear around the corner, Pamela and the two girls began talking with each other like they were old friends.

It took him about five minutes to make the trip and then he came from around the corner with my shoes hanging from his left hand, laces dangling loosely. He slowed to a walk as he came into view and we all stopped as he approached. He handed the shoes to his sister who then turned and handed them to me.

"Here you go, baby. You just let me know if he messes with you again." I looked at him darkly as she handed them to me. He couldn't even meet my eyes. Briefly I wondered how badly I could hurt him in a suicide attack before the crowd jumped me. And then I remembered that Pamela would probably be attacked too, and then maybe both of us would get our asses kicked.

Besides, my sister had just publicly humiliated the creep and his family was there to see it.

Soon the entire neighborhood would know three things. One: This guy needed all his friends with him just to beat up little kids. Two: He was really just a great big pussy. And three: My sister is one baaaad-assss!

On that day she was officially upgraded in my eyes from big sister to hero. But I learned some valuable life-lessons on that day… many life-lessons.

That one day has made me a far better man for both being jumped and the return of the shoes. From that day forward I never again let anyone lay hands on me without making them pay a price for it. You might kick my ass or take something from me, but it's gonna cost ya.

I also learned the appreciation for talk as a weapon. The sound of one's voice, timber, level, and projection were all just as important as what you said. And what you said could be uses as a weapon just as much as a fist or knife or gun.

Just lying there and taking the ass-kicking was no longer an option for me. That was the last time I got my ass kicked, outside of the house that is.

Dad still regularly used me as his own personal punching and kicking tool. But outside the house, I learned to pick my battles. Sure, I did my share of running when I was outnumbered or outgunned, but that was the last time I got beat one-on-one. I even took on whole groups of guys when occasion demanded. Thankfully, that has been very seldom.

Seeing Pamela stand in front of those thugs and the sisters undaunted, taught me worlds about confidence and about being willing to take an ass-kicking if the price is high enough. I also learned the power of determination. He who wants a thing badly enough and is willing to sacrifice the most for it, will get it.

Elevator

It was less than a week after John and I got jumped that Dad told me to go and meet Mom at the Lawrence Avenue train station. He probably wanted to get rid of me so he could get high alone.

I put on my denim jacket and left for that unpleasant trip. I didn't want to go. I hated standing around there for so long waiting as each train came and went without her. If it wasn't the junkies and winos, it was boredom.

Boredom was a child's worst enemy. It wasn't unusual for me to wait around for an hour or more for her to arrive. On my way I'd pass through gang-bangers and hangers, winos, and thieves, pimps and hoes that populate the area. It was iffy enough to pass through, but for a short, skinny kid like me to be hanging around...

It was cold as I left the lobby and after buttoning up my jacket, I stuffed my hands in my pockets and scrunched my head down on my neck to conserve body heat. Dusk had just begun to coat the sky with salmon and gray.

At the end of my block at Lakeside and Sheridan, near the parking lot where I chipped my front tooth, trouble was already waiting for me. It waited in the form of two punks hanging out with nothing to do but look for trouble.

I had never seen either of them before. One was a little taller than me. The other was a little shorter, but stockier.

"Punk!" one began as I approached.

"Faggot!" shouted the other.

"Fuck you," I shot back for lack of something better to say. Never one to wait for trouble, I passed right on by.

The smaller one jumped in front of me. Moving around him, I caught his shove on my right shoulder instead of my chest as he intended. His friend moved in from my left.

It would take years before I learned to end this type of confrontation before it started. But now it was too late. We were already into it.

I turned around with the shove and swing. My left cross just grazed his cheek below his eye as he flinched back, surprised. The other one seemed to take offense at this, moved in and tried to blindside me with a right/left combo of his own, both of which I avoided easily.

They had done this before and were good. They kept well apart and always tried to maneuver so that they would have me between them.

I kept moving. "Don't let yourself get caught in between them," I told myself. When they moved in, I moved out. When they went left, I went left faster to cut them off, herd them together. Stick and move, stick and move. I was never in the same place twice and kept working my way around them.

I couldn't afford to get locked into a wrestling match because, unlike those so-called "reality fighting" shows you see on TV today, the true reality is that on the street you never, ever want to end up on the ground. Every kid in the hood knew that. I'd seen it a dozen times, where two guys were having a one-on-one fight. And as soon as one guy hit the ground, it was open season. He got kicked and stomped on by everyone in reach. Then it was open season on yo' ass.

So my best bet was to keep moving. Surround them. Keep moving. I was all over them and they were not ready for that. I was pissed. Bullies are one thing that I cannot stand. My anger fueled my stack and I began to press them back, back, back up the street. Duck, bob, weave. Punch, kick, and move.

Now they didn't know what to do with me. They began to cast nervous glances back and forth between them. What happens when the mouse bites back? Then they turned and ran. And I chased them. I was feeling my blood pounding in my ears now. Then, to my surprise, they turned into the lobby of my building.

I came flying into the lobby right behind them and met them in front of the bank of elevators where the taller one had just pushed the "up" button. I came at them swinging.

We chased each other around the lobby, punching and swinging. During the fight none of us were able to do much damage. We each landed some decent blows to face, chest and ribs, but none of our strikes did more than back the other up a few steps before the battle rejoined. But for what it lacked in damage, it made up in speed and action. It must've been fun to watch, the three of us buzzing around each other like angry hornets.

Then came a "ding" and the elevator doors opened up. They both jumped in with smiles on their faces like they had just defeated me when, to my surprise and theirs, I jumped in the elevator with them! Baaaaad move. But once the doors closed, nobody knew what to do. I think they knew that if we got into it in these close quarters, I could do some serious damage. On the other hand, I knew that inside this little box there was nowhere for me to bob, weave, or run to.

So we all just stood there. Like idiots. Looking at the lit-up floor-indicator numbers at the top each, taking its turn to wink on in a yellow orange moment of glory only to fade but a moment later.

I felt like I should whistle or something.
"DINNNNG!"
The doors opened up at the 9th floor and they got out. I remained in the elevator politely until they exited. Then my

senses returned to me. "Hey, these guys just tried to kick my ass for no reason." Then I was out of the elevator and at them. We fought our way halfway down the hallway, past door after door, bouncing each other painfully off the walls until the short one broke and ran ahead and started pounding on one particular door.

Now I fought with a renewed fervor, because I didn't know who would come out of that door. Stranger? Family? Friends? Now with him alone, I had gotten the best of the tall one and was fighting my way through his guarding hands, pounding his face and chest while he tried to hide from me. Then the other one began shouting, "MOOOM!! MOOOOM!!!"

"Mom?" These are the tough-guys who, a few minutes ago were calling me "Faggot" and "Pussy"? Just when I began to think no one was home, the door was yanked open and a large woman stepped out into the hall.

"What the hell is all this yellin' out here!?" the furious mom boomed. Then we all froze. Then she looked over at us and froze as well. The boys waited, I waited, she waited, we all waited together.

Then the boys lowered their eyes in shame. As his angry mother stood in the doorway, fists on hips, the stocky one ducked under his mother's arm and disappeared inside. The taller one turned to follow. And the mother was just standing there looking at me wondering what just happened.

Hell, I wasn't gonna tell her. With a smile of secret satisfaction, I turned and left.

Bully

I was late for school. It was a gray, misty morning. A brown paper lunch bag dangled at the end of my skinny little arm as I made my way across the empty wet cement yard that was the playground of the John T. McCutcheon Grammar School. It was damp and chilly with a heavy fog in the heavy morning air. The iron colored sky covered me like a blanket. Happy and alone with my thoughts, I'd almost reached the far side of the playground when from a distance behind me I heard the flap, flap, flap sound of running feet smacking on the wet pavement. What I witnessed upon turning filled me with dread. So much so that I immediately turned back around and kept on walking like it would disappear if I pretended I hadn't seen it. It was Adam, the school bully. I'd seen Adam terrify and beat several children bloody this year alone. At least a head taller than me, he was bigger and meaner than anyone there. So far I'd managed to keep off of his radar and if I just kept walking and didn't notice him, maybe things would remain the same.

But judging from the sound and direction of his footsteps, I hoped in vain. For it seemed from the sound of it that his steps were not aiming him toward the door to our right, but at me to his left. With a sinking feeling in my gut, I knew what I had to do: I had to turn around and look at him again. And then even if I was right... what the heck was I going to do then?! But then I had the answer: Peripheral vision! I didn't have to actually look at him! So turning my head ever so slightly, I saw all my fears come to life. There he was, larger than life and running full steam ahead right at me. DAAAAAMN!

Whatamigonnado, whatamigonnado, whatamigonnado!?!

First, just calm down. Be cool man, just be COOL! O.K. You don't know what he wants. He could just want to know what time it is... Maybe he just wants to walk with someone. Haven't you ever felt like that?... no? So... okay, he was gonna kick my ass. Oh well, if it was gonna happen, it was gonna happen. Eddie, just do your thing baby. And remember: Fight smart.

And so in the truest Zen fashion, I chose having no Way as my Way and I waited. And waited. And I waited. I can still hear those tennis shoed feet smacking against the damp concrete. It seemed to take forever to cross that field of gray. And finally out of the corner of my eye, he came. Over my right shoulder I saw him looming above me, bearing down like a bull charging a matador. And in that last instant, totally unplanned, I sidestepped. Moving slightly to my left, I brought my tiny right arm up and across my chest. Turning in towards him, I slashed my elbow up and backwards, across where I supposed his face was going to be, and felt him smack solidly against it.

Then next thing I saw were two tennis-shoed feet rising high above the pavement, followed by a sound like a sack of potatoes being dropped on the floor. And then I turned to face him. And I waited. And I waited. And I waited. At first he didn't move. He just lay there. Flat on his back. Frightened, I didn't know what to do. I thought I'd killed him. Then slowly his head began to move from side to side. Then he started groaning. His eyes blinked open as if he'd been suddenly startled. Lurching suddenly to sit bolt upright, he looked as if he was searching for something appropriate to say. Then he stood up and faced me from a distance looking down at me. And I stood there strangely calm and silently resigned to my fate: to go down fighting. But nothing happened. We just stood there, the two of us, like two gunfighters in a TV western. Neither of us moving. Neither knowing what to do next.

Then finally he broke the silence. "FUCKER!"

I met him with more silence.

"Wha'd ya do that for?!"

Now I felt like laughing. The school bully comes running up behind you in an open yard and he thinks... What? I'm just supposed to let him jump me? Let him kick my ass? Where did this kid come from? And a funny thing happened. I found that me just standing there saying nothing seemed to make him even more nervous than my hitting him did. It was like he was used to being hit, but not being faced, being looked at eye to eye, man to man. And he backed off. A slight bemused smile tugged at the side of my mouth. Stepping back again, he said in a little voice, "Well... you better not let it happen again..." And he seemed to lose steam. Turning his back to me, he bolted towards the school and disappeared around the corner of the building.

I just stood there for long moments after he was gone. Just me in the fog absorbing what just happened. Just like that, I thought to myself. It was that easy. Finally, I looked around me as if in search of a witness, but the playground, the school windows and on the street, there had been no prying eyes into our private struggle. And then I followed Adam's footsteps around the corner and into the school with my brown paper lunch bag.

Boys' Club

The Robert R. McCormic Boys' Club was just across Lawrence Ave. on Sheridan. Uncharacteristically, Dad actually gave me the okay to go down and join when I was nine. It was where all the neighborhood kids came at one time or another. It had just about everything a kid wanted: pool tables, bumper pool, foosball, ping pong, air hockey, a gym, a swimming pool, and various organized activities like trips and cookouts, and sleepovers.

And once in a great while, I got to attend one. But for a time I would stop by after school for a few games if the lines weren't too long, or hang out with the fellas. We would joke and fight and practice with our homemade nunchaku, banging ourselves in the head, or elbows, or knees, or testicles, perfecting our flourishing fighting skills.

There were constant fights breaking out over the games, and some of them were serious with multiple groups and weapons all around. Yeah, it was a pretty rough place. You had to keep your eyes open, but it was ours.

At any given time you could buy some weed on your way in the front and get laid or blown going out the back, or downstairs or upstairs.

It was like our own little "Boys Town". Even the counselors were only a little older than we were ourselves.

I had lots of friends there, and more than a few enemies as well. I got into more fights than I can remember there, winning most and losing a few here and there as well.

There was a kind of freedom or liberation there where we pretty much got to make our own rules, establish our own codes of conduct. We even had our own hierarchy. The older kids who had been around the longest were respected and given their own space and a wide berth. Nobody questioned them or argued with them. They got respect. Then came the just plain big guys, some of whom were cool and others were just bullies who were tolerated by the O.G.s, but just barely. But even the bullies didn't bother the old schoolers.

And then there were kids like me: the smallest and the newest. To these, no one gave any slack at all and the only thing we ever got we had to fight for... and win. If you got your ass kicked, you went right straight back to the bottom of the pack where you had to start all over again earning a rep and respect. Reputation and respect could be lost in an instant. The old didn't count for shit.

Rep and Respect could be earned in several different ways, but it all came down to prowess. Be it games or girls, or fighting or singing, or casin', or rankin' on someone, you had to be good.

Gregory was still the baddest cat around. He wasn't big or loud, but he was lethal.

Zachary could run that pool table for the entire day if he didn't get bored talking shit about you the whole time while he cracked those balls around the table like he was mad at 'im. He was the worst kind of winner: loud and obnoxious.

Me? I could fight pretty well, but most fools realized it too late. At this point I wasn't the berserker that got me space later on. But I could talk more shit than Zak. But only if you pissed me off. Then you better look out. The one thing EVERYBODY had seen me do was cut someone down. And I'd do it with a vengeance. I would talk about you and yo' mamma. I'd build a case against your right to exist. And ya mamma? I'd talk about her so bad you'd wish you were an orphan.

And the more the crowd grew, the badder I'd get. I'd tell them about your high-water pants, ya' lice-infested, greasy-ass hair, yo' funky-assed shoes, and don't get me started on that booty-lickin', dookie-smellin' breath you got. And that alcoholic daddy o' yours? I just saw him! He was out bangin' some old bag lady out behind that soup kitchen he always eatin' at. I had to step over 'im on the way here. Looking down and pointing at his untied shoelace, I add, "You not knowin' how to tie your own damn shoes clown."

"Awww, shut up Eddie, fo' I kick yo' ass."

"Yeah, you can try it motherfucker, but you gonna look mighty silly tryin' to walk home with my boot stuck up yo' ass."

I'd have the crowd roaring and the poor fool who'd set me off wouldn't show his face for a week.

We forged alliances, made enemies, friends, and partners. We negotiated deals, gang-banged, and stole. It was like an orphanage for hustlers. And it was all ours.

Curtis Dies in a Vacant Lot

Violence was ever present. It permeated my life as well as those around me. It was in my family, in my friends' families, it was on the streets and even in our church. Violence, it was the only lifestyle I knew. It held both promise and action. I wonder if I'll ever be happy without it. It made even the concept of Heaven alien and hard to grasp. It made it undesirable, boring.

The first person I knew that was murdered was Curtis. He was the idol of my friend John and me, a Native American. He was also a member of one of the larger, more notorious street gangs. He was shot in the back one night while crossing a vacant lot of a demolished apartment building we used to play in. Curtis had been a few years older than us. He was only about 15 when he was killed. He was tall, proud, and strong, and a natural leader. He died alone at night in a vacant lot filled with bricks, broken glass and boards with nails in them.

John and I were walking through that same lot soon after Curtis was killed. We stood there in silent respect in his memory. On the heels of that was the thought that it could have been, or might still be... me. Lying bleeding, cold and dying. Face down with only the empty whiskey bottles and redbrick to kiss him goodbye.

Eventually, many of my friends would find violent deaths and leave family and friends in mourning. Shootings, stabbings, beatings, hangings, hit and run, and prison.

Lakeside Gang Fight

One of the first gang fights I witnessed took place in a vacant lot across from the project I lived in. The "vacant" lot in our neighborhood was never really vacant. It was filled with the rubble of demolished buildings left like ancient war-torn ruins of some forgotten civilization. Entire walls were still intact only laying diagonally across others that were now heaps of brick. We would climb over and under these ruins. Through windows and into basements, we would go exploring. Broken glass, burned wood, jagged pipe, and rusted nails were in plentiful supply for us to scavenge and remake with our imagination into new and exciting toys: pistols, shotguns, rifles, swords, motorcycles, spaceships, and robots. Here adults rarely were present to harass us. Here we would run free. The occasional hazards of a nail through your shoe or falling on some jagged point were more than outweighed by our desire to run free, shout, and sing at the top of our lungs without someone telling us to "Shut up!" or "Be quiet!" or "Stop all that runnin' round!"

On this day, Billy and I had been chasing each other with popguns. We had made them out of 2X4's with nails and rubber bands and clothespins. They would shoot pop-tops from soda cans. Ammunition could be found at our feet no matter where we ran. Mine was a double-barreled shotgun. It could fire a double burst with a total of six pop-tops. Over fifteen feet they would scatter into a horizontal oval, big enough to cover a car. It was great! I had just chased Billy out of the lot and into the alley when he came to a complete stop... staring. I stopped next to him and followed his stare.

There in front of us, oblivious to our presence, were two groups of people, all guys. Big guys. They faced each other in the middle of the alley. On the one side stood a row of young black guys much bigger than us and in their early teens. They were wearing pressed black jeans or slacks, and plaid or checkered shirts colored with gold. Dark purple T-shirts were worn underneath by some, purple baseball caps by others, and a few wore the same colored bandanas in various places On the other side were Latinos of the same age and in the same numbers. They all wore the exact same thing: white, tank-top T-shirts, navy blue work pants and black suede shoes.

They stared in silence as unmoving as we. Then, just when I started to back slowly away, it happened. One of the Latinos lunged across the divide and was sent straight down by one of the same three-foot lengths of 2x4 that I carried. "BRACK!" came the vicious sound across the space between us. The kid that had struck him down, stepped forward swinging his stick in lazy circles by his left side. The rest by his side spread out into a slight semi-circle.

They each now stood staring over the fallen body, which was lying face down in a six-inch-deep pothole puddle of water with blood streaming from the side of his face and head. For moments no one moved, then suddenly one of the Latinos screamed, dropped the pipe he had been holding and lunged for those on the other side. The two on either side of him grabbed him by his arms and held on tight while he tried to charge from their grasp. There was some momentary discussion between them while the black guys silently stood their ground.

After the apparent leader nodded his head, two guys picked up their fallen comrade by each arm and dragged him backwards, away from the battle line. The rest soon followed, backing carefully away. Once they were gone, the remaining group milled around and conferred for a while, and finally drifted away. The tension now ebbing away. Billy and I both let out the breath we had been holding. The remaining group gathered around and there was some discussion before they went off in the other direction while we went on our way.

Gar

There were two particular Vietnamese brothers that lived in my building who I did not get along with. They were new to the area and both were just full of themselves, thought they were hot-shit 'cause they knew some form of martial art or other. Arrogant braggarts, both of them. The younger brother was my age and size. Gar was his name. The older one was a few years older and much bigger. His name was Tang.

One day we (that is most of the kids in the housing project that were the same age) were playing around the building. Most of my good friends were there. We were all running around, having fun, and chasing each other.

Then down comes Gar. At first he just stood by making fun of us. We ignored him pretty much, just doing our own thing. Then he started throwing rocks at Daniel who was both younger and smaller than him.

"Why don't ya leave him alone, man?" I said. In response to my request, he began throwing rocks at me. At first I threw a few at him and nailed him a couple of times to see how he liked it, and hopefully to discourage him. This only served to enrage him. It seems I had interrupted his sport and now I was going to pay.

He began trying to intimidate me by telling me how bad he was going to kick my ass if I didn't stop throwing rocks at him.

"Well, what the hell are ya throwing them at us for?" I asked. Because he could was apparently his reason. I walked right up to him, nose to nose, and told him, "Fuck the rocks. If you wanna fight, let's fight."

He then started that circling game. You know, the one where two kids bump chests as they go around and around and around talking shit to one another.

Never one for small talk, I asked him, "Do ya wanna keep ridin' this merry-go-round or are you gonna throw a punch?" A steady stream of profanities was his only answer, so I waited. After his next revolution, I got sick of waiting and grabbed him around, the neck, threw him on the ground, jumped on top of him and we went at it.

Up and down we fought. On the ground, then on our feet, then on the ground again, we beat each other around the corner and halfway down the long parking lot.

It was one of the longest fights I've ever been in. Although it seemed to last most of the day, it was really more like fifteen or twenty minutes.

By this time a huge crowd had gathered. It seemed that the entire neighborhood was there. Then at one point while I was sitting on his chest trying to get a good shot at his face, I felt this gentle hand grab my arm from behind, calmly, gently stopping my swing, and lift me off of him.

Mom?!?

"That's enough," she quietly said.

Gar had gotten himself up off the ground and now stood panting and facing me. Mom stood between us, separating us with her arms stretched out in front of her with Gar and me facing each other on opposite sides.

With Mom there I had begun to calm down. But as I stood there looking into his eyes, I became indignant that this asshole had come down here to me while I was minding my own business and started throwing rocks at me. Fuuuuck youuuuu!

Smack! I popped him square across the face. He fell back, then came back with a blind, dazed, halfhearted attack that bumped Mom back a few steps.

Angered even further by the knowledge that it was my action that had almost resulted in getting my mother hurt, I was now furious at myself.

So I charged him again and the crowd went wild. Cheering and shouting at me to "Knock his ass out!" and "Kick his ass, Eddie!"

Then Mom was pulling me out of there again. Gar didn't make any move to follow. Actually, he seemed quite ready to be rid of me. He did, however, promise to get his big brother to kick my ass.

"Bring him on! I'll take both of you on!!" And I was just mad enough to go for him again, but remembering what happened to Mom held me back.

Neither he nor his brother ever had anything to say or do with me again.

On the way back home, Mom asked me what had happened. She knew I was never one to start fights, but was more than ready to finish one.

As I reluctantly told her what had happened, to my surprise, a slow smile spread across her face. She wasn't happy that I was fighting, but she was glad I had protected Daniel and "you guys were the same size and it was a fair fight. But you clearly won that one."

I had mixed emotions about the whole thing, but deep down, secret even from myself, I was happy that at least once one of my parents had seemed... proud of me.

She knew I wasn't a bully. I never picked on anyone who hadn't gone out of their way to make themselves my enemy.

She would retell that story every now and then to friends and family. And every time she told it, she got that same slow, graceful smile.

Herbert

There was this kid named Herbert. He was the biggest guy in the school. Bigger even that Tyrone. He must've been about six feet tall, and muscular. The guy even had a full mustache. I think I came up to about his solar plexus. Herbert and I were usually cool, but not best friends. We butted heads on a lot of things. He was used to getting his way because of his size, but of course I've never been much good at putting up with anybody's bullshit.

Well, one day it came down to us. Carla, Herbert's sidekick, who at one time wanted to be my girlfriend (Yeah, like I even knew what to do with one in eighth grade), got to talking a bunch of shit and spreading lies that I was going around talking shit and telling everyone I was going to kick Herbert's ass. Well guess what, Herbert believed her. More likely, he just needed an excuse to kick my ass.

Well on this one day it went on back and forth with Carla coming to me saying, "Herbert says he's gonna kick your ass."

"Yeah, okay," I'd reply.

What are you gonna do? Either he was or he wasn't gonna try to kick my ass. And either he would be successful or he wouldn't. I had no desire to stand around talking about it, much less send Carla back and forth between us twisting every word while she instigated the whole thing.

But again and again she would come. "Herbert says this. Herbert says that." And do you know that by the end of the day other people were running up to me saying, "Carla says this. And Carla says that."

Well, I'd about had enough. Finally I saw her again and told her point-blank, "I don't wanna hear it. If Herbert has anything to say to me, he can find me. And I don't wanna hear shit outta you again." You can imagine neither Carla nor Herbert took that too well. But frankly I didn't give a shit. I was tired of the whole thing.

Now word was coming to me that Herbert wanted to have it out with me after school. Fine. Whatever. I just knew that whatever I said they would go running back to him saying, "Eddie says he can kick your ass blindfolded, with one hand tied behind his back," so I didn't even try.

When the three fifteen bell rang, I headed outside to the O.K. Corral to have this petty little showdown over, or clear it up, whichever came first. So there I was, standing under the flagpole waiting for Herbert (and Carla) to show up when I heard this loud noise. I realize it was an approaching crowd coming from around the building.

Looking around the corner, what did I see but Herbert, Carla, and about fifty of his thug buddies. They were all carrying baseball bats, sticks, bricks and all sorts of shit, like they were about to take on an army. Fuuuuuck that! I was outta there! I went around the other side of the building and headed home.

On the way I met my friend Gar (the black one not the Vietnamese one), Everett, and their BIG brother Earnest who was in high school. When they asked me what was hapnin', I told them. They offered to back me up, but even four big guys weren't a match for fifty guys of any size. And I would hate myself if they got their asses kicked right alongside mine unnecessarily. So instead we hung out and goofed off for awhile waiting for things to cool off. Then I left for home.

When I got a block away from my apartment, what did I see? Fifty niggaz hangin' out in front. Daaaaamn! I wasn't going to go through this bullshit again. I was gonna wait for my opportunity and settle this once and for all. And sure enough, about fifteen, twenty minutes later, they began to drift away. The next thing you know there's only Herbert, Carla and a couple of other dudes left in front of my place.

Marching right up between them, I belly up to his kneecaps and asked him what he was doing in front of my place. "Carla said you said you was gonna kick my ass."

"Oh yeah? Well, Carla's a lying sack o'shit. If I decide I got a problem with you, you don't think I can find your big ass for myself?"

"Well, she said..."

"Fuck what she said! This is you and me. I'M telling you that I never said shit to Carla, or you, but if you got a problem with me, here I am. Let's go."

"Well..." We looked at each other a long time while he thought about his options. "I'll let you slide this time."

"You sure? I mean I wouldn't want you to have to come back..." Turning to the rest of them... "Anything else? Anybody?" And when no one had anything to say, they all turned around and left.

I guess word got around, because I never had any trouble with Herbert or Carla again. People were talking about it in school the next day like I was some kind of hero. But I wanted no part of it. It was all bullshit. And Carla started it all. I found that often girls would get some guy to do their fighting for them, for no good reason. Cat's paws and patsies can be found all around us.

Sometimes it's hard to see past the threat to the source. If you can eliminate that source, the threat will fall away. It wasn't so much that Herbert knew that I wasn't afraid of him that got me left alone. It was more that Carla knew that I would call her on her bullshit, make her look like a fool in front of everyone and nobody would stand up for her. That's what got me left alone. She didn't even look me in the eye after that. And that was just fiiiine with me.

glenwood

 glenwood

Finding Home

So Mom had finally had enough... again. This time I was 12 and I remember walking into the living room one sunny, Sunday morning in June to find my mother packing bags, franticly close to panic. I stood by watching, not knowing what was happening or what I should be doing. I just stood there, watching her as she finished. With two suitcases packed and a small bag, Mom and I left that apartment one sunny, spring morning. And we got on the train headed downtown. We got off just north of the heart of downtown and worked our way right back into another shitty part of town.
Eventually we found ourselves standing underneath a huge, flickering, neon cross with the words, "Jesus Saves" all in hot pink gas humming through glass tubes. There were several men hanging about the place eyeing us like jackals. I stared each of them in the eye and one by one they found other things to be interested in. Once inside the Pacific Garden Mission, the mood was no different. The woman at the front office and everyone else who worked there, right on down to the pastor who held the mandatory Sunday church service for all the "guests" treated us like some kind of lepers. I wanted to kill the woman who checked us in. She was full of

a kind of hatred that I could not even begin to fathom, but had encountered and combated several times before. We were passed through various people who kept insisting that they were helping us, but their tone, and attitudes suggested they were the wardens of our new prison. Giving us a brief, unpleasant tour they left us alone in a large room. It was lined with cots, several of which were guarded by women who watched us through lowered eyelids like animals stalking their territory. There were also a couple of baby's cribs alongside some of the cots. We parked our belongings beside three beds, which we hoped were unclaimed by anyone, and headed back downstairs.

Since no one was allowed in the shelter during the day, some of the other kids and I would run the streets stealing, fighting and getting into trouble until our parents came back and the doors were opened. When Mom got back and Pam returned from her summer school programs, we would go apartment hunting. Sometimes just Pam and I would go if she had no activities to attend.

We stayed and fought at that miserable place for the summer of '78, while all around Chicago the city played on, unheeding our plight. The Cubs continued to lose more games than they won. Phil Donahue had shows about everyone, but people like us. The Bud Billiken parade was aired for the first time on TV. Carol Burnett began making us laugh in syndication (reruns). Tom Skilling became Chicago's favorite weatherman, and the Pacer made its debut in Detroit and gave the world something to laugh about.

The summer we stayed at the homeless shelter I got to go to summer camp for the one and only time in my life. I spent ten days away from the roach motel at Camp Channing in Michigan, the glove not the fish. Mrs. Hecht got me the gig for being the "most improved" student at the school. Don't even ask me how the hell that happened. I wasn't even aware of any change in my disruptive behavior or my retaliation toward attacks or insults. Heck, maybe she just felt sorry for me and thought I needed a break, considering how much trouble I was having in school.

At camp I quickly made friends, got into fights and avoided girls. I hated that awkward feeling I always got around girls. I never knew what to do or say, or how to be.

We swam at 5:00 a.m. in freezing cold lake water. "Polar bear swimming" they called it. We just called it nuts.

It was mostly black kids. There were Latinos and a few Asians as well. And all of us were poor and from the hood. It wasn't like the summer camps on TV. Here, in between drawing classes and nature walks, kids were fighting, having sex and trying to stab each other.

I managed to get an instant rep by taking a bigger kid's best shot without even blinking. We were melting wax into our homemade lanterns in Art's and Crafts when he started in on me. When he viciously snatched the book of matches I was using out of my hands I snatched them right back.

"Don't you ever snatching anything from me," I said up into his surprised face.

Then outta nowhere the sucker just hauled off and threw a haymaker of a right hook at me. It caught me square on the left side of my jaw and snapped my head so far to the side that it made my neck hurt and numbed my entire face. I let that slow smile tug the corners of my mouth up as I got that giddy sense of anticipation that you get in the pit of my stomach. I was still smiling at him as I moved in for the kill. I was going to enjoy the hell out of this. I could already feel my fingers sinking into the soft flesh of his neck, but the counselors jumped on me before I had the chance to really have fun. By the end of the day I had more "friends" than I could count, offering to do everything but shine my shoes. And I probably could have gotten that done too.

Returning to Chi-Town there were scores of moms and dads and brothers and sisters waiting outside the YMCA where the busses dropped us off. One by one the other children were picked up while I was left alone in the lobby. After an hour of solitude, I figured that there was no one coming to pick me up. I was on my own.

I remembered Pamela had called at some point to tell me they had gotten an apartment. "You remember the one by the thrift store?" she said.
"The one by the new looking train station?"
"Yeah, that one."
"Neat!"

Now the trick was remembering enough about it to get there. Fortunately, I had taken my mother's advice and budgeted my money while I was away, and I had exactly enough money left over for one train ride. So shouldering my camping gear, this consisted of one sleeping bag (stolen by my dad), extra blankets and a pillow, plus all of the arts and crafts that we had made each day, suffice it to say that by time I reached the nearest train station at Grand Avenue just a couple of blocks away, my skinny little arms, back, legs and hands were tired.

Giving my money to the station attendant, I considered asking directions, then stopped when I realized I didn't know which station I was looking for or even which direction it lay in. So I picked a direction and got on. The only thing I knew for sure was that it was on the Howard/Jackson Park train line. That left me with a 50/50 chance of getting it right.

I got it wrong. After about three train stops I noticed that all the white folks had left the train and only black folks were on board. That meant I was heading for the South side, all black.

I remembered that the apartment that Pamela told me about was in an all white neighborhood. So at the next stop I grabbed up all my gear and got off. Then it was up and over the bridge to the other set of tracks that were heading in the opposite direction.

I was already exhausted from carrying all that crap and I considered chucking half of it in the garbage to lighten the load. The backpack was digging into my neck. My shoulders and back were killing me from the several garbage bags of stuff I carried. And my right thumb was burning from hanging onto that damned lantern that had my initials carved into it. But for some reason, I managed to hang onto everything. I kept that stuff for years until an ex-boyfriend of Mom's torched the very apartment I was heading for and we lost everything in it - but I'm getting ahead of myself.

Riding North, I kept a sharp lookout for that gray, metal, futuristic-looking train station. And ten miles later, I found it. The Bryn Mawr station. Oooh! Cool!

Excitedly I gathered my gear and managed to scramble out of the closing doors before they trapped me or my stuff. Standing on the platform high above the street, I saw a five-point intersection that looked familiar. I just hoped I remembered which of the five streets was the one I needed.

At the intersection I stood looking around me and narrowed my choices by intuition, from five, to four, to three, then two. Stuck at two, I picked one and headed off.

About two blocks down I got the uncomfortable feeling that I had made a wrong choice, so I headed back and started down the second choice. Three blocks later I was still keeping all my senses alive because I still was not sure.

Finally, after a mile of hiking, I had found the little convenience store that I remembered buying candy at when we saw the apartment. And there! There was the gas station on the corner. It was the next building! I made it!! If I hadn't been so exhausted and carrying so much stuff, I would've ran the last two blocks there.

The building was "U" shaped with entrances on the left, right, and center. Standing there in the center I had to think hard to remember which one. We had actually looked at two apartments in this building. Thinking back to my conversation with Pamela, I remembered her telling me it was the one that was empty, not the one with the old lady that was moving out. Let's see. It was... the one on the left. I was sure of it. First floor up.

Exhausted and standing in front of the door, I dropped my stuff at my feet. If this was not it, I was going to sleep right here and call the police when I woke up. Maybe they had some system for finding lost... homes? Hah! Yeah-riiiiight.

Taking a deep breath, I stepped up to the door and noticed a hole where the secondary lock should be. Peeking in, I saw, to my great dismay, the apartment was empty. DAMN!!! What was I gonna do now!?! I put my ear to the opening and listened in a desperate hope that someone was in there. Nothing. Not a sound. Shit! Resting my forehead on the door, I knocked in vain, out of habit, because there was nothing else I could do.

"Hello?" came a girl's voice from somewhere inside

Ahhh! That scared the shit outta me! Who was that? Looking in the opening again, I found it was filled with a HUMONGOUS eyeball not three inches from my own.

"Uhhhhh... my name is Eddie? I'm supposed to live here?"

"Eddie!" The latch was thrown. The door flew open and I saw that the eyeball belonged to my sister Pamela. "Hey! What are you doing here?"

"I waited at the "Y" for hours and nobody came."

"Well Mom went down there to get you. She's been calling here every fifteen minutes."

Sure enough, ten minutes later I had an elated mom (for Mom that is) on the phone trying to figure out how she missed me.

"They told me the bus dropped you off at the back end of the building," she said. "I waited there then someone finally came by and told me the bus had already gone. Then someone else said that the kids were all waiting on the second floor. So I took the stairs up and waited there thinking you had gone out for a stroll or something. After another hour or so I finally went down to the front lobby where you had been all along, and they told me you had been there but you must have just left. I've been roaming around the neighborhood ever since. My next stop would have been the police or fire department. How did you get home?"

"Remember when you told me to 'budget your money'..."?

Pamela helped me get settled in while we waited for the next hour for Mom to get back. Pamela had been taking a nap when I arrived. There were no beds; they had been sleeping on the floor on folded up blankets. We had not a lick of furniture, but we had a place. Our place... for now.

Again

A few short months after we left my dad, he miraculously got our phone number once again. He began calling on a regular basis. But I'll never forget that first phone call. It was me who answered. "Put your mom on the phone," was all he said. I was frozen. For a few, long moments my mind could not get over the shock, the terror. You can't imagine what it was like. Actually, it was like some slasher flick come to life. You know the part where the psycho chases one of the kids into an abandoned house? You think he's lost him. You think he's still outside in the woods. You breathe a sigh of relief. But as the kid backs up, out of the pitch-black shadows comes the face, then the knife, then you scream!

But this was no movie. It really was him. He had, once again, found us and was insidiously working his way back into our lives. And this was how it always started. The phone calls, the visits, Mom visiting him, him moving back in, then the beatings would start. All over again.

He began calling at all hours, would wake us up at three in the morning and, "Let me talk to your mama," would be all he would say to me.

Once in a while, Mom would bring the phone to me. "He wants to talk to you." And I would just stare at it. Sometimes I would shake my head like it was a bad dream, but the terrified look on her face told me she'd already told him I was home.

"How was school...? How's your sister...?" blah, blah, blah. The usual obligatory bullshit you say to a kid whose mom you are trying to win back. And eventually I just said fuck it. I wouldn't take the phone from Mom at all. She would just have to work with it. I figured she knew damn well I didn't want to talk to that bastard and if she couldn't figure out to tell him I wasn't home... ever... then that was on her.

Yep, sure enough, a few weeks later he had "miraculously" found out where we lived, like he always seemed to. He began stopping by at all hours and the first time I answered the door and Mom wasn't home, he tried to bully his way past me. But I stood fast. He was like a vampire, once you let him in, he wasn't leaving. He was going to have to beat his way past me. At fourteen, with a brief glimpse of freedom, I wasn't about to give it up that easily. "Where's your mom?"

"She's not home."

"How was school...? How's your sister...?" Blah, blah, blah.

"Fine... Fine... Fine..." I had only short answers for him. No smiles, no laughs, no nothing. Seeing this, he dropped the charade.

"Where's your mom at?"

"I don't know." I wasn't about to tell him she was at the grocery store. I only hoped he'd grow bored and leave before she returned.

Stepping closer, he got that deadly quiet that sometimes came before a beating.

"Goddammit, quit fuckin' around. Tell me where your mom is." But I would let him beat me to death before I ever gave him anything again.

"I... don't... know..." I reiterated slowly, steadily and looking him in the eye.

"I'll wait," he said as he tried to push past me. I'd had had one hand on the door edge and the other on the doorframe and when he came, I didn't budge. Seeing this he looked down at me with surprise. Stepping back again, he looked at me for a long moment while I waited the tantrum I knew would come.

"Eddie," he said deliberately, "get outta the way." I only returned his gaze.

Seeing this wasn't working, he changed his whole attitude.

"Boy, boy, boy," he said incredulously, laughter tingeing his words. Lightening up he turned and said, "Tell your mama I stopped by," and left.

I couldn't believe it. I listened as he walked down the stairs, out the lobby and let the door close behind him. But there was no joy in my first victory. It was a trick. He'd be back. If not today, then tomorrow, but I knew he would be back. I closed the door, locked it, and waited. Years later I read a quote from the Bible and that moment raced into mind. "Resist the Devil and he will flee from you."

And return he did. Again and again. Over and over again. But he never got inside that apartment. Sometimes he would stand outside our darkened window and scream and yell, "Susan! Eddie! Open the door!" while we cowered in the dark. Once he threw a big five-pound chunk of broken cement through the living room window. When Mom quietly called the police, it was midnight and you could still hear him in the background cursing and screaming. When the cops finally showed up, it was 4:00 a.m. He'd already left and we both were sound asleep. To make matters worse, the cop acted like we were the assholes for disturbing him. I wanted to tell him to go the fuck back to his goddamned doughnut shop and forget we'd bothered him, but I was too spent to even think.

Sometimes he would come by and if the lobby door had been left ajar, he wouldn't have to buzz the intercom and would just come on up. If I could tell by his knock that it was him, I wouldn't answer the door. But that man had supernatural patience. He would knock, and knock, and knock. Eventually he would start screaming and yelling, "I know you're in there! Stop fuckin' around and open this goddamned door!!" Sometimes he would try to kick the door in. And a few times he almost made it. And there I would be waiting.

On the other side of that solid oak door with the well-kept, just-for-him, triple locks there would be me. I would squat down low in the middle of the darkened hallway with a butcher knife in my fist. Sometimes I would wait for hours, just squatting there. I would fall asleep there sometimes, leaning against the wall. The scariest thing of all for me was that after a certain point, after the initial shot of adrenaline, after the first half-hour or so, I would want him to break in.

Squatting there I would watch the doorjamb splinter and crack, and I would actually want him to kick it in just to get it over with. In my mind I could see him charge forward as I raced forward from the other side of the door, plunging the knife deeply into his chest. Perhaps he would lock his hands around my throat and I would attack him, burying the knife in his chest again and again until he stopped moving, or I did. But THANK GOD it never happened. Thank God the door held. Thank God the locks held. Thank God the frame held. Thank God for all of us it held.

I can't tell you what price Mom paid for these visits. But she was a nervous, jittery, pale, terrified, shell of a woman. She would work from as early as she could until as late as she could, then come home and sleep. Occasionally, she would take me out to dinner or the movies. But other than that, the poor thing had no life at all. No friends, no family, no clubs, no hobbies. Work. Sleep.

But eventually she began to give in. She would tell me that he was coming by and wanted me to spend the day or night with him. Sometimes he would show up at my school and take me out of class with some made up story to feed the principal, who would usher him right in, and he would drag me around the city with him throughout the night while he hustled his way through life by various cons, threats, or thefts. Sometimes he would make me an unwilling participant in his various schemes. Eventually, I would make myself "unavailable" for these outings as well.

But after many months of strategic planning, he began to make some headway with my mother. To my horror, I heard her make a passing joke about him being here... in this apartment... hangin' out.

Rounding on her, I came close enough so that she could look in my eyes as I calmly told her, "Mom, if he ever enters this apartment, I'm leaving. And if he moves in, I'm not coming back."

She tried to laugh it off. "You don't mean that."

I repeated myself slowly and clearly. I'd had enough.

We had run halfway across a city big enough to lose anyone in and he had come walking right back into our lives with no hindrance from her whatsoever. I saw now that she had been moving in this direction all along and this was as far as I would go on this little carnival ride. It was time for me to get off.

"If he moves in, I'm moving out." As I saw it starting to sink in, I nodded my head and watched as she slowly turned and left the room deflated. It would not be the last time she invited the devil to live with us. She was free to choose that for herself, but I would never again allow it to happen to me.

Gregg and Mr. Leiss

"Ouch! What was that?!" I quickly looked at the chair I was sitting on for the source of the sharp pain I'd suddenly experienced. Finding nothing, I returned to my 7th grade science textbook.

OW! Again. Only this time it hurt even more. This time I knew it hadn't come from anything I was sitting on. It felt like somebody poked me with a thumbtack or needle, I thought as I searched the classroom around me.

There was no one nearby and the small faces of the other seventh graders around me were all bent to their science texts. The stinging in my butt, however, remained painful and real.

Focusing again on my own work, I tried to ignore the sting in my backside.

"Ouch!" This time I said it out loud. Turning around again, I said, "Who did it?" When I got no response other than quizzical looks, I tried to go along with the prank. Now I'm thinking... B.B. gun? Paperclip? Thumbtack?

"Okay, you've had your fun. Ha-ha. Now cut it out." I kept my voice calm in spite of the raging fire that was consuming my left butt cheek. I was more frustrated because I couldn't tell who it was or what it was he was doing, but I wouldn't give them the satisfaction of letting them see me in pain.

When the pain came this time, I was expecting it. Spinning, I instantly caught Greg, the tall, blonde kid, and Alvin, his buddy, before they could wipe the wicked smiles off their faces. They were both sitting at Greg's desk with their heads pressed conspiratorially together. Greg had his hands wrapped around something hiding it under his desk.

Calmly walking over to where they were, I said icily, "Alright, which one of you shot me?" When I got no response, I said it louder. "Which one?" With heads down, they snickered at each other. I was their own private joke.

When I initially approached I was just going to give them a warning – face-to-face, man-to-man. But now I felt myself along that razor's edge that I would seem to live on more and more the older I got.

Their degrading laughter, however, pushed me over. "Stand up," I said to Greg. I had no evidence to go on but my own instinct. That instinct was yelling at me, saying that Greg was the one and I guessed that he had shot me with a paperclip or dart of some kind. It was also telling me that if I didn't squash this shit right now, Greg, Alvin and even the little girls in this new class, would make me a walking duck during open season.

I was new to this class as of today. Yesterday I had been transferred mid-semester due to a fight with a student - also for hitting my teacher, Mrs. Hecht, with a box of Kleenex. The only problem was that it was encased with this heavy, plastic holder.

In that incident, Robert had stolen my lunch from my desk and was eating it right in front of me. Trying to be a good boy, I raised my hand urgently trying to get her to stop him. My family was poor and lunch was the only meager meal my short skinny ass could see in a while.

When her only response was, "Shut up, and sit down!" I said fuck that and set out to save the last handful of lunch that he hadn't gotten to yet. When he ran behind her to hide, the bitch, (well, she wasn't usually, but right now she has me pissed!) grabbed me instead. When she dug her nails into my right bicep, I hit her with the first thing that came to my left hand and that big hunk 'o plastic was it.

Back to Greg, who I had already identified as the alpha-male and Alvin as his sidekick, so I figured I was killing two birds with one stone by calling him out, establishing my position as a non-shit-taking motherfucker and repaying his insult in kind.

"Stand up," I repeated. "If you don't stand up, I'll hit you where you sit," I calmly told him. He continued to laugh, but Alvin sobered up and glanced nervously at him. Oh, well, I thought, I gave him fair warning.

Sssmack! I hit him across the head so hard my hand went numb. His face nearly slammed the desk as Alvin jumped back and away yelling, "Jesus!"

"Well..? You gonna just sit there?" I asked as a line of red rose from the back of his neck - to his cheeks - to his ears – to his forehead. But he didn't move. So I figured we were even. Then I made the mistake – one I've had to learn a couple of times in my life, but this would be the first time I would have to pay for it.

I turned my back on him. I turned my back to walk away and as I did, he jumped on me. Landing squarely on my back, he grabbed me by my curly hair. I immediately bent forward to do a shoulder throw just as he slipped off to my right side. Bent over, I spun to face him and attempted to straighten up. Unfortunately, he still had me by the hair and was pulling down hard. I couldn't move. I couldn't get any leverage to break free.

Meanwhile, he began swinging wild, frantic uppercuts, which I avoided mostly by covering up my face and head with my forearms. After I had enough of that shit, I decided to go on the offensive. Grabbing him by the waist, I rammed my head squarely into his gut and charged.

I hadn't carried him far across the room when I began to feel the satisfying sensation of Greg's body colliding with the many desks in our way. At this point he had let go of my hair and was hanging onto my arms for dear life. And I was seeing red. Like a bull that'd just skewered the matador, I was going to tear –his –ass up.

I had lost my mind – I mean literally. I still remember actually frightening myself as I contemplated how much strength it would take for me to heave him up and throw him through that Plexiglas window. The thing that really scared me was that we were on the third floor.

By the time I slammed him into the far wall, I was ready, willing and wanting to kill. Meanwhile he was sounding like a walrus with asthma, fighting for breath. Grabbing him by the throat, I straightened his limp body up and slammed him against the wall again in preparation for a murderous right hand that wanted to drive his head through the cinderblock before heaving him through that high, wide Plexiglas.

But halfway between my shoulder and his face, something brought my forearm to a complete and immediate stop.

Looking over, I saw a huge hand engulfing my little bicep. Following it up, I saw it was attached to the enormous girth of Mr. Leiss' full 300 pounds. Pulling me away from Greg, he stepped in between us and raised his huge arms like toll gates to keep us separated.

"What's going on here? What is the meaning of this?" He seemed incensed at our disruption of the class. I began telling him our story as Greg recovered and the more I talked, the more I remembered. The more I remembered, the angrier I got – I was pissed! How dare him – I was just sitting there! Minding my own business, doing my work. When out of nowhere this fuck-head decided to start fuckin' with me! To cause me pain!

I saw the prick looking down at me, face pink, breathing hard, jaws clenched. He looked like he wanted some more. So...

Sssmack! I bitch-slapped him right over those separating arms. Man that felt good, because now the entire class was watching. I slapped him so hard it felt like I had burst a watermelon. The teacher's jaw just dropped as he stared at him. Meanwhile, I watched as Greg recovered his balance. When he looked at me again, it was almost funny. His lower lip was stuck out in an unusual fashion. His hair was as tousled as a haystack. His pink face bore my handprint, tomato red, over the entire left side. His nose was running and tears streamed down his face.

Crying out loud, he charged and started kicking at me. Then suddenly, and much to my surprise, I found myself airborne. "HowTheHellDidIGetHere?!?" flashed through my mind and just before my feet touched down, it followed through my mind, indignant, "Why the hell did Mr. Leiss hit me?" Instead of Greg the instigator, he chose to swat me through the air like a badminton bird. Catching me in the chest, he flicked me across the room like a cigarette butt.

Fortunately, I landed on my feet. Unfortunately, my backwards momentum was such that I stumbled back off balance for several steps. To make matters worse, I then collided with a desk, whereupon both the desk and I toppled over backwards. As if that weren't enough, when I landed there was still enough momentum to flip me completely ass over end.

By the time I stopped rolling, I was ready to kill... EVERYBODY!! Furious! Enraged beyond all reason or control, I launched myself off the floor and like a guided missile aimed straight at the one person who started this whole mess: Greg! The way I saw it, Mr. Leiss had every right to do what he did just as I had every right to be angry at Greg for getting me into this. If he'd only stopped after the second one...

"AAAAAAAAAAA!!!" When I let out that primal scream it made everyone jump and when I charged, they scattered. So now tears of rage were streaming down my face and I was howling like a banshee while I knocked desks over like bowling pins.

Mr. Leiss at first stepped back with his mouth hanging open. I guess he thought I was trying to kill him. Realizing I was going for Greg, he recovered himself and jumped in front of him with arms outspread in an effort to keep me from him. By this time, Greg, eyes wide, had begun to panic and was now hiding behind the expanse of the teacher. He was now just a target in my crosshairs and I was going to make him pay! Pay for the pain, the humiliation, my degradation, and my shame... I was going to MURDER HIM!!!

But first I had to get around Tubby. Brillo (as I then began to refer to Mr. Leiss for his short, wiry hair with silver sidewalls) was D-ing up on me like Rodman at the hole. But I was quicker and much smaller, and wound up chasing Greg around him like playing tag around an oak.

Faking right, I went left as Greg skittered around him counter-clockwise. Lunging around, I reached out and just missed his collar. I felt satisfaction build in me as I visualized my fists smashing his mouth into shards of white, pink, and red.

Brillo had spun around behind me and managed to grab a hold of my right arm with his left. While holding on with his left hand, he tried with his right arm to catch me around the body. Spinning around to our right, I managed to avoid his right arm, but he still had a firm hold with his left. For a time we strove with each other: him trying to restrain me and I trying desperately not to be caught.

But no matter what I tried, I could not break that grip. It couldn't have been more than a minute of struggle, but already he was starting to tire. His face had grown red and sweat sprang up on his brow while my fury had turned into pure survival against this mountain of a man.

Then my luck ran out and he somehow managed to snag my left arm with his right, and I wound up wrapped up with him behind me, and my arms crossed in front of my chest with him pulling tight. But I was not done yet. Not by a long shot.

Stepping back, sinking, and bending forward, I attempted to throw his enormous girth over my right shoulder. Okay, so I'm not a Judo champion nor am I a rocket scientist. How did

I know what a hernia was in seventh grade? All I know is I came damn close to giving myself one with that little attempt.

Once the pain in my gut subsided, I tried throwing my right shoulder under his right armpit. I straightened my left hand pulling down and out while simultaneously leveraging up with my shoulder. That one worked. My trapped hand slipped free of his grasp. Adding to its momentum, I twisted my hips and slammed my now free arm, elbow first, viciously into his midsection. Doing ab-so-lutely... nothing.

And right about then is when I came to my senses. I finally figured out that I'd pretty much done my worst. Maybe it was time to quit before I made him mad. Just about that time he grew impatient and picked me up in a squeezing but harmless bear hug, and said, "James, will you please calm down!?"

"Fuck You!"

- I hated it when he called me James. He would call me James all through the rest of that year and the next until I graduated. Probably revenge for the Brillo thing. When on graduation day he called James Edward Thornton to come across the stage, I stage-whispered, "That's Eddie, Brillo!" And to his credit, red-faced he said to the crowd, "Excuse me, James Eddie Thornton," finally getting it close enough for me to let it go. -

"Please... calm down," he said.

Finally caught and catching my breath, I figured what the heck. "Yeah, sure," I told him and he set me down.

"Now what is the matter with you?" he asked incredulously.

"I don't like people messin' with me," was the only explanation I could offer. Anger was still in my blood and I was still looking at Greg's hiding figure like a wolf eying a rabbit. Not knowing what else to do, Mr. Leiss took me down to the principal's office where I spent the remainder of the day.

The next day, Mom had to take a day off of work and come down to the school, not the first time and not the last time, and begged them out of expelling me.

And that was pretty much the way things went for me where fighting was concerned. You can see why I was always reluctant to get into it with anyone. Because once I did, there was no middle ground for me. I was always in a blood-rage. I always knew there was something wrong with me. I just didn't know what it was or what to do about it.

None of my teachers or counselors was prepared to deal with this sort of problem I faced on a daily basis. Even when I was arrested for disorderly conduct or disturbing the peace or assault, or vandalism, the police had no helpful advice. They would just shake their heads and walk away.

It wasn't until many years later that I decided to stop waiting for someone else to fix me and do it myself. Eventually, I did find others who were equipped to help guide me in my quest for balance. Out of all my searching, all my learning, all my growing, I've learned one thing:

No one makes it through this Life unscathed.

High

I was 12 the first time I got high. I was playing at John's house. I had spent the night at his house and I found a joint behind his couch. I showed it to him and he guessed it was his mom's because she and some friends had been getting high and partying there the night before. He asked if I wanted to smoke it.

Now at this time in my life, EVERYONE got high, drunk, fought, cursed and had sex. So I said sure. And so we two children smoked this joint and we giggled and laughed because it was silly, we laughed because it was funny, we roared because it was hysterical.

Then I realized it wasn't that funny, because we couldn't stop. I tried to stop laughing, but it was hard. It was very hard. In that instant it felt very wrong. I told John and he just laughed and laughed. I needed some space, so I went into the kitchen. John laughed and followed. I needed some air, so I went outside. John roared and followed. "Where ya goin'?" So I ran to get away. He ran to follow. Then we ran just to run, and we ran until the laughter died, then I stopped.

"Where ya goin'?" he asked, concerned.

"No place. Let's get somethin' to eat," I said.

My First Pistol

The first gun I shot was a nine millimeter, blue steel semi-automatic. I was at John's when George came by with this piece he had taken from some apartment he had burglarized. He asked John to hold onto it for him, because he didn't trust it not to be found and taken by his dad or brother. John agreed to keep it for him for a few days.

"Lemmee see that," I said to him. To my surprise, he handed it right over like he didn't want anything to do with it. I loved the weight of the thing. It felt heavy and solid in my hand. The combination of precision machining and worn steel made it a work of art to me.

The next afternoon at John's, I asked him if he wanted to fire it. Surprising me again, he said no.

"Let me," I said to him.

"Sure, I don't care," he said and handed it right over.

Feeling the weight once again in my small hand, I anticipated firing it. I had never seen a handgun fired up close before. To my mind came images of the boom and kick of Harry Callahan's .44 Magnum.

Ejecting the clip, I found it had a full magazine. Taking out all the bullets, I then put one back in and reinserted the clip into the handle. Sliding the safety onto the safe position, I secured it into the waistband of my jeans and we were off.

Cruising up and down the dusky alleyways of the next neighborhood over, we finally selected one that was more secluded than most and allowed plenty of escape routes.

For a target I selected a telephone pole about fifty feet away with the broad side of a brick building behind it. The building had no windows and in case I missed, the bullet would ricochet upwards with its energy spent. However, I didn't think I'd miss. I'm pretty mean with a BB gun.

"Alright, keep an eye out," I said to John, who sat astride his bike behind and a little to my right. As he checked the entrances to the alley, I took the safety off, ratcheted a round into the chamber, and drew a bead on the center of the pole and about fifteen feet up. From my perspective, this was dead center of the brick wall.

Spreading my faded, black, size six All-Stars, I anticipated the booming, Clint Eastwood recoil. Turning my face slightly away, I aimed, cringed, and pulled the trigger.

I didn't feel a thing. A dud? I thought. I mean I felt a little jerk, but no real recoil. And as for the concussive boom? Nothin' but a lil' ol'' pop.

Looking at the pistol I saw a wisp of smoke rising from the barrel. Turning to John, I said, "Now, ain't that some shit?" But he was *gone*.

At first all I heard was the spinning of his bicycle chain away to my right. Turning further, I saw his ass-end fading into the distance as his legs spun around like the Road Runner in a hurry. Shit! He's leavin' me. Then I figured it wasn't such a bad idea.

Hurriedly, I put the safety back on, shoved the nine back in my pants, then quickly had to readjust it as the hot barrel had begun to warm my dick up a little more than was comfortable. Pulling it to the side and snuggling it at an angle, I hopped on my bike and began the ride back home with John nowhere in sight.

georgia

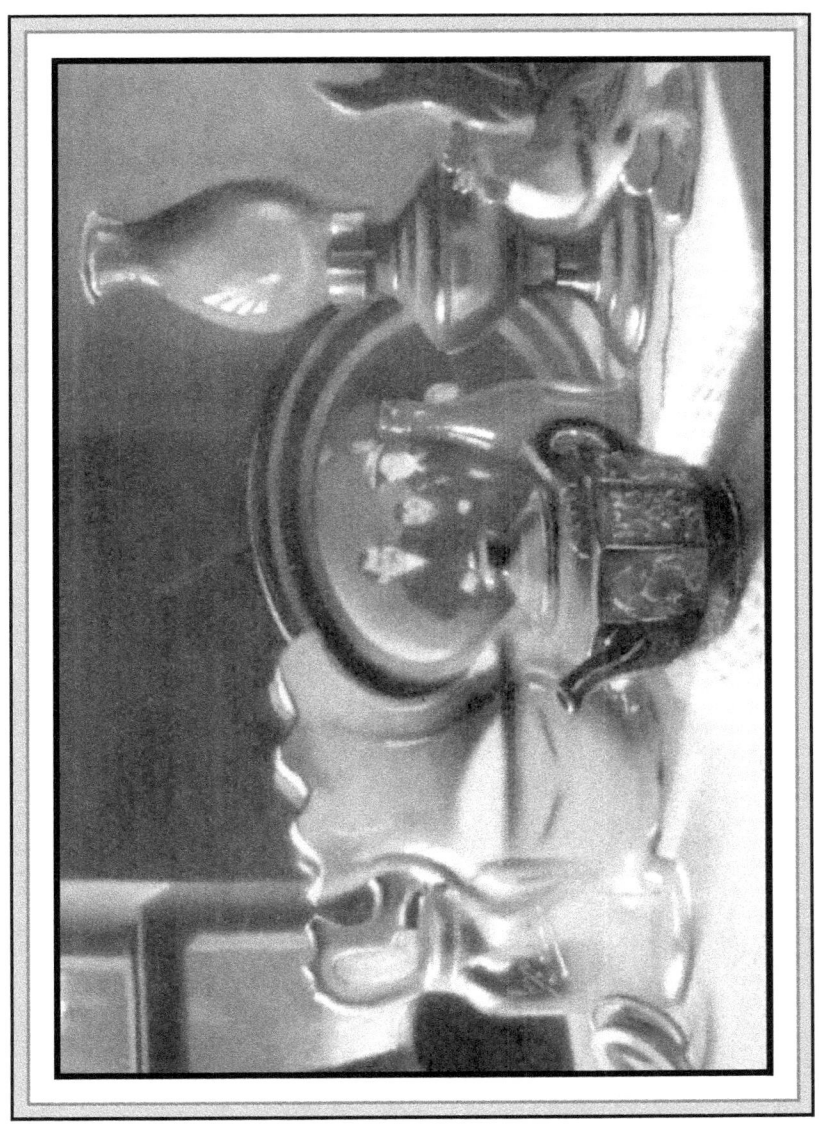

 georgia

Georgia Summers

My summers with my grandparents were like a reverse looking glass, like coming out of a twisted Wonderland, a perverted Oz. Almost every summer from the earliest time I can remember, Mom, Pamela and I took a trip south to the northern hills of Georgia where my grandparents owned 140 acres of land. We would either rent a car and drive the 800 miles or fly when we could afford it. That was the sole thing we looked forward to, well, actually two things: 1) It was far away from the madhouse that was the mean streets of Chicago; and 2) It was far away from my dad.

He almost never came for one reason: he was afraid. He was a black man afraid of my white mother's parents. He was afraid of the South. He was afraid of not being around a readily available supply of heroin. He was afraid of the strength my grandparents gave to my mother, Pamela and I. As if he feared we would suddenly rise up against his cruel oppression and banish him from our midst. So he did it himself.

Thank God.

The land was basically a basin with hills, ridges and ravines within. There were flat areas and steep hillsides.

There were trees of every sort, several varieties of pine, oak, hickory, maple, and walnut. The soil was a rich orange color where it was uncovered. In the denseness of the forest, the ground was perpetually covered with a carpet of pine needles or leaves. Rocks of all kinds were found there: marble, quartz, isinglass (fool's gold), granite and many others I cannot name. There were parts of the forest that were open and the sun came through in bright ribbons of fire so that the red clay was reflected on everything around it. Other areas had a canopy so dense that beneath there was a mysterious, permanent twilight.

The land was about 50 miles south of the Tennessee border and 120 miles north of Atlanta. The nearest small city was Gainesville, which was twenty miles away, and the nearest small town was Cleveland proper, which was ten miles away. And once you left the highway, it was a mile over a steep, twisting, hilly, rutted, rocky, dirt road before you saw the rusted tin roof of their house.

Actually it was more like a shack. You remember the opening scene of "The Beverly Hillbillies"? Well, ours was about twice the size of that. Literally. It had been a barn originally before Papa added rooms, a kitchen and a bathroom, living room, dining room and three bedrooms. The boards had long since turned gray with age. He built it in 1941. It was hot in the summer, and in the winter the temperature dropped to ten degrees Fahrenheit at times. There was an attic for storage and instead of a basement there was a pit dug in the earth underneath for plumbing access and storage. There was a storm shelter across the dirt road and an outhouse a hundred feet to the east.

Yes, I said outhouse, "Shithouse" as the natives called them. We, by the time I was born, had an indoor bathroom we used just as often as the outdoor one. But the water pressure was so low it took about fifteen minutes for the tank to fill up. And in the winter it was only a few degrees colder outside so if someone was in and you had to go, there was hardly any difference at all except the walk.

Our water source was a spring about a quarter of a mile up the nearest mountain. Papa had dug it himself and run hand-spliced rubber and plastic tubing all the way down to the house. Let me tell you something: there was nothing sweeter than the taste of that water straight out of the earth. I used to fill up gallon jugs and bring it back home to share with all my friends back in Chicago. Forget corn liquor; just give me some of that sweet, Georgia Mountain, spring water.

There were all types of wildlife to be found on our land: deer, bear, fox, coyote, eagle, hawk, owl, raccoon, opossum, rabbit, groundhog, and skunk. Of snakes there could be found the copperhead, king snake, and rattlesnake. Insects like millipedes, scorpions, lizards, huge horned beetles, and every type of stinging, biting insect could be found there as well.

While Mom and Pam spent their time with friends and relatives getting reacquainted, I had work to do. My "job" was helping Papa in the sawmill that he owned and ran at the top of his property. My grandpop was a true pioneer. He had numerous sources of income. Both Granny and Papa were on social security later in life. In addition, while nearly seventy, Papa still operated the saw mill with his last surviving partner. He still raised thousands of chickens at a time. There was the corn farm, a vegetable garden, the pigs he raised, the mules he kept, and the cows he fed. He had given up moonshinin' while he was still a young man.

We were expected to pitch in around the house. I did so gladly, because it hardly seemed like work, even though I hated the gardening and especially hated raising the chickens and the pigs. I hated it because they were being raised only to die. Even at my young age, I still found that quite morbid and unfair. But my favorite thing was "sawmillin'", "lumberjackin'". It was a wonderful process that, unlike the other work, I got to see from start to finish in one day.

Papa and I would go scout out trees of suitable number, variety, height, shape and integrity. Then we would cut them down with a power saw and trim the branches off with axes. His partner would then back the tractor up to several of the fallen trees and we would hammer spiked chains into the end of them with sledges, and the tractor would then drag them back to the saw mill and pile them up in a big heap. Some days the pile could be as big as eight feet high containing dozens of logs. The saw was powered by a tractor engine and driven by a belt. The diameter of the blade was about five feet across. Once the machine was tuned and running right, we started rolling the logs with the peavey, a pole with an iron tip and an iron tong attached near the bottom. If the logs were stacked high and heavy enough to prevent us from rolling them from the bottom of the pile, we would have to climb up on top of the pile and roll them down from there, all the while watching for the log you were standing on to come out from under you and bury you in an avalanche of tons of wood and bark. And when the pile had been left over night you also had to keep an eye out for snakes and scorpions.

It was just you and nature. No anger, no hatred, no revenge for some imagined slight. Here if you got killed at least it made sense. Eaten by a bear? He was hungry; had a family to feed. At least it went for some good.

When I wasn't working or hanging out with Granny or Papa, I was in the woods. I would take one of the rifles and go target shooting. I'd go climbing. I practiced with my bow and arrows. Sling, sword, martial arts, you name it, I would be doing it. I would go running up and down through the woods for exercise. I loved to explore. I could roam for hours through those hills. As a child I lived a rich fantasy life where I was an explorer, a pioneer, hunter, tracker, soldier, and ninja. I would stalk animals through the woods and sneak up as close as I could downwind before they would finally pick up some sound I'd made and bolt. Then I would chase them as far as I could. I have followed deer for miles. When I got older, if the wind was just right, I could get close enough to spit on one. And then they'd be off like a flash. I would try to catch the smaller ones. I never even got close.

When I was younger I was afraid EVERYTHING. I was especially afraid of the dark. So in order to get over it, I would wait for night to fall. When there was a full moon you could see the shadow of your fingers on your upraised hand. But when there was none, it was pitch black. You could barely see your feet. Then in the darkness of night I would set out with no knife, no flashlight, no walking stick and set off straight through the thickest and darkest of woods. I would walk until I figured I was at the far edge of the property line and then I would just stand there, or sit in the nestling leaves. I would listen to the abundant night sounds all around me until the threatening sounds of wild, stalking animals sneaking upon me in a ravenous feeding frenzy became merely the sounds of the forest breathing, living.

After a while you learn to pick out the individual sounds of insects and animals. The brief fluctuations of shadow and shade became just the denizens of the dark going about their nightly business. Raccoons, opossum and other dwellers of the deep woods would soon accept me as simply a part of their environment and after a brief inspection would move on past me.

Yes, it was strange being a child of mixed race living in the Deep South. Yes, I encountered my share of racism. Many a closet Klansman has plotted my demise. I've even been shot at. Beneath that genteel Southern charm lies a sickness that some have recognized and begun to deal with. Others remained willfully blind. And they are even more dangerous than the outright racist. At least they don't fool themselves into thinking they are something they are not.

Believe it or not, I've been called Nigger in Chicago more times than I can count. And as unbelievable as it sounds I have NEVER been called ANY racial slur in the deepest southern woods of Georgia. Sounds strange, huh? Yet another stereotype shattered. And by the way, I've had to fight for my life far more in our country's liberal north than in those Appalachian Mountains.

Papa

Papa was a mountain man. He was a part of the hills, mountains, streams and trees of his land. He was 82 years old when he died. I was 23. He died in his sleep of a heart attack and it was just his time. Papa, my grandfather, was more like my father than my dad was. I learned some of the most important life lessons from him. He didn't teach so much as live his life. There were no "talks" or "lessons" so to speak. It was just him.

He was about 5'9" and skinny as a rail the way old people are. His head was bald as a baby's ass and Granny swore that all his hair fell out the day after she prayed it would. He was always a quiet man, but he sure loved to tell a joke. And he was good. It was not so much that the jokes were that good, it was just that it was funny listening to him tell his stories. They were always about some regular guy who would say or do something incredibly stupid. It was the kind of thing you hoped you'd never do. Or at least you hoped no one caught you doing it. Once he got to telling you the story, it usually cracked him up so much remembering it you were usually laughing before he even finished.

Papa was a real mountain man. He spent far more time outside the house working on the farm than he ever spent indoors. He was skinny, but he was strong. At 80 he was about as strong as I was when I was about 18. He was around 70 when I was on the swim team, track team, cross-country and lifting weights, and he was just about as strong as I was. I helped him and a friend of his lift a plowshare out of the bed of a pickup and they had it on their own until I offered to lend a hand. I was staggered by how much it weighed and thrown off guard by how light they made it seem before I jumped in.

He owned 140 acres deep in the North Georgia Mountains. It was mountain land with a kind of valley and a basin smack in the middle of it. In the basin was where the house and farm were. The acreage covered the hilltops all around us. He would regularly walk the perimeter of the land checking animal traffic as well as human. He would take note of all the flora and fauna that affected his kingdom. Papa could name every one of the hundreds of plants and trees that were on his land. Could tell you how many different things it was used for as well. The altitude of the mountains, combined with the steepness of the slopes and the ruggedness of the terrain, managed to keep him in great shape. It always took me a few days to adjust to the altitude and the exertion it took to trudge up those Rocky Mountains.

Every summer we would go walking in the woods and he would point out each tree and tell me the different names for them. And each fall as I returned to the guns and gangs of Chicago, I would forget. My desire for remembering them was quickly replaced by my need for survival. And that would sometimes occupy all my time and attention.

All the peace and calm that I absorbed down there throughout the summer I quickly lost upon returning to that hostile city. I loved being in the country... for a while anyway. The peace and tranquility was hard to get used to. I used to hear the silence so loud it was deafening. No cars, no sirens, no arguing, no fighting, no gunshots... nothing. It would ring in my ears so loud it hurt. When I would go to sleep in the back bedroom there would be no light. Nothing. I mean literally I could not see my own hand in front of my face. It was like being dead.

Then, slowly over a few days, I would start to relax. I would begin to hear sounds in the stillness of the night, the crickets, the screech owl, and the wind. It was beautiful. Then suddenly what had been my nemesis became my friend. With the silence came peace. Instead of trying to look harder into the darkness, I began to feel, to sense, to be.

Papa wasn't a talker like Dad. He was a doer. You would rarely hear him talk about "what I'm gonna do." The first thing you usually heard about what he was "going" to do was after he'd done it. He'd just get up, put on his hat, and walk out the door.

The coolest thing was that neither he nor Granny ever laid a hand on me. Sure, they threatened to, but they never did. Every now and then they would threaten to "git out the hickory and lick ya good," but they never raised their voices even in arguing. They would just express their anger then go on with life. Nothing was ever that big a deal, no matter what I'd done. It was nice to see that I didn't have that big an impact on the universe, that it wouldn't be the end of the world if I had forgotten to do a chore or mouthed off. It really was okay And in respect to that, I never did anything contrary to their wishes on purpose.

Usually when I'd pissed them off, it was an accident. Sometimes the words would be out before I knew what I had said. Then I felt bad about it. But they would just go on with life. Thank God. So many adults put so much pressure on their children to "behave" then yell, scream, spank or beat them when they get it wrong, instead of just calmly explaining why it was wrong then getting on past it. It's like they think children just sit around all day thinking up ways just to piss them off. I got a newsflash for ya: children spend far more time thinking up ways to have fun and NOT get into trouble than you seem to remember. At best, it's hard to be a kid.

When Papa was younger, he wasn't the best of fathers. But by the time I came around, he'd mellowed considerably. In fact, almost forty years in retrospect, I believe he was the best example of a father I have ever seen. He would invite me along with him in whatever he did. He never told me to do anything. He would go quietly about his work and trust that I wouldn't do anything too far beyond stupid. He kept an eye on me, but you'd never know it. I never felt watched, but he would always give me a warning before I got into trouble.

One time our old German shepherd, Charlie, was napping on the porch and I decided to stick a broom straw into his ear. Pop, who was sitting on the porch also, saw it and said, "He's gonna bite ya if you keep that up." I didn't understand why and Charlie seemed okay so far, so I kept on going. Then outta nowhere he swung his head around lightning-quick and snapped at the hand that was holding the straw. That scared the shit outta me! Charlie had never snapped at me before! So between him and Papa, I knew that I was the one who had messed up, not Charlie. Pop just sat there. Didn't say a word.

Another time we were on the back porch. He was looking for something stacked back there. I was out there enjoying the view and opening a can of sliced peaches with my little Case pocketknife. I would jam the point in the top of the can, then slice down an inch then repeat the process along the perimeter of the top. "You'll cut your hand off doin' that," he said.

"I'll be careful," I said as I continued. Sure enough, about ten seconds later, "OUCH!!" The can had slipped in my hand. The blade folded in on my finger slicing me a deep, inch-long gouge, which immediately began to bleed profusely. Papa came over and paused briefly as he looked down at it. Then he continued on back inside the house. Never said a word.

Granny

Granny was the matriarch of the house. Definitely. She was short and portly. About as wide as she was tall. She used to joke that she didn't sleep so much as roll and tumble in the bed. It was no surprise. Her identity was centered around food. Man that woman could cook. Anybody who walked in that door had to be fed. Had to. Fried chicken, mashed potatoes, string beans, biscuits, and cornbread were the staples, but I never got tired of them. She cooked what she grew. She would help Papa with the garden beside the house. She was warm and motherly/wife and mother. And that was the extent of her universe. She didn't propose to have understanding of the world at large. She knew Jesus, she said, and that was enough.

Granny never strayed far from home. As I got into high school, she seldom left the farm. She never rode into town for groceries, never visited friends or relatives. She was an artistic soul. She could knit and crochet like no one else. People who had visited her house would write from across the country and beg her to crochet something for them. On the living room wall there was a reproduction of the Last Supper that was finely detailed. It was about five feet long and two feet high. She had done portraits of Queen Elizabeth and the Sistine Chapel.

Not too long ago I was visiting my mother, who now lives on the farm, and I was listening to a song by Enya sung in Gaelic. Then Mom floored me by saying, "That sounds just like Mother used to sing to me when we were children."

"What?! This song? In this language?"

"Yes."

I hit the roof! "You mean to tell me my grandmother could sing Irish music? In Gaelic?!" Laughing, she told me of how she used to sing to her. How could I know a close relative for almost thirty years and not know something like that about them?

Granny was a part of those hills, the mountains, the trees and the soil. She was like a part of that house: inseparable. So much so that when I first saw her in the hospital before she died, I was shocked to see her out of the element I'd seen her attached to for so long. It was like suddenly coming across the Empire State Building, uprooted and planted in the middle of an Iowa cornfield. I felt as if I was looking at a heap of dusty Georgia clay resting on that stainless steel.

Then, as today, I feel proud and incredibly blessed to have had Granny and Papa in my life. Poor, ignorant, red-neck, racist, lovely, loving, wise, giving, funny, kind, and mine are all words that do not begin to encompass what they were to me.

"Chicken Chokin"
(It's not what'cha think)

I've only killed two chickens in my life. One I shot, the other one I wrung its neck. Well, kind of.

It was the time of year when all of the chickens had matured and Papa sold them off. Soon the men would come, pickup trucks full of 'em. Late at night they would tear through Papa's chicken houses, herding them into corners and snatching the panicking creatures up two at a time and then shove them into wooden cages with bars like prison. They would be packed in there like slaves on a ship.

We would work silently, far into the night, hustling crates and stacking them high upon the trucks. Hundreds of 'em. They seemed a mile high with white-feathered balls of clucking agitation.

Papa couldn't help because his asthma was so severe the dust and feathers that they kicked up would have killed him. There weren't enough inhalers in the world to keep him from dying in that environment, especially at his age. But I always had to be part of the action in spite of my mixed feelings.

When they left, both of the normally teeming chicken houses would be cavernously empty, leaving only sawdust and feathers to mark their sweet, soft existence. The thousands of once tiny, chirping, balls of dandelion fluff, now grown large and bold, were all gone.

But before they came, Granny would have her pick to kill, pluck, cut up and freeze for our future dinners, suppers, and breakfasts. When I heard where the chickens were going, I was curious to see the process from start to finish. So in the dark of night, off we went.

It was a short walk down the sloping drive to where the chicken houses lay. Because they all got the same exercise and ate the same amount, they were not surprisingly, all the same size. It was kind of anticlimactic actually.

Holding them by their feet, upside down and squawking, we had one in each hand, six ready to go. Once outside the chicken house Papa, turned one around so that he held it by the neck and with one, two, three deft swings, built up enough circular momentum for centrifugal force to snap its neck. Then he did the same with the other one.

Now don't ask me why, but I just had to try it. There was something intriguing about the technique. They both laughed and Papa said, "Go on." Handing one of my two to Granny, which by the way was almost as long as I was tall, I took the other by the head in both hands and began to swing.

Weeeeeell, let's just say things didn't go as smoothly for me as they had for my grandfather. First, the thing was so heavy I could barely swing it hard enough to get it over the top. The downswing almost ripped it out of my small hands. Second, the damned thing was squawking and flapping and kicking and thrashing about so that my semi-circle soon became an erratic, uncontrollable kind of... mess.

Finally, just as I was really starting to feel bad for this poor, frightened, in pain creature, it kind of exploded... from both ends. And in an instant I was covered from head to foot in yellow chicken puke and brown... y'know... chicken shit!

Yeeeeeeeeuck! At this point, I abandoned the endeavor completely and focused on trying not to vomit myself. So there I stood, all three and a half feet of me, painted yellow and brown, arms out at my sides holding that damned chicken as far away from me as possible with a look of absolute disgust on my face. And there stood my grandparents, laughing their asses off. They were laughing so hard I thought they were both having coronaries. They whooped and howled and slapped their thighs, each other's backs, and stomped their feet. Granny's eyes were tearing up so much her glasses were wet and she had to take them off to see.

Ain't this a bitch? I was so mad I didn't know what to do. Eventually, I got tired of waiting for them to laugh themselves out. They clearly had far more stamina than I previously gave them credit for, and more lung capacity too. Stomping over to Papa, I handed him the now irate offended chicken and headed off for home still holding my arms out at my sides like Jesus crucified. Like somehow that was going to keep me from getting more vomit and shit on me. Like I could possibly have more vomit and shit on me. I don't see how unless you could somehow layer it up.

Well, that was enough for me. I was through for the night. I went home, peeled off my overalls and flannel shirt, kicked off my boots and climbed into bed.

I heard them come in ten minutes later. They were still laughing... both of them.

Wayne's World

Near the end of one particular stay with my grandparents, we were visited by a family friend of theirs named Wayne. Wayne was a good ol' boy through and through. He was a long-haul truck driver in his early thirties. Standing about five six, he was stocky with short brown hair that had a light salting throughout. His eyes had that slightly droopy quality like he was constantly on the verge of taking a nap.

He was funny. He had the driest sense of humor this side of Don Rickles. And smart too, though you wouldn't think it to look at him. His pot belly had traveled across the entire face of the continent and visited others as well. But he was just as comfortable in a recliner with a can of Pabst in his hand.

Wayne and I hit it off immediately and when he found out I was from Chicago, he said he had a run to make to Michigan that would take him right past Chi and I could hitch a ride if I wanted.

Once Granny and Papa gave us the okay, I couldn't wait for the next week to pass and our adventure to begin.

After hasty, afternoon good-byes, I was anxious to be on our way, to start on the new adventure. Wayne drove us out to his house in the pickup. Then we climbed in his Peterbilt tractor-trailer and struck out for the nearby town of Gainesville and its lone poultry plant.

It was my first time inside and it was an eye-opener. Walking through the front office and into the main body of the plant, the first thing that hits you is the stench. It's a kind of... well... wet-chicken smell. Like rotten eggs.

Men and women marched silently past dressed in long, white lab coats like some white garbed regulators out of the old west. Dozens of them. Unspeaking and on a mission.

Then there's the noise. The noise of machinery. All kinds of machinery. And chickens. Like some sort of terminator factory, above my head wound a chain all around the factory. There were hooks dangling from the chain every foot or so. Some were empty, but most had live chickens dangling from them. They hung upside down from their feet, some flapping, some squawking, and some doing both.

I followed with my eyes the twisted path the chain led them on, when it passed another just like it, only this one carried dead chickens. Chickens with their heads cut off. Now my eyes followed that chain back to its source into a big box-like machine. And into the opposite side of that box flowed the chain of live chickens. Somewhere in between, a ghastly mechanism guillotined them and disposed of their silent heads.

To make matters more macabre, directly beneath the entire bending, twisting path of that chain ran a pit about six inches deep filled with blood. A river of it. Flowing slowly. Silently.

And then we were out the back. Bursting out into the fresh air and sunshine, and free of that abattoir. The charnel house. That cold, dead place. Here Wayne made arrangements for the loading of his truck and then we plunged back into the depths of chicken-hell and were spat out the other side again where we moved the truck. We then waited about an hour or so while it was loaded up with the packaged product of that place.

Then it was on the road for real.

The first part of our journey took us up a wide interstate through the North Georgia Blue Ridge Mountains and the Great Smokey's, part of the Appalachian Mountain chain that stretches from Alabama through Georgia, and then on up into Canada.

The mountains, ridges, and foothills all made for a rollercoaster ride in that bouncing big rig, swaying down that winding-ribbon road. To the left and the right of the road it would alternately rise before us as undulating hills revealed the rock beneath the soil, trees and plants as the highway had been cut through with dynamite and earthmovers. Or it would plunge beneath us leaving us to look down upon the tree tops far below. Boulders and streams and fields would sometimes stretch out for miles.

Wayne's CB handle was "Blue Ribbon" and he, like all truckers and most southerners, kept it on constantly. Its squelched, static-y babble blended in with the hum of the retreads, the rumble of that big 435 cc engine and the plaintive wails of the bluegrass that played on the radio.

Heading north out of Kentucky, the hills began to smooth to undulations, eventually becoming the Great Plains of the Midwest.

Around midnight we finally pulled into a truck stop for some desperately needed sleep. In spite of a mattress and a claustrophobic sleeping compartment behind the seats, I had been unable to do more than doze for ten or fifteen minutes at a time, unused to the rumbling and bouncing of the truck along with the various hisses, buzzes, and whines the monster produced. I was looking forward to the stillness.

Unfortunately, Wayne was going to occupy the tiny, single mattress in the tiny, single sleeping compartment. So now I was stuck trying to get some sleep in the cramped front passenger seat with the dashboard creasing my shins along with the hard back wall to rest my head against. No sliding the seat back, no reclining, no tilt... just... damn. It was like trying to sleep on a park bench built for one.

As Wayne climbed into the sleeper, I settled into my box seat and tried to get comfortable 'cause for the next four or five hours, I was stuck. I wasn't having much luck, however. So I sat there fruitlessly trying to hurl myself into the depths of sleep, to no avail. The bitch of it was that once we stopped, I wasn't sleepy at all. Damn.

Giving up on sleeping, I decided to make the best of it. Sitting up, I took in my surroundings while the ever-present murmuring static of the C.B. kept me company. Like a true trucker, Wayne even listened to the damned thing in his sleep. But hey, right about now I was thankful for even the sporadic conversation that came from it.

Taking in my surroundings, I noticed an artificial twilight of neon and mercury vapor. As it was nearing 2:00 a.m., I was surprised at the amount of activity going on around me. We sat smack in the middle of several rows of rigs that sat back to back and faced opposing rows. Nose to nose, tail to tail.

All around us figures moved in the semi-darkness like zombies on the prowl, roaming, lethargic through the night. There were mostly men with a few women here and there, alone and sometimes in pairs, either with drivers or drivers themselves. Flannel shirts, blue jeans, cowboy boots, cowboy hats, cowboy shirts. There were work boots, big belt buckles and lots of tobacco. As the slow activity continued, they got in and out of cabs, checked their tires and engines, wires and hoses. And some just seemed to be doing nothing but coming or going. But to where?

On the C.B. there were more women than usual with a sharp, clear signal. They had names like "Mamma Hen" and "Honey Bunny". As I sat back listening, I began to notice they were taking orders. And "Beaver" seemed to be the order du jour. That's when I noticed the women who weren't truckers were doing most of the to-and-fro roaming. Aaaaaand they were clad more skimpily than the average southerner. Contrary to the "Dukes of Hazard", "Daisy Dukes" were NOT accepted by respectable, church-going, bible-belt-living south-of-the-Mason/Dixon dwellers.

Not that I needed this to confirm what I already knew was going on, but every now and then a bouncing head, bouncing cab, flash of moon on flesh, or thrashing silhouette left nothing to the imagination.

Eventually I drifted off to an uncomfortable half-sleep that lasted until dawn. Then I just sat there in the now cold, empty parking lot waiting for Wayne to wake up. I was looking forward to stretching my legs, getting something warm in my tummy and hitting the road.

And after all that was done, we were on our way. Sitting warm and full in the front seat, we pulled in the merge lane and he hit the gas. Running up through those gears, we built up speed slowly but steadily as the lumbering beast moved on.

On the side of the road to my right and just ahead there was a snow-white dove standing on the shoulder like a hobo looking for a ride. But just before we got to him, he decided to launch himself into the air.

Forward and upward it began to fly ahead of us, slowly and steadily rising on a long, shallow, upward parabola. And on he flew just like that, like he was leading the way for us as we gained speed. We began to catch up to him and I smiled, as he was just a few feet ahead and below the level of my window. I was looking forward to the next few seconds when he would be close enough to me that I could almost reach out and touch him.

That poor bird was doing fine until he decided to make a left turn. Right into our path. THUMP! He never had a chance. We hit him with the grille about three feet below me and a spray of blood splattered our windshield. Strangely, a handful of pristine, white angel feathers flew up and were glued to the windshield by its own blood.

Horrified, I look over at Wayne who looked at me with a droll expression on his face and said, "Well... he won't do that again." And with that he flicked on his windshield wipers, which smeared the blood and feathers across the entire surface before washing them away.

Damn. Life is like that sometimes. Sometimes it smacks you on the ass no matter how fast you run. I just hoped I wouldn't make that sudden left turn when my time came.

Somewhere around the bottom of Indiana, between the purgatory and perdition of endless nothing, we pulled into a truck stop for a well needed breakfast, rest and refueling.

I had been restlessly dozing since early morning and was looking forward to stretching my legs. As I stepped down from the cab, I was greeted by a crisp, chilly breeze, which helped chase the cobwebs from my head. Standing there, I filled my lungs with that cool morning air, stretched my arms out wide, expanded my chest, and stomped my feet to get the blood back in them. Then finally, I began to feel alive again.

After a few minutes of staring at the flat, green fields to the east, I became antsy and decided I needed to look at something I hadn't been staring at for the last half of eternity. I walked around to the other side of the truck to see if anything different was happening over there. Hoping, hoping, hoping.

And boy was it! It actually scared me. It was huge. It had eaten up the entire sky ahead of me. It seemed to take up an entire half of the planet Earth. On a horizon so flat you could see the curve of the Earth, one BIG, black, flat storm covered the globe like a terminator of the moon. It was a funeral shroud draped on a world ignorant of its own funeral. Suffice it to say, I had never seen anything like it.

In our neck of the woods, in the North Georgia Mountains, the sky you saw was always cropped at the sides by the encroaching trees and mountains that rise up all around you. You didn't see a storm until it was just about on top of you. We only got about a thirty to forty degree field of view. Anything beyond that was not thought about.

In Chicago, the cement and glass and steel towers rise so high that it seems you can only see about three square feet of sky straight above you.

But here the entire planet was laid out, naked before you. Whereas every other time I drove through it with my mom and sister the sky was endless blue or had intermittent soft, fluffy, white clouds, now it was terrifyingly ominous. There was power enough to cover nearly all of our existence and power enough to destroy it with wind or flood.

What was even worse was that the mass of antimatter was moving towards US! Below the layer of black was a lesser black of pouring rains and mists that seemed to swallow up everything beneath it.

Quickly catching up to Wayne, who seemed oblivious, I drew his attention to it. "Uuuuuh, Wayne?"

"Yeah?"

"Uuuuuh... what's that?" I said, pointing into the blackness just a few miles distant.

"Storm," he said.

Storm. Storm. That's it. Just storm. "Is that normal?" I asked like I was speaking to a retarded child.

"Ayeah," he said, and then went back to hooking up the diesel feed from the pump. "See 'em all the time."

More than a little dubious, I was anxious to get inside to safety. That thing was moving pretty fast. I guessed it would reach us before we'd finished eating and didn't know which would be worse: to be stuck inside this speck of life on an otherwise barren planet for the duration, or be caught out on the road in the truck when it hit.

Inside the tiny eating area, I grabbed us a booth with an eastern-looking window and posted watch, ignoring the waitress that came by to see what I would be having.

Later Wayne found me still staring out the window, fascinated. It was awesome to watch. As it approached you could see the few lone trees at first begin to sway in a strong breeze, then suddenly they would jerk as if from a nuclear blast, then recover, only to be blasted again until darkness overwhelmed them.

I wasn't that hungry, so after we looked at the breakfast menus I decided on a small glass of O.J. and rather than a half-order of pancakes, I thought their "Silver Dollar" pancakes sounded like a cutely light and appealing little snack. I pictured about six of these inch-across thingies covering my plate like some kind of fluffy Chicken McNuggets.

But instead, what arrived at my table was a platter that took up most of the table. It was blanketed with a covering of HUGE pancakes. Like a ten-gallon hat.

Damn.

I cut a wedge out of the center of that deep stack about the size of my fist, set it on a saucer and put the platter on a nearby table in case my eyes weren't bigger than my stomach. Then I covered them with syrup, took a deep breath and dug bravely in.

About twenty minutes later, I had gotten about half way through 'em when the storm hit us. It was like someone turned out the lights. One minute I was watching the dark edge moving towards us, the next we felt the pressure change around us as the glass was belted by the first, sudden gust of wind. And it was black outside, a kind of Stygian blue-blackness that you could swim in.

For a moment we held our breath wondering if the storm front was going to shatter that glass and come ripping through the building, blowing us along ahead of it. But it held.

Once the initial impact had passed, it calmed down and turned out to be just another bad storm, not the horses of Armageddon.

After finishing breakfast, we tooled around the gift shop/store. They had the most oddball collection of knickknacks to sell to the truckers. And you could definitely tell which way their tastes ran: South. Even though we were technically in the Midwest, we were, in reality, still in the Deep South.

There, locked up behind glass were Texas longhorns, cowboy hats and boots, model trucks and Indy cars. Products bearing various tobacco companies' logos dominated the shelves. Caps, mugs, watches, jackets, key chains, beer bottle openers, pocket knives, beer-cozies and belt buckles all bore the logo of some type of sucking, chewing, or spitting product. Of course there were also those same items with gun manufacturer's logos, beer logos, or just plain naked lady logos.

There were bumper stickers, beer mugs, cigarette lighters, license plates bearing German crosses, Nazi SS symbols, and, my personal favorite, the rebel flag. It was like I was visiting a mausoleum dedicated to the confederate dead

To them, they tell me, that flag is a symbol of their heritage, their independence. But to every not-white human being on the face of the planet, it means the same thing as the Nazi flag means to a Jew: murder, rape, robbery, lynching, burnings, torture, and enslavement. Yeah, something to be really proud of. But they don't seem to mind at all. But when I bring up Malcolm X and any flag or hat bearing that simple Roman numeral, oh, well that's different. Yeah, then they have a shit-fit. And Malcolm never advocated any of those aforementioned crimes against humanity, white or otherwise.

Well-fed and awake, we made a mad dash through the wind and rain. Once back in the truck we laughingly brushed the water from our shoulders and hair, and pulled back onto the long, straight highway that was still black with the storm, which hung a left at the same highway and followed us through the morning.

The afternoon brought sunshine and dry roads followed us the rest of the way to Chicago.

normalcy

 normalcy

The Aranus Family

The Aranus family seemed to have everything. Even though they lived in the hood like we did, they never seemed touched by it. It was like they had been touched by God. They were intelligent, articulate and well spoken, in spite of having English as their second language and being recent immigrants. Both of the parents worked... hard, and still managed to find time to be a family. They went on picnics, camping and to Great America. They had nice stuff in their apartment. Big screen TV, nice stereo and good food. They were always cooking. The Aranus' were a Filipino immigrant family, a mother, father and three sons: Jeffery, Romel, and Glenn.

Jeff was my best friend and we were the same age. He was good at everything. He was smart, handsome, strong, athletic and nice. Everybody loved him. He had that bad-ass Bruce Lee charisma thing going on. Usually he was the captain of whatever sport we happened to be playing. And he would always, always pick me first to be on his team. And I'll always be grateful to him for that.

Back when we were kids in grammar school, I was always the last picked. I sucked at everything. Being short and skinny there were only two things I had going for me: I would try the hardest and I would try the longest. Whenever we played tag or catch-one-catch-all, I was always the last one caught. I was always crafty.

Romel was a couple of years younger than us. He was good at everything too, but he was also a brat. Young as he was, he was stronger than me, and better at everything as well. In high school I once saw him (as captain of the team) catch a kick-off and run for a 99-yard field goal. It even made the papers. The only time I could expect to make the papers was for some crime I committed.

Glenn was younger than all of us, but he and I were a lot alike in that he also was short, skinny, awkward, and shy. Poor guy never outgrew it. I haven't either, but I fake it well.

When they moved to the suburbs, I think Jeff and I were in high school. I used to go out and visit them. I thought I'd died and gone to heaven. It was a small house, but it was a NICE house. It was beautiful. They actually had a lawn! Fresh paint on the walls (and no holes in them). And then they got even more nice stuff. A synthesizer, toys, all kinds of stuff. And Romel got into electronics. He got into this home schooling for it. His parents supported this expensive hobby of his with what seemed like no limits. He even started building remote controlled airplanes and helicopters. We would all go to the airfield and watch him fly for a couple of hours, crash them, and come back and build another.

Whenever I would go out there, I would be so happy I felt like crying. It meant peace. Yeah, yeah, Romel and I would fight all the time but it was like a couple of brothers, not like mortal enemies. And my dad wasn't there abusing us and my mom wasn't there letting him. There would be PEACE. When I spent the night, I would sleep like a baby. I didn't care what we did. We could just sit around and talk. Sometimes we watched TV or sat around the yard and watched the sun go down. I never got tired of being there, never got bored.

I remember once we were driving back from their place and it was evening, nighttime. I was so happy that I was singing the theme song from Grease. I think I must've been in my freshman year. I think Mom even rented a car for the trip. Sometimes she was like that. She would go out of her way, above and beyond the call, to do something nice for me. Something like spend a ridiculous amount of money, like renting a car just to take me out to Jeff's place.

They lived far, far away from the ghetto we lived in. I think they wanted to get as far away as possible to erase the memories. They were so far out that it usually took us about two to three hours of bus-train, train-train, bus-bus-bus to get there. We would wake up early, leave as soon as we could, and be back home by midnight when I didn't spend the night. And I gotta hand it to Mom, in the beginning she would make that trip all the way down there, drop me off, only to turn around and come back to pick me up. It was like a full day of work for her. But after the first few times, I would go by myself and usually Ricardo, Mr. Aranus, would give me a ride back home, which would take him about forty-five minutes to an hour.

But they took me in. I was at their place every chance I got. I never said no. Even so, I would only get to visit every couple of months or so. And they never said no to me.

I kid you not, the Aranus family was THE single family that I had knowledge of that never laid hands on one another in anger, never called each other filthy names, and did what they said they were going to do. You could TRUST them. You could COUNT on them. They were the only indication that there was some "normalcy" in the universe. I could hardly believe they existed. It was like a unicorn. Something that does not exist. Yet here they were. In the midst of all their arguments, their disagreements, their poverty and hardships, I never heard a foul word out of them. They were my HOPE. Hope that there was something better in the universe, something worth living for. A real FAMILY.

The Forrester's

The first time I met the Forrester's, I thought they were Nazis. Not because they were creepy or anything, but because they had these thick German accents. But hey, when you're seven years old and all you know about Germans comes from TV, what can you expect? Anyway, the Forrester's were the only people I had ever met that showed me the face of God. Sure, everyone was telling me what God was like and what He wanted me to do, and what He expected from me, what He did like and didn't like, and so on. People were always telling me about God, but they were the first of a very select few "Christians" in the world who showed me. I mean they really walked the walk.

Mr. John and Mrs. Greta Forrester were the Sunday school teachers at the Peoples Church on Lawrence Avenue near Sheridan, just around the corner from where we had recently moved to in Uptown. It was a huge church run by the world-famous Dr. Preston Bradley who was a small, gentle old... old man. His sermons were aired each Sunday on the radio as well.

When our stepfather moved back in with us and the horrors started all over again, Mom started taking us to church as an escape, a weekly ritual to rid ourselves of the demon who plagued our lives from Monday on. And even though Dad never had any qualms about snatching us out of school or work or hospitals, he never, ever set foot inside that church. This comes as no surprise, as he quite frequently cursed God and Jesus at the top of his lungs with a venomous vengeance. But having never frequented churches before, it was a new experience for me. I had a hard time adjusting to being in a place where I clearly wasn't wanted. As far as I was concerned, I would rather be running the streets with my friends or even at home... at least there no one would tell me I didn't belong. But Mom was insistent, and so bright and early every Sunday, off to the concentration camp we went.

That church was like some kind of throw-back to a lost age. It was full of mean old white people with accents who dressed as if they were rescued from the Titanic before it went down. They seemed to be completely unaware that they were in a welfare community, surrounded and outnumbered by Blacks, Asians, and Latinos. It was starkly obvious that they were only prepared to "tolerate" all these little brown kids running around the basement of "their" church. They were always shushing us. "What are you doing here?" "Where are you going?" It was always something! They could never let us be, telling us to "Be quiet!", "Stop running!", and "Sit still!" Stop breathing! Lie down and die! I swear to you that if we were standing still and quiet, they would find some reason to criticize us and tell us we should be somewhere else doing something different.

Aside from the harpies that harried us there, there was another insurmountable problem: It was BORING! More boring than anything I had ever experienced until that point. I can remember only one single item of any importance from all of the many sermons I ever attended: wanting to be free from the torture. It was an experience too painful even to sleep through. Make no mistake, I tried! I tried! I tried! I tried if only to escape the vicious, venomous, savagery in the hisses for silence every time I shifted in my hard, stiff, miserable, wooden seat. Even there in the midst of a Godly message, they seemed to spend more time wanting us gone than wanting the Bread of Life.

After church we children would go downstairs for Sunday school, which was taught by Mr. and Mrs. Forrester. Each was in their 70's and they were the first white people that were kind to me, but in my skeptical mind, I knew it was all a sham. They had to be holding back their true feelings for a reason. I knew they hated us like all the rest. They had to want something from us, but I didn't know what. Maybe they were a couple of perverts? Child molesters that would wait patiently until an opportunity arose to get one of us in the back room alone where no one could see or hear what was going on. Then the real Forrester's would emerge. Yeah, I would keep a good eye on them. I treated them with the same suspicion, the same cool, detached, uncaring attitude I treated everyone.

One day, Mr. Forrester called on me to follow him. While I reluctantly did so, he led me deep into the dank, dark bowels of the basement. Exposed pipes, cobwebs, dripping water and naked, dim light bulbs marked our passage. I marked them like breadcrumbs. When we stopped, I kept my distance, waiting, waiting for some trickery to reveal itself - I was ready for him, ready to punch, kick, scream and hit him with any and every weapon that lay nearby. An ashtray here, a length of pipe over there. While I was waiting, he was searching. Searching among a stack of boxes until he found the one he wanted.

He said, "Come here" as he opened one up. Reaching in, he pulled out a handful of dusty, damp, yellowed magazines with yellow borders on each of them and extended them to me. When I didn't move to take them, he said, "I thought you might like to read these. You can take them outside if you like."

Reaching out carefully, gingerly I took them from his hand and stepped away. Looking at them from a safe distance, I saw on the cover, animals and mountains and people from around the world looking back at me from the covers of ancient National Geographic magazines.

"Thanks," I told him.

"You can put them back when you're done and get another stack."

Wow. These were cool. Once out in front again, I paged through each and every one of that first handful and I was hooked. Going back, I saw that there must have been hundreds of them lying around and in boxes. I kept looking over my shoulder and listening behind me to make sure no one snuck up on me while I marveled over my newfound treasure. And for the rest of my years there I had my own private stash and retreat, because I never saw anyone else back there.

The Forrester's had infinite patience. In the many years I knew them, I never once saw them lose their temper, act or speak inappropriately, or even speak ill of someone. Not once. And believe me, I gave them lots to be angry about. See, I knew that everyone there despised me and my family, because none of them even bothered to try to hide their contempt for any of us. So I figured I didn't owe them anything. Further, being a seven-year-old, I followed their example. Why should I hide my dislike of them? It took me no time at all to start showing them exactly what I thought about their rude comments. Being loud and obnoxious became my primary response when offense was given, lacking the communication skills to tell them to fuck off in proper fashion.

Fighting was always a problem in the hood. In a church in the hood there was little difference. But even then the Forrester's were shining examples of Godly Love. I remember getting into a fistfight with Nate over a toy that he had snatched out of my hands while I was playing with it. The other kids had picked sides as we fought, formed a circle, and started cheering us on. We were about evenly matched, but I had just started getting the upper hand when out of the corner of my eye I saw Mr. Forrester come running down from the stage. I was prepared to face both his anger and Nate at the same time. If he raised his hand to me, I would slug him just as fast as I had slugged Nate. But when he reached us, instead of angrily yanking us apart he, in the gentlest fashion, took me by my shoulders and pulled softly backwards and away from Nate just as I had knocked him down. Having my blood up, I turned ready to fight him as well, but to my puzzlement I saw not the fury or rage that I was accustomed to seeing, instead I saw the most perplexing thing. It actually made me stop. The anger flooded out of me when I looked into those faded blue eyes. I saw love. Love and sadness. He then removed his hands from my arms, looked me in the eyes, and gently said, "Come with me," and turned and headed for a storage room. Following reluctantly I was ready for him to even attempt to hit me before I would strike out as fast and as hard as I could. But when he turned, he gestured to a big box of toys and said to me, "Someone just donated these toys to the church. I thought perhaps you would like to open them and try them out before taking them out to the younger children." I was still waiting for a speech or something even as he turned and walked out, closing the door behind him. Is he going to try to lock me in here? As soon as he left, I tried the door. It opened. Well, I'll be damned. I couldn't believe it. And that was it. He just left me in there to play with the new toys, take them out of their packages and give them out to the other kids. He never said a word about the fight. Nothing. Not once. Not ever.

In my entire life that had never happened. There were always repercussions. Always a price to pay. Always. And here for the first time in my life, I was forgiven. No yelling, no screaming, no cursing, no punishment, no hitting. Nothing. Just... love? What was that all about? It was a trick. It had to be. I knew it was. See, I always knew my mother and my sister loved me. And vice-versa. We just never said it. We never showed it. The only thing we could do was refrain. Refrain from hurting each other. Refrain from damaging each other the way my stepfather had. But the absence of abuse doesn't equal the presence of love.

Love was something we did not know how to do. We could only hope to avoid all that opposite stuff. For a healthy life, that is not enough. But with the Forresters it was something else entirely. They loved in a positive, active, proactive way I had never seen or even heard of before. Each time they greeted me, it was with warmth and a smile. A smile that worked its way up from the depths of their beautiful hearts, through their eyes, and into their faces. And it wasn't in that touchy-feely, huggy-kissy kind of way. It was just in their presence. You could feel it envelope you when you walked into the room and they became aware of you.

The Forrester's would take the Sunday school on field trips to the Brookfield Zoo, Morton's Arboretum, White Pines Forest and many places that though relatively close to our homes they were a world away. They showed us things we would never have investigated on our own, either through awareness or access. Sometimes they would have my mother, sister and I over to their house, which they opened up to us as they had their hearts. Even after we moved far from the neighborhood, they would still offer us goods, clothes, and food that were donated to the church for the poor. They even took us out to lunch or dinner where we would sit for hours just enjoying each other's company. No expectations, no performances, just... us.

the yard

 the yard

Joan F. Arai

Joan F. Arai was a junior high school on the east side of Uptown. It was called a "middle" school for some reason that we could never figure out. Nor for that matter could we figure out why there was a need for a "Jr. High school". But it really was a prison. Make no mistake about it.

I actually watched them build that thing. It looked like a building foundation that got out of hand. The plain, dull brick just kept growing... up. When they finished the thing, I thought it was a prison. Literally. It had industrial steel gates on the front of the "Yard" and only a few, sparse, narrow, tinted windows. Black. No name, no signs, no ornamentation whatsoever. I was in fifth grade at the time and can you imagine my surprise when I found out that it was a school? For KIDS?! Yeah, right. The man just wanted to keep the monkeys in their cage.

Can you imagine my shock when I found out that I was going to be the one going to that "Wonderful, New" school? I was chosen against my will by lottery to attend and I was torn from my comparatively safe grammar school, which for the last few years had been John T. McCutcheon further north.

The teachers all tried their damnedest to convince us that it was this great, new thing. But c'mon! Exactly how stupid did they think we were? I mean, do you honestly think that any parent would design, let alone build, a "school" like that for their kids? And then actually let them attend it? Every day? With other kids from Uptown? IN Uptown!? PLEASE!

The building itself was actually laid out like a prison separated into three designated "Houses". House 1, House 2, and House 3. There was a central cafeteria, complete with security guards looking on while we ate. We felt like specimens in a zoo.

Inside the houses were all the little juvenile criminals in the making. Here was where they practiced their arts of intimidation, extortion and so forth. Knife fights and beatings were regular occurrences. Now the gangs were present in real numbers and they were a *presence*. Black eyes, broken noses and dark bruises were always apparent on my classmates.

There were hundreds of students there. Some of these kids were hitting puberty while I was miles away from it. In fact, my real growth spurt didn't even come until high school. And here I was coming in at the lowest grade, a sixth grader locked inside with the "Big Kids", the seventh and eight graders. Most of the folks there towered over me. Even the girls. Some of these kids were as much as four years older than me. I felt like a minnow in an ocean of sharks.

Now, even though I'd had to deal with certain realities on the streets, the worst of it hadn't yet made its way into our insulated little classrooms at John T. McCutcheon Grammar School. Sure there was foul language and fistfights, but knives, guns, drugs, and sex were not yet part of my daily public education classroom curriculum.

But welcome to the "Yard." Here I saw it all. Now the roving wolf packs were inside the walls and among us.

And of course in this environment my violent upbringing was allowed, even encouraged, to flourish, though it hadn't yet reached the peak of its refinement.

So here was where talking shit really came in handy. Doin' the dozens served many purposes in ghettos around the country. It was a great anti-boredom tool. It sharpened minds and creativity. It let people know just how far you were willing to go, how down and dirty you were willing to get. It was also a means of intimidation. If I was gonna stand up in a classroom of thirty students and tell them all "Yo' mamma's so stupid she glued her food stamps to an envelope" or "she's so fat we had our family picnic in her shade," you probably weren't going to want to be seen for awhile, let alone have anything to do with me. "Don't fuck with me baby. You'll regret it," was the message I was sending out there.

Beatings were no real threat to me at that time, because almost daily it seemed I was beaten with hands, fists and feet by a full grown man who was an ex-soldier and a killer for sure. So getting beaten up did not hold the great dread for me that it did for some of my friends. However, it was still something to be avoided at all costs. If I had a chance at winning the fight, I didn't care a bit about fighting. However, once someone started in with me, I was there for them 100 percent. If they were bigger than me, no problem. If there were two of them, all right. But once the numbers got up there, four, five, six big gangsters, I was outta there. I had no problem running from a fight if there was absolutely no chance I could win it. With those odds there was no shame in runnin'. If you didn't, you were just stupid. However, once you were cornered, you had to take it like a man. If you didn't, the whole neighborhood would hear about it and you would have a hard time living it down. And if you got your ass kicked while kicking some of your own, you at least kept your respect in the hood and by the cats you were fighting with. Yeah, you heard me right. See, when some guys front you, it's just because they want some easy action, an easy victory. But if you make them pay for it, they will be forced to find easier prey next time and avoid you. They don't want to be walking around with busted lips, black eyes and bloody noses talking about "Yeah, it took all five of us, but we sure showed him." "Where are the other guys?" "Well, two of us took one guy to the hospital and the other one's home in bed nursing his wounds." That only makes all five of them look like punks. On the other hand, who wouldn't mind being known as the guy that single handedly fought five gang members to a standstill. Nobody sees it is going to be messin' with you for a very long time.

Sears

We were all about 14, still stumbling through life not caring a whit for our futures, because no one else did, let alone shown us how to do it ourselves. We had no future.

Autumn was well underway so it was cold, but no snow had yet fallen. It was about two in the afternoon when the six of us sauntered into the Sears store on Lawrence Avenue. John, J.J. George, Brian, Dave, and I had nothing to do and nowhere to go. So on this day we would go to the store and eyeball all the bikes and toys we could never afford, and the roller-skates and skateboards no mothers or fathers would ever buy for us. We wanted, just for a moment, to pretend we were like normal children.

We would laugh and joke amongst ourselves. We were constantly teasing and horsing around everywhere we went, but we never hurt anyone who wasn't trying to hurt us. As we moved through the far end of the store, there was a counter that served burgers, fries and sodas. It was free of diners, but the guys each grabbed a handful of straws with paper wrappers and started to shoot spitballs at each other.

It was getting a little rowdy, so I told the guys to chill out. They didn't hear it, because they were too busy having their fun. "I've had enough of this," I said. "I'll be over here when you guys are done fucking around." And I thought to remove myself from the insanity by browsing through the aisles. I didn't even touch anything. I just wanted to get away from them until they were back in control of their facilities.

So there I was, walking through the aisle where the nails and screws were kept, when I noticed this tall, fat, balding, white, obviously plain-clothed security guard standing at the end of the row pretending to read a wrinkled magazine while watching me like a hawk. Ignoring him, I continued to kill time while I waited for the guys.

Five minutes later and three rows down, this asshole was still following me. I was used to being followed around stores by white guys, but this one was getting to me. I found it ironic that this bastard was following me around while I quietly minded my own business and looked at brooms and mops while five other much lighter-skinned guys made a wreck of the food court while screaming at the top of their lungs. Two rows later, I told him that exact same thing after I'd finally had enough. He called me a smart-assed bastard, walked to the next aisle and continued watching me.

Another five minutes went by before the guys were done screwing around. When they found me, I pointed out the racist asshole to them.

"Fuck it. Let's get outta there."

"Yeah," I said and we began to file out of the revolving doors. I was the last one out and the asshole actually followed us out the door.

"Little fucking nigger," he said, looking me in the eye as I was walking away.

"Fuck you," I said, and then made my mistake. I turned my back on him.

John at the front had looked over his shoulder a moment later and a worried look came over his face. "Eddie, look out!" I took off as soon as I heard the warning, but was stopped in my tracks.

I began to run even as I heard it. Turning, I saw that the fat bastard had just caught the corner of my coat. Spinning, I tried to yank it from his grasp. It didn't work. He reeled me in like a fish on a string. With his free hand he tried to get a hold of my hands, neck, or collar, but I kept managing to be just out of range. But he still managed to hang onto my coat.

I didn't have the time or the space to shed the coat to get away. Not to mention it was the only winter coat I owned. If I lost it, it would be one long, cold and possibly deadly winter. As soon as he became frustrated with trying to catch me, it moved quickly from a wrestling match to a boxing match. My four feet, eleven inches and eighty odd pounds did next to nothing to his six feet of height and 300 pounds of girth. The good news was that he was too slow to hit me. The best I could hope for was to tire him out.

Then things went from bad to worse. Through the glass doors I saw a shorter, younger, stocky plain-clothes security guard come running towards us.

I put up a last-ditch, desperate attempt to free myself that proved unfruitful. And then there were two of them on me.

Somehow I managed to fight them both to a standstill before the fat fuck finally landed a solid blow.

It was a vicious uppercut that caught me squarely under the point of my chin. It caused me to gray-out momentarily and my legs turned to Jell-O. It stunned me just long enough for them both to grab hold of me and get me handcuffed.

The two of them each took an arm and lifted me from the ground and carried me bodily through the store. I kicked and raged, and struggled all the way.

They dragged me down into the dank, dark security office downstairs in the back. Once down there, the stocky one lifted me up high while the fat one handcuffed my skinny little arms over a hot steam-pipe, and left me dangling there with my feet clear of the ground.

Tears of animal rage and humiliation ran down my face for a while and then my fury dimmed and I slowly pulled myself together.

I must have hung there for about twenty minutes before anyone else came down. Several people came in and eventually there were four other men in that office, and they just went on about their business as usual while I hung there in pain.

An hour or so later, the two men that I fought with came down and started talking shit. They got in my face and started yelling and calling me names.

"Bet you're ready for me to let ya down from there, aren't ya punk!?" the fat one said with a sneer full of rank breath. But I was ready for him this time.

"No. I'm fine where I am," I said calmly with the best, bored air I could manage. I regretted letting him see me with tears in my eyes and swore it would never happen again. I was determined to let my arms fall off before I'd ask any of these people for a damned thing.

They soon grew bored with trying to get a response from me and left even more pissed off than they were before.

I don't know how much time had passed, but eventually two police officers came down to the office ushered in by the asshole.

Immediately the officers became upset and asked, "What the hell is he doin' up there?"

"Well... er.. he was giving us some trouble..."

"Get him down from there," one of the officers said.

I was actually weary of the officer's kindness, because I was so unused to it. I figured they had something even more devious in mind, but I was determined to take it like a man.

"This little guy giving a big guy like you trouble?" the other officer remarked. As the guards faces grew red, I gave him my best smirk and he roughly unlocked the handcuffs while his partner held me up.

They exchanged the pair of handcuffs I had worn for a pair of the officer's. My legs almost gave out on me when I hit the ground. They had partially lost their feeling. But the first officer grabbed me by the arm before I could fall. I didn't even feel it, because my arms and hands had lost all feeling completely. Try as I might, I couldn't get them to move.

After they each signed and exchanged forms, the two officers escorted me outside. It was dark out as they put me into the back of the paddy wagon. They handcuffed me to the benches, which were made of diamond-plate steel, as were the walls. Each bump and pothole jarred my teeth and my bones, especially my spine. Occasionally my head would bang loudly against the wall until I gave up on resting and just leaned forward.

I watched through the tiny ventilation holes as we made our way through the darkened city streets and back alleys. We drove for so long I began to think that they were seeking an isolated spot to give me another beating, after which I would be left lying broken and unconscious in some gang's territory. The police in our neighborhood perpetrated such things upon us far too often. We had all seen friends of ours come back from a visit by the police with black eyes, bloody noses and sore ribs. We were living in occupied territory. But eventually we pulled into the precinct station.

Once there I was put in a rank cell with chipping paint, cold, damp, graffiti-stained walls, and wet stains on the floor, where I waited briefly before a detective could process me.

After an hour or so, a plainclothes detective let me out, put me back in handcuffs and locked me to a bench opposite his desk. After I'd settled in, he began his paperwork. I gave him answers that were short and to the point.

"Name? Last name first. Date of birth?" and so forth.

When he'd gotten all my statistics down, he asked me, "So what happened?"

"I got jumped," I said simply.

"What?"

"Got beat up by a couple of fat-assed security guards."

"Yeah, but what were you doing before they jumped you?"

"Nothin'."

"Pffft. Yeah, right! These guys got nothin' better to do than to beat up on a little guy like yourself?"

"Apparently not," I replied, disinterested. I knew that he wouldn't believe me or wouldn't do anything about it even if he did believe me, which was highly unlikely.

I had told the other cops what had happened when they asked on the way to the car. The only thing they said was, in defense of the asshole, "Yeah, well, some of these security types are pissed off because they wanted to be something else."

"So somebody should tell 'em to quit," I had responded and gotten only silence.

"Yeah, but they had to have a reason?" the detective prodded.

"Yeah, he's a racist asshole," I said, starting to get angry at the fact that everybody seemed to have an excuse for them, but here I sat in jail under arrest... for losing an unfair fight.

"That's not how they see it. According to them you were shoplifting and starting fights with customers. When they asked you to leave, they say you refused and started the fight."

"Yeah, that's exactly what happened. See that's how I get my kicks. I go around starting fights with guys four times my size and wait for them to get help beating me up." When I get angry the smart-ass comes out.

But instead of the detective getting angry, he started laughing. It was a good, honest laugh. And soon I was laughing right along with him. After a pause, he said, "If I take those off you, do ya promise not to go starting any more fights?"

"Sure," I said with more laughter.

In all of my many experiences with police, I had never shared a joke or a smile with one. "Officer Friendly" is something we only joked about, like Santa Claus or the Tooth Fairy. They were always something to be avoided. So this was a surreal experience for me.

After he had taken the cuffs off, he sat back down, leaned back in his wooden, swivel chair and said, "Why don't ya tell me what happened in yer own words?"

It took me several moments looking into his eyes before I decided that this wasn't a trap or a trick to get me into further trouble. Then I began the story from the moment we walked in the front door until the point where I'd told the uniformed cops what had happened.

When I was finished it, was his turn to search my eyes for something. Nodding his head when he thought he'd found it, he said, "Ya know, I believe you."

"But?"

"But unfortunately it's his word against yours."

"So that's it? They get to go around following people who are minding their own business through the store? They get to beat up on little kids and hang them from steam pipes and

I'm the one that gets locked up?!" I said, getting angry all over again.

Sadly he shook his head. "Yeah kid, that's how it works. I believe you when you said you were minding your own business while your friends were screwing around..." And then he said something that changed my view of everything. The way I view myself, my friends, the world, and how they all view me. "...but unfortunately kid, ya hang around with shit, ya smell like shit."

And just like that I knew he was right. I was fortunate enough to learn a lesson at fourteen years old that I have constantly seen repeated and missed all around me still, decades later. I'll never know why I heard certain lessons, but I am constantly thankful for them. But that would not be the last lesson of the night.

We talked good-naturedly for a while longer before the detective said, "Well, I suppose it's time we got somebody down here to get you out. Picking out the receiver on the old, dirty, grayed, beige phone from the cluttered mountain of files and folders on his desk, he dialed my home number while he told me the latest joke he'd heard.

My mom picked up in the middle of the punch line and surprised him. "Mrs. Thornton! Hi ma'am. I'm Detective (?) from the precinct on Foster and I'm calling about your son..." he said around our laughter. "...Well ma'am, we uhh..." And for lack of getting the right words out, he joked without thinking, "...we uhhh... We shot 'im!"

Fresh laughter began and then died in the same exact moment. Instantly we both sobered up as he sat up in his chair. "No. I'm sorry ma'am. Bad joke. He's okay. But we've got him down here at the station and we'll need you to come and pick him up. Here, why don't you speak to him?" he said, extending the phone. As I took the receiver, he grabbed a file and hurried off to another corner of the station.

She nervously asked if I was okay and I assured her that I was, and she could come and get me whenever she could. When I hung up the phone, the gravity of what just happened fully sank in. I realized that in all of the bullshit I'd been getting into, I didn't care whether I lived or died. Pain, Death, and Prison were the only three things I really knew were certain in my future. Nothing else existed in my future. That was it. But for the first time in my life, I was shown that what happened to me had a bearing on someone else. In a perverse way that moment was the first time in my life I realized that in a way I did matter.

How ironic that this was the only way for a child to know that he mattered to his mother, that his existence mattered, that whether he lived or died, mattered! How fucked up. I think that was the first time in my life I saw past my thoughts of survival and was able to see something, anything, else.

Mom came and got me, as usual. And she had nothing to say about it bad or good, as usual. But nothing would be usual for me again. You see, I knew a secret: I mattered.

I regret to this day that I didn't remember that detective's name. Because wherever he is now: THANK YOU! Your lessons have taken me safely this far and they are lessons I live by today and tomorrow.

E.J.

E.J. was a knucklehead. He was one of those guys who were always talking shit. Incessantly. Always going on about what he had, what he did, where he'd been. And he was always threatening to kick somebody's ass. Mine, yours, your mama's... everybody.

For some reason, when we became teenagers there came a time when kicking ass becomes really important to a boy. Unfortunately some of us never grew out of it. A lot of the guys were scared of E.J. because he was a big talker and just a little bit bigger and heavier than everybody else, especially me. E.J. lived in the same neighborhood as my best friend, John, and they hung out together so, consequently, I had to put up with him quite frequently.

I've never been one of those cats who have to put someone down or push people around, or even talk much shit. I was usually kind of quiet between random ideas and jokes. I believed in live and let live. So you could talk alllll the shit you wanted, it was your prerogative, but nobody put their hands on me. And one night E.J. put his hands on me.

On this evening in particular, he decided that I was to be his target. So it seemed every other comment that came out of his mouth was aimed at me. Some little barb or snide remark made indirectly at my expense. I took it for awhile. I just figured he was havin' a bad day. Figured after a while he would get bored because I wasn't giving him any feedback and move on to something else. But he didn't.

We had been out running the neighborhood being the usual nuisances that we usually were to our neighbors. Eventually we found ourselves on Clark Street just around the corner from Foster. We had been running, racing each other down the street just burning off youthful energy on a typical Sunday evening.

We had all stopped and were gathered in front of the Ann Sather restaurant. I was just appreciating the warm smell of dinner coming from within and peering through the low window watching all the people with money eat warm, beautiful meals.

When I turned around, E.J. was staring right at me about three feet away. I had just opened my mouth to ask him what, when he took a quick step forward and putting his hands on my chest, he shoved me. Hard. I flew back a step before my hips struck the bottom edge of the window where the brick, wood and glass met. Instantly my hands instinctively flew down sensing the only stable place to take the impact was the brick below the window about hip level. That made me top-heavy so that the remaining momentum took my shoulders and the back of my head and slammed them into the window. Fortunately for me, my head and shoulders smacked hard, not glass, but the thick wooden cross braces between the panes of glass.

I remember seeing that stupid, smug, idle grin on E.J.'s face just before the guys who had missed the whole interaction took off up the street for another footrace. When they took off, E.J. went with them.

As soon as I had recovered my balance, a myriad of thoughts raced through my head: shock, hurt, and anger. No... fury. I was furious that this little fuck had felt the need to reach out and hurt me for no reason. No reason at all. And here I was the runt of the litter. Oh, that made me MAD!

Instantly I took off after E.J. and within a block I had caught up to him at the back of the pack. Grabbing him by the sleeve of his windbreaker, I spun him to a stop. Looking down at me, he had the nerve to say "Fucker! What's your problem, asshole?"

Seeing the look in my eye, he knew what I was all about, so he stepped back and put his fists up and went into a boxer's stance. "Oh, you wanna fight, huh?" Then he opened his mouth to start talking shit. I'm sure he was about to say how he was gonna kick my ass all over the place or some such shit, but he never finished.

We had come to a stop in front of a furrier. It had floor to ceiling plate-glass windows with all these mannequins wearing these big, fluffy, full-length fur coats from different kinds of animals. When E.J. stepped back, I went with him. And when he stopped to tell me how he was going to kick my ass, I kept going.

As I reached him, he tried to take a swing with his right hand at my head, but I put both hands on his ribcage and using my legs, heaved him up and back, sending him through the front window of that shop knocking over mannequins on the way in.

When he landed, he lay there stunned and I stood oblivious amidst the broken glass with shards still raining down on me. I was dimly aware of an alarm going off in the store and there were people all around looking and talking, but it was like watching something on TV. It was all background. All I saw was E.J. I was waiting for him to get up and charge after me so I could tear him apart, and I didn't feel anything about it. It was going to be like tying a shoelace.

When he finally started moving, he rolled over onto his side and started mumbling and slowly shaking his head as flakes of glass fell off of him. Then he sat up and asked me what happened.

Expecting a trick, I ignored him and placidly awaited his attack. Struggling to his feet, he stepped towards me. When I smiled at him, it brought him to a stop and he circled far around me. Once back out on the sidewalk, he brushed glass from his hair, shoulders, arms, and somewhere inside of me I was amazed he wasn't cut to ribbons.

"What the hell did you do that for?" He tried to sound indignant, but neither of us believed it. Looking down I saw that his right hand was dripping some dark substance. Following my look, he raised his hand into the light and saw that it was red from a two-inch gash on the outer edge of his hand.

"Holy shit!" he said as he held it away from him. We heard police sirens in the distance and he looked both ways before looking back at me.

"Well, uh, I guess we better get out of here." I saw that there was no fire left in his eyes, but I was still wary. I couldn't believe anyone would let that pass. Then I realized that he was afraid of me. Lil 'ole me.

"Go ahead," I told him. I didn't think was going to do anything, but I still wasn't going to let him get behind me.

When we finally caught up to the guys, they asked us what happened. I looked at E.J. awaiting his explanation. I was as curious as they were to hear what he had to say.

"I fell through a window," he told them as he sheepishly glanced down at me.

By now his hand was pouring blood. It had sprinkled onto his jacket, pants, and shoes. Looking back, I followed its trail down the block.

"Shit! Man, you better go get some stitches."

"Yeah man, you better go to the hospital."

E.J. still seemed dazed. "Uh, yeah. I guess I better," he said before setting off for home.

The next time I saw him, his hand was bandaged up and the guys told me he'd had to get seven stitches. He kept his distance from me after that. Which was just fine with me, because that meant I never had to listen to any more of his lip.

It's funny, sad really. Some people have to get themselves hurt before they start paying attention to warning signs. They have to pay a price before they realize the value of a thing.

God help me keep my eyes open.

northside boogie

 north side boogie

"Kill the Niggers!"

John, Raymond, Cesar and me. We were going to a friend's house just a few neighborhoods away. It was summer in the middle of the day, in the middle of the week.

Raymond, the only white dude among us today, was a tall, blond, buff, California surfer dude and as mellow as they come. But he could take care of himself. John was Native American, part Chippewa, part Menominee Indian. He was cocky with a "don't give a fuck" attitude. Cesar was a Spaniard, short and stocky and just as crazy as they come. He carried the arrogance of his homeland. As a Commando style warrior, he was always fighting and he was also my main competition. Then there was me, short, skinny and cunning. I was always the "nice guy" until you crossed me. It might take me a week. It might take me a year. But I'd settle your score. "You never want Eddie mad at you," I had heard friends say of me. But, ironically, with the gang, I was usually the peacemaker.

We had passed through several gang territories without incident, all the way from Ray's place up by Loyola to John's about a mile behind us. We picked Cesar up along the way. Taking a shortcut, we climbed the high wall at the St.

Boniface cemetery where we goofed off and chased each other around on our way through. At one point we were all racing each other and I came in dead last due to a chest cold. I felt like my legs were made of lead and I eventually stopped running altogether. I had no energy and couldn't breathe.

Ray had found a piece of wrought iron that looked like a really cool spearhead. He hung onto it and fiddled with it in his hands while we walked and talked.

Eventually we climbed out the other side of the cemetery on Lawrence Avenue near Dover. We were just crossing into an all-white pocket of holdouts that still lived there in hopes that "the S'ath shall rise a'gin."

A few minutes later we were all standing at the intersection of Leland and Dover. There was some discussion as to the shortest route: left or straight.

As they discussed direction, Ray was absentmindedly holding the spear-tip by the point and end with his index fingers while he revolved it on its axis by his thumbs. I stared mesmerized, lost in thought.

Ray casually looked right and then left, then shouted "BOOK!!" And like an incantation, a magic spell, he disappeared. He was gone. Just... wasn't there. In the space that Ray just occupied there was only the floating spear-tip. Like Wiley Coyote off a cliff, it just hovered there, in space, revolving for a moment before beginning to fall.

Looking up I found myself suddenly alone. The sound of running footsteps drew my eye down Leland Avenue where Ray, Cesar and John were three diminishing figures. Looking over my left shoulder, I saw what I thought was the source of their concern. Three white boys about a block behind us were running full bore towards us. One had a baseball bat and another had a length of slat wall.

"What are you running for? There's only three of 'em," I shout to the retreating figures from half a block away. Then, looking over my right shoulder, I saw it.

"It" was the rest of the gang. Rebels 20 strong were pouring down the street right towards... ME! And they all had weapons: bricks, knives, sticks, bats, pipes, you name it.

As soon as I spotted them, the uproar began. "NIGGERS!" "GET 'EM!" "KILL 'EM!" "GET THEM MOTHERFUCKERS!" "KILL THE FUCKIN' NIGGERS!"

So I figured, hey Eddie, now might be a good time for you to run. And I... was... GONE. I ran as if my life depended on it. Because, well... it did.

A few bricks were sent flying past me, shattering at my feet. Shrill whistles broke out behind me among the shouts like a kind of Morse code. "Tweet-tweet tweeeeeeet! Tweet-tweet tweeeeeeet!" Then I really began to worry.

See, it was the middle of summer. Everybody in this all-white, Klan-infested neighborhood had their windows wide open. I scanned windows and rooftops as I sped along in anticipation of gun barrels, thrown bricks or other flying debris in answer to their call. I also had to be wary of the few random pedestrians I passed lest they strike a blow for the "cause".

Then hope of salvation caught my eye. It came in the form of a black-and-white police cruiser parked at the end of the next block. Questions piled into each other inside my head, each struggling to come out first: "Is there one cop or two?" "Could even two stop this lynch mob?" "Would they even try to help?"

The Chicago Police Department had so far proven itself more an enemy to be avoided than a help in our lives. I hadn't seen a friendly officer since Officer Friendly, and that was back in the second grade.

And then all the questions came to a quick and hopeless end, because not only were the police not in their car... they were nowhere in sight! DAAAAAAMN! So I kept runnin'. And then somehow, miraculously, I had caught up to the guys! Now I was at the front of the pack! HowthehelldidIgetuphere?! Just a few minutes ago I was too sick to move, now look at me. Lesson learned: fear of being killed is a great motivator. And there's no telling what you can do when you have to.

Ray looked over at me with such a look of shock that I was afraid he would stumble and fall with Cesar and John running right over him. He recovered and at the following corner he broke right with me, Cesar and John following. I snatched a glance back up the street and was astounded to find the whole rebel clan so far behind us. Their shouts had ceased as breath was as hard to come by for them as it was for us. We were just a whole lot more motivated.

Ray led us down the street and into a vacant lot occupied by the remains of a demolished brownstone. We were spent as we came to a stop. Instantly, each of us began searching through the wreckage collecting weapons. Bricks, broken bottles, sticks, pipes.

Then we waited. If we were going down we were determined to take as many of them with us as we could. Lining up, we put our backs to the closest wall and waited, listening for the sounds of footsteps. I held a piece of slat wall in my hand. It was no match for a baseball bat, but it was better than nothing.

"Their territory ended at the last block. If they crossed it, they were in another territory," Ray said. "They won't cross it… they shouldn't cross it," he repeated to himself as we waited breathlessly. We each silently hoped he was right.

After a silent eternity, we found out he was right. It was a good thing no civilians came around that corner, because the first head to show itself would have been split open. We decided to git while the gittin' was good. Heading though the rear of the lot, we made our way onwards, hanging onto our weapons. Just in case.

Friday Nights

I used to think I had the best mom in the world. I bragged to all my friends that my mom let me do anything. Complete and total freedom. No rules. No boundaries. No repercussions.

When I was 12, we left my stepfather, spent a summer at a homeless shelter in downtown Chicago, and then moved to the North side Edgewater neighborhood. And I cut loose. Nothing was said. I just went. After the brutal oppression of my stepfather's household, I took total advantage of my newfound freedom. I took to the streets and stayed there.

Soon, "home" became the place I sometimes stayed. In between running the streets and getting no sleep at all, I passed the early hours in jail for curfew violations or disorderly conduct, or vandalism, or staying at one friend's or another. In all, I probably spent less than half my nights in our little one-bedroom apartment.

So, by the time I turned 13, I had gotten drunk, high, laid, and almost died. Several times. I'd been shot at, stabbed at, clubbed at, arrested, almost drowned, and kicked out of school on at least half a dozen separate occasions. And Mom said not a word. I thought that was sooo cool. It made me feel like an adult. I didn't have to "ask Mom" as lots of other schmucks did.

My cutting loose, it didn't happen all at once. I don't remember anything that abrupt. No, what I remember is being driven away. After years of living under an insane dictator, I had what seemed a few days of peace. I knew not to count on it, though. She had left him before.

He would show up unexpectedly to shatter my very existence. And soon it began to happen again. Phone calls at first. "He wants to speak to you," she would say and hold the phone out to me.

"I don't want to."

"Please." It was the pleading in her eyes. It said if you don't talk to him, I'll have to pay for it. What I wish I had been mature enough to tell her was, "No, I'll be the one to pay, and pay, and pay."

But instead, I just took the phone.

Then he began stopping by.

"Oh shit! How'd he find out where we lived?!"

"He must have followed me home," she would lie.

At the door he would tell me, "Grab your coat. We're goin' out." And with that, my existence wasn't my own again. We would usually be out all night, combing his various bars, whorehouses and hangouts. Sometimes he would bring me back home, and sometimes to whatever dump he was staying in. Sometimes I would awaken on the floor and he would be gone, leaving me to walk the many miles back home if I didn't happen to have bus fare. Fortunately, one good thing Mom did was teach me how to get around. I never got lost in Chicago.

Somewhere along the line a pattern began to form. The way it unfolded was this: At first I would often miss school on Monday, Tuesday and maybe Wednesday. But somehow Friday would usually find me in class. Coming home from school, I would park myself in front of the TV and I wouldn't budge. Waiting. Waiting to see if she would call or come home. She never did. This sadistic torture of my young soul would eventually prove more lingering a wound than all the years of physical and mental abuse by my Dad.

My mother was a workaholic. She always got to work early and stayed late. It was her means of escape. What could Dad say if she said her boss wanted something done before she left? She was the sole means of financial income. He would have jobs rarely, but always seemed to have cash. So he depended upon her paycheck to pay for his fix.

So on Friday I would sit and watch and wait for my mother in that cold, cruel, lonely city. I loved Chicago, but she had been robbed several times by gun, knife and fist. I was both victim and participant of almost daily violence in its gang-filled streets. So when 8:00 p.m. struck and she was still not home, I would concentrate on not worrying, not caring - 9:00, 10:00 and still, no Mom.

I began to come up with contingency plans. Call the police? And say what? "My mom's late?" Call the hospitals? Which ones? There must be a hundred between home and her job. By midnight I couldn't avoid the thought that she was with him. To my damnation, I found myself hoping, wishing she were with him and not laying bleeding, dying in some alley. On Saturday morning I would rise early and go to her bed, praying she came home while I was asleep.

I hated seeing her bed still made. It was, to me, a statement of uncaring, of my worthlessness.

Then, if there was food in the house, I'd get to eat for the day. If not, I would go hungry. Sitting in front of the television again I would lose myself in cartoons or comic books, awaiting a phone call from her or the hospital or the police. Rarely would any come. And that was even worse. By noon I couldn't stand the waiting, the not knowing anymore, and I would leave. Friends would occupy my day and I'd be back home by 8:00 to see if she had returned.

Sunday would pass much like Saturday, only there was less food around. By Sunday night it would be even harder to get to sleep. So I would stay up even later.

On Monday morning I would wake up late and drowsy from staying up all night. Anger and fear rising up within me, I would pick up the phone and call her at work. When her voice would come over the line, I would breathe a sigh of relief and a curse of hatred and resentment, and just hang up the phone. Sometimes I would say, "Hi." And then she would just babble on like everything was juuuust fine. By the time I hung up, I was even angrier than before.

Eventually, I would just skip the weekend altogether. I would wait for her on Friday until about nine and when she hadn't called, I would take all my pent up pain and rage with me into the streets. I would run myself ragged with the thrill of danger. A reckless, almost suicidal drive to... go, Go, GO! Go until I dropped.

And then on Monday I would find my way to a phone and call her at work. I didn't want to hear anything she had to say. I just wanted to make sure he hadn't killed her in some heroin-induced frenzy.

The Wooden Nickel

I've lost count of the times that it happened. But for as frequently as I spent the night at John's place, it seems like we never slept. There was always something going on. Inevitably one thing was a constant: We would get a call from the Wooden Nickel.

It would come about two, three, or four in the morning. We would get a phone call. It would be some pissed off bartender calling from the Wooden Nickel telling us to come get his mom, Gertie.

The Wooden Nickel was a real shit-hole. It was right smack in the middle of Uptown, across the street from Truman College, It served as a second home to the local, alcoholic population, mostly Native Americans, of which there were many, many in Uptown. It was a boisterous, bawdy, dangerous place that was constantly swimming in piss, vomit, salt, sweat, beer, and blood, and each battled constantly for your senses.

We loved to go down there with his mom or one of her friends to hang out, drinking ginger-ale and Cokes, and listening to the adults swap stories and tell dirty jokes. We would shoot pool, well, mostly we watched as the older men cleaned the tables on us, sinking ball after ball as we stood by idly chalking our sticks. Once in a while, if they were drunk enough, we would actually win one and get to play each other if we had enough quarters.

Fights. There were always fights. Guys against guys, women against women, and women against men and men against women. They used beer mugs, pool cues, cue balls, knives, and pepper spray. For us it was always like going to a three-ring circus. We would be watching one argument brewing when the blows of another would sound out behind us.

But usually the call would come because it was his mother that was starting the fight. She was a hellcat. Big, tough, and didn't take no kinda' shit, real or imagined. And if the bartender couldn't get her outta there, someone would give 'em her number. They would call the house and, lucky us, we would be the only ones home. And since John and I were usually home alone, we were the ones who had to come and talk her down and drag her out of there.

Sometimes, in the time it took us to walk the couple of miles or so down there, she would still be fighting, dragging some poor guy around by his hair or scratching some poor woman to ribbons. She'd still be cussin', spitin', and yellin'.

I gotta hand it to John, he wasn't afraid. While I was still looking for an opening, he would just wade right in there, right into the middle of the fight, grabbing his mother by the arm or around the waist and talk her down. He would just keep talking to her. "Ma! Ma. C'mon Ma. We gotta go. Ma. Ma. MA!" And he would just keep at it until she finally wound down and let us drag her, still yellin' and cussin', out the door.

Mostly we would all walk back. But on a couple of occasions she was so bombed that a couple of her friends chipped in to get her a cab and once we got her calmed down, we would put her in the back seat and walk on back to the house in order to be there as soon as we could after the cab dropped her off.

If we were lucky, there would be enough money for all of us to ride home.

Once at the house, it took both of us to pull her out and try to hustle her up the front steps before she woke up the entire neighborhood with her cursing and yelling before she fell over. No small feat considering she weighed more than both of us put together.

In the coming years that woman would go through hell and in the end would come through shining. Eventually she would, at more than forty years of age, take herself back to school, earn a college degree, meet and marry a good, strong man, and be promoted at work.

I would find in her many years later, the strength and courage it takes for an older adult to drag themselves back to college, to learn alongside younger, stronger, more energetic, stylish, hip, cool, smarter youngsters.

At the ripe old age of thirty, using Gertie as a role model, I would take myself back to school to earn my third degree.

Help

I was sound asleep on the night I got that desperate phone call. It woke me up at about two in the morning. George was panicking on the other end.

"Eddie, you gotta help us! You gotta come get us! They got guns! They've got us surrounded!" Suddenly the phone dropped to the floor and I heard shouting in the background. Another voice came on the line. This time it was John.

"Eddie, they're all over the place. We can't get out. You gotta do something!"

"Where are you?" He dropped the phone and there was more yelling. "John? John!" Then George was back on the line.

"What should we do? We're trapped!"

"Who are they? How many are out there?" I asked.

"Hang on, I'll go see." About thirty seconds later he came back on. "There's about ten of 'em out front. But there's some more behind the building."

"How many guns?" I asked, sitting up.

"I don't know."

"Where are you guys?"

"Lisa was babysitting earlier and we came over... Lisa! What's the address here?"

He gave it to me. "You guys got any weapons?"

"No."

"Go to the kitchen. Grab steak knives, butcher knives, hammer, anything. Then lock all the doors and windows and wait for me to get there. It'll take me about fifteen minutes," I told them. "Keep your heads down. I'm on my way!"

I rolled out of bed and into some black jeans, black sweatshirt, and a black watch cap. It was about two miles to the address, and the police and several gangs roamed in between. Normally you never left the house without packin' something, but I couldn't risk being arrested for some weapon possession this time. Getting locked up wouldn't help the guys, so I left the house empty-handed, knowing that in the two miles or so of back-alleys I would have to travel through to avoid being arrested for curfew violation, I would be able to find plenty of makeshift weapons on the way.

So I was off and running. Literally, dodging cop cars and a few gang bangers along the way. And, can you believe it, I found nothing! Not a brick. No pipes, no sticks, no chains, not even a whiskey bottle. Must've been garbage day.

About twenty-odd minutes later, I arrived at the end of their block and there was shouting and guys were running around in front and on the sides of the apartment building I needed to get into. The guys were Assyrians, a local gang of Immigrant-Americans that regularly fought the Mexican, white, black, and Asian gangs around them.

There were only a couple of them in the alley, so I headed to the back end of the block and cut through the gangway across the alley from my target. Waiting for an opening, I shot across the alley and into the backyard, and into the shadows. In a few moments the two left the alley, and I took the opportunity to kick a few sharp slats out of the picket fence to use as weapons for us. I left the nail points sticking out of them. Then I managed to find a three-foot saw blade (don't ask me why it was there) and a length of pipe under the porch. Pay dirt!

The building had an enclosed stairway, which was locked at each level, so I had to climb up the outside all the way to the third floor where I slipped over the porch railing. Once there, I leaned out over three stories of empty space to gently tap on the rear, kitchen window. That managed to scare the shit out of everyone in the place and they all came running with weapons drawn. George finally saw it was me and rushed to let me in.

Once inside I distributed the weapons, giving one each to John, J.J., George and Lisa. I kept the pipe for myself. Rummaging through the garbage can, I found some bottles to use as missiles.

"Are they still out there?" George asked.

"Shit yeah."

"How many?"

"All of 'em, I think."

"Aw, shit! Oh man. We're screwed!"

Everybody was pretty spooked, but there was more than just panic in his voice. He was usually not this panicky.

"What've you guys been doing?"

"Nothing, just havin' a few beers," John told me.

"Those fuckin' bastards are always messin' with us," George said. "They won't leave us alone!"

Now he was working up a full head of steam, switching from terror to indignation. I knew what was coming next. Next thing you knew, now that I was here, he would be inviting them up for a free-for-all.

"Turn those lights out," I told them. "Everybody stay away from the windows." Low to the floor and in the corner, I crept slowly forward until I could see the street in front of the apartment. Peering over the ledge, I spotted about eight guys in the middle of the street talking animatedly to each other and looking up at our window.

Then suddenly George just walked right up, threw the window wide open and shouted at the top of his lungs: "Hey you fuckers! We got Eddie with us now! We're not afraid a you!"

I was speechless, trying to comprehend this lunacy. I couldn't believe it! I tackled him to the floor with my hand over his mouth as everybody else frantically told him to shut-the-fuck-up!

"What the fuck is wrong with you?! Do you want to get us *all* shot?!"

Up close he smelled of beer. And with George it didn't take much. DAMN! I thought to myself. These drunk-asses are about to get us all dead.

"Naw man, I ain't scared of them fuckers. One of 'em pulled a gun on Lisa. Tried to break in here. Tried to rape her!"

I looked over at Lisa who was looking me in the eye, shaking her head slowly from right to left with a "He's full 'o shit" look on her face.

"What happened?" I asked her, moving us into a quiet corner of the kitchen.

"I know one of the guys. He was over here earlier trying to get some. I told him no, but he was being an asshole. He showed me this gun and I told him to fuck off. So he left. I called George to come over here in case he came back."

"Did he?"

"He lives across the street. George and John saw him and started talking shit. Now they're all out there."

From the living room I heard John and George shouting again. "I dare you to fuck with us!" I heard them shout as I came rushing back in. Grabbing them both by the back of the collar, I yanked them away from the window. The voices on the street were now raised in shouts of anger and there were more of them. Several glass bottles shattered against the brick wall just below our window. Apparently we were too high for them to hit... just yet.

A safe distance away from the window, I faced everybody.

"Obviously there's been a miscommunication. Apparently you two want to fight guys that have guns and outnumber you by five to one. Knock yourselves out. I'm goin' home." And I walked towards the back door.

"No!" "Wait!" "You can't leave us here!" came in chorus from each of them.

"If you guys want my help," I said to them, "then SHUT THE FUCK UP!! If one more person sticks his head outside that window or says ANYTHING to them, I swear to God... I'm leaving!"

"Okay, man, okay."

"Just tell us what to do."

"Take George in the back room and keep him quiet and *away* from the windows!"

Lisa and J.J. hustled George out. I gave John a warning glance as I walked cautiously to the window and stuck my head out in plain sight. They hadn't started shooting yet and I was banking on the theory that they wouldn't until we came out looking for trouble.

Keeping an eye out for flying brick and glass, I waited silently until the guys outside quieted down. When I had their attention, I began in a neutral voice, loud enough for them all to hear.

"Yo! What's goin' on, guys?"

"That motherfucker's about to get himself shot!"

"Yeah!" a chorus of shouts confirmed this sentiment.

"Yo, we got more guys on the way!"

Taking a good look at them, I saw some lean, hard faces. These weren't the wannabes. They were the real deal. Gangstas. Drugs and guns.

"Guys... I gotta apologize." They didn't know how to take that or where I was going with it. "I got a problem. My man in here, he's drunk." As if that could ever explain George.

"No shit you got a problem. He's about to get himself killed."

"Yeah? Well sometimes I want to kill him myself," I told them honestly. "How about this: Why don't I take him in the back and get him sobered up and you guys can get back to enjoyin' your Saturday night? I know you got better things to do than hangin' out arguin' with his drunken ass."

"Yeah, well... you just better keep him in check or I ain't gonna be responsible for what happens to him," he said without much conviction.

I let him have it. "Aight man."

After I closed the window, the crowd began to mill around and then began to dissipate as I watched from the shadows. We headed back to where George was at and then I addressed them all.

"They're leaving. We were lucky, because they had enough manpower to bust this door down, kill us all and gang rape Lisa. If you get 'em started again, you're on your own. I'm out." And without another word, I left.

It was that night that I began to realize the power of keeping your mouth shut. The life you save may be your own. On the walk home I got to thinking about similar experiences. What they all had in common was this. Out of all the trouble I've seen in my life and the lives of those around me, the vast majority of the trouble we find ourselves in is due to our own efforts. Usually, in some way, we have invited that trouble or those people into our lives the way George had stirred up that crowd. I have no doubt that had we not been able to shut him up, the situation would have escalated beyond all of our control.

"Niggers Shot Curt"

Nicholas Senn High School was literally a block away from where I lived. We had moved to 5814 N. Glenwood when I was in eighth grade and we left Dad for the last time. It was a huge school. It took up a patch of land about four square city blocks. It was four stories tall and held about three thousand students. The school was uniquely comprised of approximately 25% White, 25% Latino, 25% Black, and 25% Asian. I say approximately because there were also large numbers of Native Americans, East Indians and other ethnicities. There were also a large number of gangs that were comprised of every culture under the sun. In addition to the predominant races, there were also Filipinos, Vietnamese, Korean and Cuban groups that had become their own de-facto gangs.

I never belonged to a gang nor had it ever even crossed my mind to join one. Nothing about it ever appealed to me. To me it was for those followers who needed something to belong to or someone too afraid to fight their own battles on the fair and square. Sure there were some bad mo-fo's in those gangs. And I knew many of them personally. The real deal. But I also knew a lot of pussies that needed someone else to front them when shit went down.

I chose to fight my own battles. Never once did I run to someone else for help. I either stood or fell on my own. Thankfully on a couple of occasions, the cavalry arrived to pull my ass out of the midst of a good ass kicking. Most of my friends thought like I did. They would handle their own beefs. If we were together there was nothing that would separate us, but when we fought, we fought one-on-one. Either we won or lost on our own. We were just as fierce alone as with a group. We didn't butch up and start shit with other people when we went out in numbers. We just wanted to be left alone to have our fun. We didn't bother anybody, but if someone was determined to start some shit, we were more than happy to sort that shit out.

There were several entrances to the huge school and each one was the hangout of one gang or another. They were always sitting outside those doors looking for someone to fuck with. And there were many victims they found to harass or rob. But if you stood your ground and showed them you wouldn't take any bullshit, they usually left you alone. All except for the stupid ones. There was always at least one little fuck in the group who talked all the bullshit and started all the shit knowing his boys will back him up. But only if they thought they could get away with it. There have been several times I was surrounded by guys with some little fucker with a big mouth egging them on. Most times it came down to three choices: run, let them kick your ass, or my personal favorite, let them know you mean business.

"Ain't you guys got anything better to do than hassle me?"
"Naw muthafucka!"
"All right. You gotta do what you gotta do."

And with that I would get in my battle stance, pick my first target and get ready. But once they saw that I wasn't going to go down easily, they usually found some excuse not to fight, something else to interest them and they would be on their way. A couple of times the fight had already started by the time they figured out I was serious and they decided to break-the-hell-out. It's the weirdest thing in the world to see a bunch of guys running from one little dude. But you gotta let them keep their dignity. After all, the next time they might be ready for you. So I wouldn't talk shit. Just pick up your stuff and be on your way, Eddie. Walk, don't run.

Sometimes you just gotta run. I recommend a diversion. Like a punch in the face of the nearest, biggest one, then run like hell and don't stop. Guys determined to kill me have chased me for blocks. But let me tell you, there is no motivation like knowing that if you stop you're dead, dai-ed, ded, or just plain d-e-a-d. That'll keep ya going for days. And for the guys chasing you? They are rarely as motivated to kick your ass. Even if you really piss them off like I sometimes did, provided you don't have a severe asthma attack or anything, the will to survive will usually keep you just out of their reach. Again, just don't stop. Cause then they know they got ya. But the farther you go, the greater your chances are. Sooner or later they will fall away one by one.

Look at it this way. Even if they eventually catch you, which would you rather have, five big strong well-rested guys kicking the shit out of you? Or five weakened, tired, winded, worn out, exhausted assholes throwing halfhearted punches and kicks at you? I'll take my chances with the latter, thank you. And I have. There's no comparison. But thankfully 19 out of 20 times I would get away. And the more I did it, the better I got.

So the real threat comes from surprise. AWARENESS! It will save your life. It is ALWAYS preferable to see danger coming a mile away and avoid it than to have to walk into the middle it and then try to get back out again.

J.J. and I were just heading out of my place when we spotted Fitch and a friend of his working on a car across the street.

"Egg up, egghead!" we greeted him.

"Whassup!" Fitch replied.

We hung out and shot the shit for a while. He didn't introduce the other white dude, who just stood looking on with an oil-stained adjustable wrench in his hand. They had been working on replacing the water pump, so we all tucked our heads underneath the hood to see what was going on. Fitch climbed back underneath while the new guy was on my left.

From the next block up, across the street from our high school, we heard CRACK! CRACKCRACKCRACK!!! Then followed the echo, bouncing off the stone canyon walls.

Looking up our side of the block, we saw two black men in their 30's standing in a doorway. One of them was waving a nickel-plated revolver and shouting something.

There were about ten white gangsters running around across the street from him in front of the school. Stepping out into the street, we saw one of the white guys lying face down in the street not moving. "Here we go again," I said as we got back to looking at the pump.

This kind of stuff was constant in the neighborhood. Always some drama, some bullshit, somebody getting into something they shouldn't. Shootings, stabbings, beatings... run of the mill. Then I heard this cat J.J. and I didn't know mumble something about niggers. I stood up, turned around and faced him. Putting his face down, he couldn't even look me in the eye. Then he turned away and pretended to be looking in the car for something. After staring at him for a minute I decided not to pursue it and went back to watching Fitch who had crawled under the car again. As I was watching from above, I heard J.J. calling, "Eddie, Eddie, EDDIE!" very persistently.

"What dude?"

As I looked up to him, he said, "C'mere. Let's go take a look," nodding his head in the direction of the guy still lying in the street where a crowd had begun to gather.

"All right dude, relax," I said.

When we were about a block away, he said to me, "The reason I called ya is that asshole who was standing behind ya with a wrench in his hand looked like he was trying figure out if he was gonna hit ya or not."

"Motherfucker!" I stopped and was deciding to go back and have it out with him when I heard someone in front of the school shout, "WAR! This is WAR!"

The guys who had been out front when the shooting went down were still hanging out there.

"Don't say that!" one of his friends hissed to him. By now there were about fifty white people... and I gathered in this all-white neighborhood. And more people were coming by the second.

Now two squad cars pulled up and four officers were just getting out when we heard voices and sounds of running feet coming from between two buildings adjacent to the one where the shooters were. Then rounding the corner, a pack of about eight gang bangers. The one out front had a chrome .45 semi-auto in his hand.

He didn't even get a chance to raise it. Those cops had their guns drawn and pointed before he even came to a stop. All eight of those assholes froze and the leader s-l-o-w-l-y held the .45 out by two fingers and offered it to those officers.

Minutes later as the officers questioned the gang members, an ambulance arrived. They placed the shot guy on the stretcher and put a yellow plastic sheet over him and elevated it on its telescoping legs. As they wheeled him to their vehicle, one of his arms plopped loose from the straps and fell down. It hung there as they rolled him out and one thin red line of blood trickled drop, drop, drops of blood to mark his final passage.

Then they were gone. Minutes later the cops disappeared into the apartment and then emerged with the black man handcuffed. The white guys started shouting and cursing at him and his only response was, "Come to my house again and I'll shoot me another one." With him and the white guy who had the .45 in custody, the police departed as well, leaving a sea of angry white faces and me.

"Niggers!" I heard one of the gangsters shout.

"Fucking niggers shot Curt!"

"Yeah! NIGGERS!!!" another one yelled.

He began to repeat his chant and others joined him in circling the front field of the school. Now that everyone had left, the crowd was starting to work itself up. Now that the police had taken their enemies away and disarmed them, now they found their bravado, their useless false courage.

"Fucking pussies," I said to myself. To J.J. I said, "Let's get the fuck out of here."

Just another day in paradise.

Gokes

There was a burger joint on Petersen and Broadway, down the street from where I lived in the all-white area of Chicago called Edgewater. In this burger joint they had a couple of pinball machines and one foosball table. It was on the outskirts of one gang's territory and the beginning of another's, but it was a kind of no-man's-land where Mexican, Black, Asian, and white kids hung out and ate and played. It was just down the street from our high school.

I didn't associate with too many white kids back then, because the ones I met were usually affiliated with one of the white, racist gangs. Needless to say, they didn't want much to do with my dark ass anyway. Tensions usually ran high at the burger joint. No one knew when some shit would break out. I got to be pretty good at foosball and after a while I would hold the table, taking on all comers.

There was this white kid called Gokes. Gokes was a member of the local white gang, but he didn't seem to have a problem hanging out with me. I was cool with anyone and everyone who was cool with me. He was about my age and he and I would usually play each other to a standstill on the foosball table. Just to be nice, we would usually quit after three loooong, close games just to let other folks have a chance to play. He and I became pretty close there. He was the first white friend I had met in a long time.

Then he just stopped showing up. And after a couple of weeks I found out that he had been killed. Three guys from a rival gang had snuck into his apartment, shot him in the chest with a twelve-gauge, and then took the time to cut his throat.

I have to say that even though I didn't know Gokes that well, I considered him a friend and would have fought on his behalf. He was a nice guy, one of the few. And that was one of the more vicious killings. It saddened me deeply. Death was usual and savage killings were usually reserved for those whom everybody knew would get it. But Gokes? It just didn't make sense. And even though little made sense in the hood, it's in humanity's nature to try to make sense of it anyway. But if you stop to spend too much time on it, it will drive you crazy. Little by little, I've seen it happen.

Jerry

J.J., his brother George, John and I were sitting outside Jerry's apartment with Jerry and his brother Thomas. We were just hangin' out talking shit. Chillin' and smoking dubies and downin' some suds. It was about ten o'clock on a Saturday night. My guys and I ranged in age from 14 to 16 years old. Jerry and his brother were each about 20 years old. Tom was an okay guy, but Jerry was kind of a dick. He thought because he was older and bigger than everybody else, that he was the man. We let him think so, because he was no threat and he was the guy with the drugs. Right now it was his bud we're smoking and our beer they were drinking. They were small-time. Not really dealers so much as they shaved a little off their own stash and sold it on the side.

Jerry could be a real asshole when he got high and right then that about said it all. We tried to ignore him as best as we could. Everybody wanted to have a good time, right? Well, everybody but Jerry, that is. It seemed he was devoted his evening to telling everybody what a big man he was. Talking even more shit than usual, he was getting on everyone's nerves, especially J.J. and George. They had been going back and forth for the last hour or so, and it was getting to be a drag.

Then we started giving each other that look. The look that said which one of us was going to have to do something about this asshole? Why didn't we just leave? There was nowhere else to go. This was where we were and this was where the drugs and drink were, but our patience was being tried, tried… tried.

Then finally we couldn't take it any more. "Ya wanna get outta here?" I asked.

"Yeah, let's book," said J.J.

"Hold up. I wanna get a nickel bag from this guy," George told us. So we waited while they worked it out. With said baggie in hand, George and J.J. decided to roll the joints up before we left. So they broke out the rolling papers and got to work. Then about four joints into it, J.J. shouted out, "What the fuck?!"

Come to find out there were only four joints in this five joint bag that Jerry just sold George. George asked Jerry what was up and Jerry smugly said to the brothers, "Ya must've rolled 'em too big." Then he went back to tokin' his own joint.

I took a look at the four rolled joints and said," Dude, you shorted them."

With us all standing there looking at him, the asshole just shrugged. Can you believe that? Now we had to figure out if one of us or all of us was gonna kick his ass.

And before we could make a move, up pulled this big white Buick. J.J. and George's cousin Steve, "Moose", as his fellow gang members called him, saw us and stopped his car in the middle of Winona Avenue.

While J.J and John were still arguing with Jerry, George and I walked over to Steve to see if anything was happening. No, he was just cruising through the hood when he saw us.

"What are you guys up to?" he asked us.

"We were just trying to figure out which one of us is gonna kick this guy's ass," I told him.

"Which guy?"

"Jerry, the big one up there."

"What for?"

"He just shorted George on a nickel bag on purpose."

"No shit?"

"Yeah!" George told him. "That fucker's always pullin' shit like this. I'm tired of it!"

Looking at me, Steve asked, "What's this guy about?" He wanted to know if Jerry was normally cool or was he always an asshole.

"About being an asshole," I told him.

And with that, Steve opened his door and lifted his huge frame out of the car. At sixteen years old, he was not a tall guy, but at about 300 pounds, he was built like a fucking tank. It might look like it was all fat, but that fat covered a whole lotta muscle.

George and I gave each other that "Oh shit" look. Steve was not the guy you wanted to have mad at you, even if you were a bad-ass, which Jerry was definitely not.

With Steve leading the way, we followed him up onto the front stoop. Stopping in front of the front step that Jerry was sitting on, he looked right at him and said, "What's up?"

Jerry spared him barely a glance before he went back to his pot. "Nothin'," he responded in his best 'I'm too cool to care' voice, "what's up with you?"

Steve just drew back that big ham hock hand of his and SSSSMMACK!!

The open handed blow caught Jerry across the side of the mouth and knocked him off the top step and flat onto the porch. He didn't know what just happened, but he was mad.

"What the fuck!?!" he shouted, rising from his prone position.

"I heard you like rippin' people off." BAP! Bending over Steve had popped him in the mouth in an almost casual fashion and Jerry landed flat again.

"Hey man! Fuck you!" he said, trying to rise again.

Krack! The first kick caught him on the other side of the face.

"C'mon man!" His anger has quickly turned to doubt.

Krack, krack, krack! Slowly, methodically, the kicks and punches fell down on his covered face, head, ribs, stomach. The sickening sounds were punctuated only by Jerry's screams.

"Please!"

Bam!

"Please, man!"

Krack!

"Stop!"

We all stood around silently and watched. I had mixed feelings about this. On the one hand, one joint wasn't worth an ass-kicking. On the other hand, if this matter wasn't dealt with then, we'd all have to deal with Jerry from then on out. His thinking that he had, and can continue to, get over on all of us present was a real problem. And after all, we did try to reason with him. And in the streets you've got to handle your business. And while it should have been George, Steve worked just as well, cause George would've stabbed 'im.

When Steve was finished, he stood there looking over the trembling, crying form for a few moments. It was like a cat eyeing a mouse before he eats it.

"Think about this the next time you decide to rip someone off." And just like that he turned and headed back for his car. George and I walked him back to the Buick.

"Thanks man," George said to him, "I'm sick of that asshole fuckin' with me."

"I don't think it'll be happening again, but if it does, just let me know."

We said goodbye and he was gone. Like some twisted lone ranger on a white stallion, the Buick drove off up Winona Avenue. George and I walked back up the steps to the stoop where Jerry was still lying and crying, and bleeding. Everything else was silent.

"Clean yourself up, Jerry. It's over," I told him quietly.

"I've never seen a grown man cry," George said with loud contempt.

"Shut up, George!" his brother snapped at him. "You'd be cryin' too."

We all sat around for a while to allow Jerry the dignity of pulling himself together before we moved to leave. If we had left while he was still lying there crying, that would have been the only thing people would have remembered when they thought about him. But as it was, we left him standing. Because after all, getting beaten down isn't a crime. It happened to everybody sooner or later. Even Steve. But how you take it becomes extremely important.

When he managed to stop crying, brushed himself off and got back up, we slowly got to our feet, said goodbye and left.

Jerry didn't talk much shit after that. Matter of fact, we didn't see too much of him or his brother. We didn't mind. It's not as if we were all that close to them. But it just goes to show you, we all get ours in the end. If you're gonna screw somebody over, it never pays to gloat. Everybody gets screwed at some time or other. But when you rub their face in it, it usually adds up to a sure-fire recipe for revenge. And then you've got enemies, and you always have to look over your shoulder. And that's no fun at all. Trust me.

Jim

Jim was a social worker who had just been assigned to George while the guys were staying at my place. Coincidentally, Caesar had also been assigned to him a couple of years before.

George had only met Jim once and he gave him the creeps. J.J. wasn't around and George did not want to have to go to his appointment with Jim alone, so he asked me to come along with him.

When we got to Jim's "office" it turned out to be his little one-bedroom apartment. But you'd have thought you'd stumbled into Hugh-fucking-Heffner's place by accident. This asshole was standing there in the door wearing nothing but a raggedy, half-opened bathrobe that barely covered his narrow chest, pot-gut, and skinny legs.

He had the kind of controlled ooze that the guilty-but-looking have. He had a masculine "butch" front with a secret "fag" oozing between the seams. He always gave us fleeting glimpses of it, intermingled with the "don't fuck with me" strong, black male thing.

In the room behind him were three other sullen teenagers sitting quietly on various pieces of furniture. And over all, hung the sweet, stale odor of already-smoked weed.

"Awwwww-shit." What the hell have I walked into, said the fly to himself.

But George had to go. And I wasn't about to let him go in there alone. So I slid my left hand into my pocket and onto my knife, and shook his hand with my right, and we went in.

I didn't like the sound the door made when he closed it.

It wasn't a meeting as much as it was a feel-out session for George, and I was just an added treat. Like two chickens being eyed by a hawk. Jim asked the usual, "Staying out of trouble?" questions for George, plus a whole lot more. He took his sweet time too. Asking us repeatedly if we wanted anything, food, booze, pot, or blow.

For a "social worker" he was waaaaaaay too interested in me. He wanted to know aaaaaaaall kinds of shit that was none of his business. Shit like who was I dating and what kinds of girls did I like. I answered them all with short "Uh-huh, uh-huh" answers.

If he hadn't been someone who could have George locked up with only a word, I would have told him exactly what I wanted to do to him and walked the fuck out. But it wasn't that kind of party. So I just chilled and let George do his "interview" thing.

In the hour or so he kept us there with his bullshit, there twice came a knocking at the door. And each time a new boy would come into the already crowded "playpen".

Each one would be greeted with an almost gleeful smile before being led unhappily, glumly, into Jim's bedroom. Once inside Jim would close and lock the door, and they would remain sequestered for over a quarter of an hour.

While they were inside there would be an awkward silence. Each of the teenagers in the room would sit with bowed heads while George and I exchanged an "I'm in the fucking Twilight Zone" look.

Chill Eddie. Juuuuuuuust chill. There is nothing you can do here to help anyone, especially George. Let's just get through this without killing anyone or getting locked up.

I thought about how this son-of-a-bitch had these kids over a barrel. Either do what Jim wants or get sent back up.

And I started to get mad. Cutting that bastard's throat apparently never occurred to these guys.

Yeah, well… if he made a move on one of us, the police would be chasing my little ass clear across state lines. And if one of these punks wanted to try and stop me, I'd send him on his way too. I didn't know shit about Canada, but I knew it was a hell of a lot better on teenage runaways than Mexico was. Hell, it damn sure wasn't any colder than Chicago.

The more I thought about it, the better it sounded.

Chill Eddie. Juuuuuuuust chill.

When the bedroom door was again unlocked and opened, Jim would emerge grinning like a Cheshire cat and the boy he'd been in there with would make a silent b-line for the front door, with his head down and in a mean hurry to be gone.

When our business was finally done and over, we couldn't wait to be gone. But Jim juuuuust kept on. Oblivious.

Staring deeply into my eyes as he squeezed my hand goodbye, he gushed about how wonderful it had been to meet me. He made sure to tell me I was welcomed to stop by anytime, day or night. "My door is always open to you," he said with all due sincerity. He managed to keep from drooling while he said it. Yeah, I thought, your bedroom door asshole, no thanks.

By the time we finally got out of there, I felt like I needed to shower.

Deep down I was fuming. I was furious that they let a corrupt, drug-dealing, pedophile like that be in charge of a bunch of kids.

George was mad as well. "I hate that motherfucker! Fuckin' faggot!"

"You need to call them up and get you another case worker," I told him. "That motherfucker is poison."

To his credit, George did drop that dime. He didn't go into why, just told them it wasn't working out, that they had "problems". The government employee in charge of it couldn't give a shit. Basically, he told George he was shit out of luck. Told him he'd better go back to Jim.

Several times over the next few months George would plead with me to come along with him to Jim's. As much as I despised being in Jim's lair, I couldn't bring myself to let George go in there alone. Those other boys there were like vampire's familiars. No telling what else they would do at Jim's command.

Then one day George, J.J., and Caesar came home all out of breath and in a rush. While J.J. locked the front door and Caesar headed for the fridge, George headed for the bedroom and began rooting around in there.

I thought they were being chased. "What's up?" I asked.

"We just ripped off Jim," J.J. said matter-of-factly.

A slow grin spread across my face as I began to chuckle. "It couldn't have happened to a bigger asshole."

J.J. was like a sapling. You could yank his chain, but the farther you pulled, the harder the slap when he got away from you. I just knew Jim had finally gotten to him.

"That motherfucker just kept fuckin' with me. I told him to lay off. Askin' me if I liked boys an' shit! Fuckin faggot! At first he was cool. Asked us if we wanted to do a couple of lines with him. So I said 'what the fuck?' Then he broke out some weed and we started up a joint and he started in on me. Talkin' about how cute I was an' shit. FUCK that man! Shit!

So the next time he took one of those boys in the back for his blowjob, I had George watch the door, Caesar watched the guys, then I grabbed up all his shit and we booked."

"That's fucked UP man," George jumped in. "Fuckin' havin' sex with boys an' shit! Man, that shit ain't right!"

"Yeah man, no shit," I said. Then figuring out what George was doing in the bedroom I told them, "That's some pretty fucked up shit. But yo man, you can't keep that shit here."

"Aw, c'mon!"

"Aw, c'mon, my ass. He's got our phone number and address!" I said. "Just how the fuck long you think it's gonna take for the cops to get here?"

"He ain't gonna call the cops, Eddie," Caesar said. "What's he gonna say? 'They stole my stash'!"

"He ain't gonna call 'em'," George piped in.

"No, fuck that. You know some 'o them cops are friends of his. He works with 'em for chrissakes! All I know is, you can't keep that shit here. HELL naw. 'Sides, what do you think they'd do to my mom? Huh? They come here, find you three juveniles with warrants AND all that shit?! HELL MOTHERFUCKIN' NAW!"

I guess that put it into perspective for them. And once they knew I wasn't fuckin' around, George went and dug out a big bag of weed with a couple of little packets inside with cocaine and pills of various colors, acid, uppers, downers, and 'shrooms. Several hundred dollars worth of shit.

Oh yeah, that DEFINITELY had to go. I thought they'd been talking about a dime-bag, not the guy's entire fuckin' supply.

About three days later I was home alone reading comic books when there came a knock, knock, knockin' at my front door. And guess who it was. Detectives! Knockin' at my front door. After asking for their badges and checking them through the peep-hole, I opened the door.

"What can I do for you?" I asked innocently, looking up at their towering figures.

"We're lookin' for George and J.J.," and said their last names. No mention of Caesar. The stockier detective began to barge right into me as I stood in the doorway with a half-opened door.

But I wasn't havin' it. I wasn't going to move. If they wanted to they could knock me down, cuff me, and walk in over me, but I wasn't going to just stand aside and let these two assholes just barge into my home. Besides, there was no tellin' how many illegal substances there were in my house besides the illegal weapons I did know about.

When he finally came to a stop, I could smell the aftershave he had rubbed onto his chest. I couldn't tell if the booze I smelled was coming from the clothes he wore or the breath pouring down from his nostrils. There was a surprised look on his face. He shared a brief, bemused look with his partner, then he stepped back and said, "We need to see 'em… now."

Steadily returning their stony gaze with my own, I said, "They're not here."

"C'mon kid, we know they live here."

"I know 'em, but they don't live here," I lied.

"Mind if we look anyway." It wasn't a question. And to prove it he began to press forward rather than wait for a response.

"Sorry," I said, holding my ground and gaining a certain satisfaction at this David and Goliaths' stand-off.

"We could make you let us in, you know."

"Yeah, you could try that," I admitted.

And then they stood there and thought about that one. I stood there thinking about them thinking about it. And then, just like that, I knew they wouldn't when he said, "You know what this is about?"

"Jim."

"Yeah, Jim. He says they ripped him off."

With a smile that told them I knew something they didn't, I asked, "He tell ya what they stole from him?"

Again the glance. "Yeah, stereo equipment." It was his turn to lie.

"Weed," I replied. "Weed, pills and blow," I said, knowing he wouldn't act on the information.

"Yeah well, it's his word against theirs."

"I'll take theirs. Toss his place. You'll find plenty."

"We can't do that." But I knew that they could do that. And would, IF they wanted to.

"You know those kids that were hangin' round?" I gambled. "D'he tell ya he's fuckin' 'em?"

And again the glance. "Well... we don't know anything about that."

"I'm telling ya now." When they didn't respond I knew they wanted no part of that mess. "But a pedophile screwin' a bunch 'o kids...? You guys don't care about that do you?"

Yeah, I was keenly aware that they might just decide that they'd had enough of this smart-assed little kid telling them how to do their jobs and decide to beat the shit out of me. But I didn't care. I was mad.

Here they were, hounding two broke, homeless, victimized little kids. Trying to punish them for not allowing themselves to be victims, for not bashing Jim's twisted head in like they should have. Trying to lock them up.

But the predator? The real threat was let go to run rampant, unchecked, covered, destroying lives and families and generations, undaunted.

"You see 'em, tell 'em we're lookin' for 'em," he said finally. And with that they made their exit, their power turned to impotence.

They never did catch the brothers on that one. But Jim? Oh, Jim's just fine.

For years afterward I'd pass the asshole on the streets, in the neighborhood. At first he tried to get me to come visit him. Then he would complain about mean ol' George and J.J., after all he'd tried to do for George. Shame on them. Poor ol' pedophile Jim.

Lawrence Avenue Assassins

About ten o'clock on a weekend evening, J.J., John, Axel, Caesar, Tony and I had decided to infiltrate the Lawrence Avenue train station. It was part of our regular but infrequent routine when there was nothing going on. We would find an elevated train platform and find a way to climb up, in, over, around, underneath or through it, then ride the trains across the city until we got bored with that, then ride back home.

Lawrence was an easy one. We had done it before a few different ways. J.J. went first this time and we watched him go over the edge and step onto the tracks. But instead of crossing them and climbing onto the platform, he headed parallel to the platform, right in the middle of the tracks. And speeding towards him from the rear was an oncoming train.

"J.J.!" came the first harsh whisper from John. Then when we realized he didn't hear John, several of us shouted out loud, not concerned with blowing our cover.

"J.J.!!" Turning, he paused and after seeing us gesticulating wildly, he headed back towards us.

"What?"

"Whooooosh!" the express train hurtled past him so fast that he didn't even hear it until it was completely by him. It scared him so much he nearly fell when he turned around.

With our hearts back in our chests, we watched him turn around and this time take a more direct path to the platform after first looking both ways. Once up there, he gave us the "all-clear" signal to let us know we would be unseen and we followed by twos. Up on the deserted far end of the platform, we gathered together and discussed which train we would take.

Suddenly we heard a scream. It was a man's scream. It was a mortal scream. It was the scream of a man looking death in the face for the final time. Now I've seen men die and I've heard men scream, but I've never heard a scream like it before or since.

It was impossible to tell the direction it came from as it echoed through the cement canyons of the city below us, but it was close.

Slowly, reluctantly, we spread out to get a view of its horrific source. Abandoning our curiosity to our better judgment, we did not go down there looking for trouble. We decided to stay put. It was a good thing too, because we were soon distracted by a more immediate and more personal peril.

Making our way towards the middle of the platform, we joined the rest of the waiting passengers. It was not unusual to wait up to an hour on the trains, so we goofed off while we waited. After about fifteen minutes I got that little tickle in the back of my neck that I always listen to. The one that shouts "danger!"

Stepping away from the crew, I looked around and tried to sense from whence came my discomfort. At the end of the platform we had climbed up from, there were two men in the shadows dressed in jeans, denim jackets and baseball caps. Each was about twenty or twenty-five. Both had sandy brown hair. One had a mustache, one a biker goatee. And they were what was setting off my alarms.

Turning back to the guys, I told them about the two other ones. "These guys are checking us out. I'm gonna go see what they're up to. Keep an eye on 'em."

With that, I decided to stroll past them to see what they would do. As a train pulled into the station on the left side of the platform, I strolled casually down the right side. Passing the exit, the enclosed stairway took up the center of the platform. The walkway on either side of it was only about three feet wide and an old woman was standing against the middle of the structure taking up half of that space. I stepped gingerly around her, trying not to fall or bump into her, and made my way to the far end.

The closest of the guys tried hard not to notice me as he meandered in my direction. Bingo. He was definitely after me. Now let's see why. I kept walking as if to go past him. If he came at me, I was confident enough that I could knock him down or fight him off and be gone before his friend, thirty feet further down the platform, caught up to us and joined the fray. But I didn't get the chance to pass him.

"Hold it motherfucker!" he shouted as he ripped his jacket open and snatched at a big-ass, nickel-plated revolver that was jammed down into the waistband of his jeans.

Oh, I thought, that's what he has planned. Well never mind.

As he yanked that big cannon out, I was already turning and bolting in the other direction.

Shit! The old woman who had been out of the way against the wall of the stair structure was now smack in the middle of the walkway heading away from me, blocking my exit. To make matters worse, there was also a train approaching on my side of the tracks so I could not jump down to escape.

Fuuuuuuck!

I made an instant decision not to knock the poor woman over in my flight, hoping he would not open fire and choose instead to try and chase me down. I did a ballerina-tap-dance on the outside three inches of platform available to me just above the tracks. As my toes skipped across the edge, the rest of my feet bobbled over open space that awaited the oncoming train. Incredibly, I managed to defy gravity long enough to get past her without falling into the train's path or hearing the pop, pop, pop I feared.

As I neared the gang I saw that they had indeed not been watching and the sounds of the breaking train had covered his shout.

"Break! Break! They got guns!" I shouted as I neared them. Seeing me in full flight they all froze for a moment, then bolted into the just opening doors of the first train. That looked like a bad idea to me, because those doors would stay open for a few minutes. They'd be trapped in there just long enough for them to walk in and pop all of us. Not for me kid.

As I drew even with the exit, I threw out my right hand and grabbed onto the doorway and hooked around into a 180 so fast it nearly pulled my shoulder out of the socket. I was now heading full-tilt towards the top of the stairs.

It was a loooooong stairway broken up into two sections. Launching myself into the air, I hit the first section about halfway down praying my ankles would survive the landing. What I hadn't planned on was skating down the rest of the way on my heels, four steps at a stride.

Stumbling hard onto the bottom landing, I heard the guy above me shout down, "Joe, he's comin' down! He's comin' down!" before his footsteps hit the stairs behind me. In the back of my mind I was thankful my friends weren't being shot like fish in a barrel above me. On the other hand, I was now alone and the guys with the guns were coming after me!

Grabbing the doorway at the bottom, I hung another "U" and burst through the doors into the pay area. What I had planned to do was dodge and/or fight my way past "Joe" and whoever else was with him, jump the waist-high turnstile, and ghost. What really happened was that I came into the pay area and slammed full on into the iron bars that made up the newly built revolving gate.

Surprise, surprise. Urban renewal at its best. Covering up as best I could, I hit the rotating gate like a hotdog falling into a bun. WHAM! I let the gate swing me around and spit me out the other side.

There were about six people milling around and I eyed their frightened faces as I caught my balance. None of them seemed to want to have anything to do with me. I figured Joe was outside the entrance waiting in ambush. I figured I'd ambush the ambush.

Heading straight for the double swinging –doors, I hit them head-on at full speed and hard enough to knock down any two people that might be waiting for me on the other side. I didn't slow to see if I scored. Then I was out into the night and flying like the wind.

Shooting across the flowing traffic of Lawrence Avenue, I dodged a couple of cars and shot straight into the alley across the street and kept on going. There were plenty of gangways and garages to dodge through or into if they came after me. If they had a car and were going to circle the block looking for me, I had no idea what they were driving. So I took all the darkened side streets and alleys I could find the whole two miles home.

When I got back to my apartment, the guys were all there sitting around eating and talking animatedly.

"Eddie! What happened to you?" "Where'd you go dude?" A chorus of questions hit me as soon as I walked in the door.

"Did anybody come after you guys?" I asked them.

"No, they all took off after you."

"Yeah dude, they must've wanted you pretty bad." "Who were those guys?" they asked.

"Never seen 'em before. I was gonna ask you the same thing. So what did you guys do?"

"Nothin'. The train took off and we just rode it home. Got here about ten minutes ago."

"Well, why the hell didn't you come after me?!"

"We talked about it. Then we figured, 'Eddie can take care of himself.' So we came back here to wait for you to show up."

Damn. I wanted to be pissed at them for not coming after me, but then those guys did have guns. What could they have done to help? I'd like to think I would have done something if our roles had been reversed, but on the other hand, it flattered me that they had that kind of faith in me. Oh, well... what are you gonna do?

And we never did find out who those guys were.

Meeting with god *on the train tracks*

I met God at the Loyola train station.

I have not always been a believer in Christ. Quite the opposite. In fact my stepfather tried his best to make all us sworn enemies of God himself. He used to rail against him at every opportunity. Spewing poisonous hatred, he would use any excuse to make Him the cause of all the world's woes. Like it was God that made my stepfather beat me, my mother and my sister, curse us, and try his best to destroy our very souls. Of course it was! It was, after all, God who went out of His way to make my dad's childhood so messed up. Y'a know, I wonder if my dad thought it was God's fault he was beating me.

I figured if there was a God, I didn't want any part of one who would allow my sister, my mom, and I to be subjected to the kind of shit we had endured.

One day I finally got the chance to meet God. Well, it was Him or one of his messengers, but it was definitely someone on His side. Unfortunately, He didn't stay to chit-chat. Guess he had other lives to save. But I gotta tell ya, it was really scary-cool.

One dark, cold night, me and the gang were out fuckin' up, as usual, doing something we shouldn't have been doing, being someplace we should not be. But hey, it was how we lived. Just sitting around the house talking got pretty old. We didn't have money for going to clubs, or movies, or shopping, or travel (legitimate travel anyway). I read a lot, but I'm a social creature. I needed to be well-rounded. I had not yet discovered the whole "school" thing; clubs, sports, classes, etc.

So around eleven or twelve o'clock we all left my apartment in search of... well... trouble. It was the only fun, the only "recreation" we had. This frosty December night we all decided to go train-hopping. In our version of the game instead of just running and jumping over the turnstile to ride the trains without paying, we would actually climb up the outside of the elevated train platform, trying not to fall and kill ourselves, and trying not to electrocute ourselves on the multiple electrified rails. Are you beginning to get the idea that trying not to die, made up the bulk of our time?

With me were John, J.J., George and Caesar. Caesar was my road dog. We were birds of a feather, daredevils both of us. We spent much of our time trying to outdo each other, pushing each other. We went head-to-head on everything from martial arts to climbing. Everything but women. And he and I shared one or two of those. It was great to be pushed and have someone to push. Everyone should have a friend/rival like that in their lives.

We had already infiltrated just about every train station on the north side. Loyola station was one that we had not hit yet. It just sat there waiting. Calling out to us... cliiiiiimb me, cliiiiiimb me. This particular platform was about two stories above the street. And unlike the other elevated train platforms, which were made out of steel girders and I-beams, Loyola was made of cement, one solid wall that ran the width of four sets tracks with the station itself in the middle. We knew it was going to be tough, but what the heck, it was not like we had anything better to do.

Bundling up in my all-black stealth outfit, we hit those glistening, snowy streets. Walking the long, cold couple of miles down there, we regarded the monolithic structure as we approached it. Then we made our rounds.

We had made our way entirely around the thing, several frigid blocks of walking, and had no luck in finding our egress. We were standing there by a darkened, shadowy alley, stumped, when J.J. said, "Fuck this man, let's get outta here."

"Let's give it one more circle," I said and we headed off again. We had gotten maybe three quarters around again when Caesar piped in, "Man, we ain't ever gonna get up there."

That's all I had to hear. Anytime anybody tells me "you can't", it just makes me more determined. I say, "Ah, but let me at least give it a shot!" And then inspiration struck. "There!" I said.

About a block away from us, I saw my opportunity. Across the narrow alley from the where the stone wall of the platform curved around into the distance, there was a two-story apartment building. And attached to that building was a one-story garage. "There!" I said pointing it out.

"We can climb up on to the garage, then climb onto the roof, then jump across."

"You're crazy," J.J. stated.

Caesar was equally skeptical. "Yeah, right, lemme see you do it."

Well, you know that was all I had to hear.

"Go for it, dude," John said.

"Keep a lookout," I told them and approached the garage.

From a distance of about ten feet, I started at a run. About four feet away, I launched myself up with my left leg and hit the brick wall of the garage with my right foot, launching myself up. That got me up high enough to grab the rain gutter at its roof. Continuing my upwards momentum, I first pulled up, then pushed down with my hands until I was shoulders and chest above the roof. By leaning my head and shoulders forwards it brought my hips and legs higher up. First I swung my right knee up and hooked it onto the edge of the roof. Then my left knee followed it and rolled me over.

In a moment I was on my hands and knees. Getting my feet under me, I stood up and surveyed my surroundings. I scanned for movement and listened for sounds that might indicate that I had been seen. I found a drain pipe running up along the alley side of the apartment and I used this to climb the rest of the way to the top of the building.

Once I had gotten to the top of the building, I took a moment to look down. I always got that feeling of electric tingling in my knees and lower belly whenever I got up to a height. This is no surprise as I'm afraid of heights. Maybe that's why I seek them out.

At the bottom the guys were busy checking the streets for cops. Every now and then they would look up and check on my progress. But now that I was standing there on the edge, they all watched to see if I would make the jump.

It was maybe nine feet across the alleyway, and the roof I was on was several feet higher. Here is where the giddiness hits you. When you are standing there - actually making the jump in your mind. The adrenaline was already hitting my bloodstream in full effect.

Well, let's do it, I thought. Looking down at the guys, I stage-whispered, "Clear?"

With last looks they came back at me, "Clear!" This was it. There's no taking it back once you stepped off that edge. And I went.

With a running go, I took off across the roof with measured steps. I had to make sure I was slightly head-forward, since I would be catching myself with my hands before my feet hit. With the cold, crisp wind in my face, I launched myself outward and felt gravity take over. Mixing with momentum, it arced me downward. I hit the wall simultaneously with both hands on the edge and my left foot on the wall, then my left foot landed and I had a secure hold.

I had braced myself for the impact with my chest against the wall. My main concern was not letting my hands be jarred loose from their purchase. If I slipped, the fall could easily kill me. If I was lucky enough to land on both feet from that height, I might only get me a few broken bones and a trip to the police station by way of the hospital.

Safe, I held on firmly by my fingertips while I caught my breath. I checked in with the guys just to make sure the coast was still clear. If I absolutely had to jump down, now was the best opportunity. It would take me a while to get up and over that edge. Then I had to look around, and then poke my head back over the edge to let them know the platform was clear. Looking down at the tops of their heads, no one seemed agitated, no one was staring fixedly, so I determined that all was well.

Carefully, I began to pull myself up until I could get first one elbow then the other over the edge of the platform. Then I leaned forward with my upper body in order to bring my legs over. Then I had a curious moment.

As I leaned forward it brought my face to within four inches of one of the rails that the express trains run on. What brought my attention to it was the cold. I could actually feel it radiating from the steel like a furnace spewing cold instead of heat. As the waves of cold emanating from it hit my face, it made my cheeks, lips, teeth and nose instantly about ten degrees colder than the rest of my head. They felt slightly numb, strangely like... putty. It was a curious thing. I had never experienced anything quite like it. In that instant I looked at it... really looked at it. I took in the bluish gray. The microscopic grooves scratched into the top surface from the speeding steel of the train wheels grinding across it. I saw the tiny pockmarks and I briefly wondered if it were due to impure steel, improper smelting of impure molten metal? Or was it grit pounded in by the wheels burdened by tons of metal and flesh.

And then, in the span of the next few heartbeats, five seconds at the most, the purpose and direction of my life were instantly and irrevocably changed. Forever.

In the next instant I heard the one word that would change it all: "Eddie".

It came from high above and behind my right shoulder. As soon as I heard it, I froze.

My first thought was that I was in trouble. What immediately came to mind, because it was an adult voice, was that it was a coworker of my mom's who had improbably recognized me from one of my visits to her workplace. I looked in the direction from which the voice had come and saw...

Nothing.

Thin air. There was no window on that side of the building. In fact there was no building up there at all. The rooftop was slightly below me. I thought it odd that I had gotten the direction wrong, because I was usually pretty good at directional hearing.

I swiveled my head over my left shoulder and found... the same kind of nothing. Then I looked back to my right and two stories below me to where the guys waited, watching the street. I hesitated briefly before asking them because of two things. First, the voice had been distinctly adult. Second, unlike the guys who called me "Ed", it said, "Eddie" in a crisp, clear voice that was insistent and would not be ignored. And third, it came from high above, not down below. But what the heck.

"What?" I said down to the top of their heads.

All of them immediately looked up confused.

"What??" J.J. said. I could barely hear him.

"Who called me?" He consulted with both John and Cesar, both of which shook their heads to the negative.

"Nobody," he said back up at me, bewildered.

Now they were all looking.

And that was it. Right shoulder, left shoulder, down, "nobody".

Five seconds. That's it. That's all. Just about the right amount of time for me to get right up onto the middle of the tracks on my hands and knees. Just enough time to look up and see a bright, shiny death coming right for me with blinding lights and a greeting gust of air.

For as I turned my face back to the track, I felt that gust. From that close it was like a punch in the face. It blew my hair to the right then swirled in frenzy like a dervish about my head and shoulders. And right behind it was the train.

I didn't even see it coming. Didn't feel a trembling in the platform, didn't hear it rumbling through space. I didn't even see the lights coming around that curve. Nothing. Just a blast and a rush and then nothing.

Time seemed to freeze everything but that train. It just kept going and going and going, blasting ahead like one long, huge, steel serpent. And then it disappeared from my sight, like it had never been. It snaked on around that curve and behind buildings blocks away. Finally all that was left was the shimmering, keening ring of wheel grazing track, block after block. And when it was done, when all the train cars had disappeared from view around the long, gradual curve, I was left behind, still frozen.

Just Frozen.

"Ed... Ed... ED!" J.J.'s voice snapped me out of it. "What's the matter?" he said.

When I looked down, they were all three staring up at me with worried expressions on their faces.

I only thought of telling them what had happened for an instant. And then I realized that they would think I had lost my mind if I told them that a voice from above just saved my life.

"Nothing," I replied.

Then looking both ways, I made sure no trains were coming and pulled myself on up onto those tracks.

I checked the passenger platform to make sure there were no police or C.T.A personnel around. Then returned to the edge, checked for trains again, and told the guys all was clear. Ten minutes later they had followed me up and we stood on the platform awaiting the next train away from there.

For the rest of the night and into the morning, we rode trains and joked around. Just before dawn rose, we made our way back to our respective homes and into bed.

But all through all that time I had something else on my mind: What was so special about me that some celestial being a) knew me by name; and b) wanted me alive. Why?! What for? And why me? It kept me awake long into the morning.

That night began my quest. A path that I would travel for years. A journey that would never really be over. I was out to find out who that voice belonged to and what they wanted with me.

Over the years I have found God, Jesus, the Holy Spirit, and their angels. And I have begun to find out what I am here for, why I had been spared.

The journey is still on.

I'm just a little farther down that path.

George + Knife =

George and J.J had been living with Caesar, Mom and I for several weeks now. I asked Mom if Caesar could stay with us when his mom kicked him out of the house for being too much of an adult. J.J. and George moved in recently because their dad had taken to smacking them around on a regular basis and going into whiskey hallucinations. Frankly, I was afraid they were going to kill him one day.

I had two hard rules in my house. Aside from the usual courtesy and common sense things, there were these: 1) No drugs in the apartment under any circumstances. I wouldn't jeopardize my mom or her possessions just so somebody else could get high; and 2) On work nights if they were going to sleep there, they had to be in the bedroom for the night by 10:00 p.m. Mom slept on a rollaway bed in the living room and no matter where you were in the apartment, any light or noise was only about fifteen feet away and would keep her awake. She was too passive to say anything about it, but I knew it bothered her.

One night it was about a quarter to ten and none of the guys were home yet. I knew that they were at Missy's basement apartment about two blocks away, so I figured I would take a walk and see what they had planned for the night. It turned out that by the time I got there, Missy's place had become a full-blown party. There were about eight people there and the music could be heard half a block away.

Missy saw me knocking at the knee-level kitchen window. When she opened it I said hey to everybody, then to Missy, I said, "Hey, what's the occasion?"

"Nothin'. Just havin' a party. C'mon in."

Everybody was having a good time and it was tempting, but I was going through one of my infrequent phases where I was actually trying to get to school once in a while.

"Naw. Thanks. I gotta get up early. Are the guys stayin' over here tonight?"

"Nope. Mom's comin' home early tomorrow."

J.J. came walking by and he looked to be in a bad mood. I shouted over to him, "What's up dude?"

"Nothin'," he said sourly.

"You hangin' out tonight or are you comin' back with me?"

"Yeah," he said and left the room. Yeah, what? I thought.

When Caesar drifted by I asked him the same question and he said, "Yeah, lemme get outta here," and proceeded to climb out the window. When I asked George, he spent five minutes trying to argue me into letting him come home drunk and ornery whenever he wanted to.

"No dice," I said. "If you want to stay here, that's cool. Maybe she'll let you crash out down here. Or maybe John will let you stay there. But if you wanna stay at my place, now's the time. We gotta go."

George walked into the other room and I heard him shouting and cussin' angrily. I decided to give him a minute. Looking around I saw all the empty beer cans and I thought, Oh great, George and beer, what a wonderful combination. He was a mean, ornery drunk.

There was a hole in the wall opposite the window and surrounding it there was a light spatter of blood in a circular pattern.

"What happened over there?"

Missy told me, "J.J. was fuckin' around and punched a hole in the wall. Then George tried to be a copy-cat and do the same thing, and he hit a stud." She and I both laughed together right at the moment when George was coming around the corner. I felt bad, but not too bad, as he had already pissed me off.

"Fuck you!" he shouted at me in particular.

"Whatever," I replied.

Then, lightning-fast he snatched a nearly full can of beer off the counter beside him and hurled it at me, a fastball special. That thing struck me full in the chest while I was squatting there, and it nearly knocked me over. The beer sprayed all over my face and coat and down my neck.

"Motherfucker!" I couldn't believe he just did that.

Then, like quicksilver, George was across the kitchen and out the window and charging right at me, and in a delayed reaction I heard Missy say, "Look out! He grabbed a knife!" Then my brain caught up with my ears and I remembered the sound of metal sliding against porcelain.

Then in the darkness, I saw it. It was a twelve-inch butcher's knife, swinging in ice-pick fashion from high above his right shoulder. Before I knew it, George and I were standing face to face in that dark gangway.

We grabbed a hold of each other in the same instant. His left hand grabbed the lapel of my coat tight, while I grabbed that wrist in my right hand. My left held his other wrist up high over his shoulder. And while George stood there panting through bared teeth, I was holding my breath. No, that's not quite right. I was breathing, but it was in s-l-o-w motion. I wanted no sudden moves to set this ticking bomb off.

While George was born with a knife in his hand, he was a little smaller than I was. Then again, that was little consolation to me with the world's biggest knife not a foot away and aimed at my neck. Ya ever have one of those moments when you ask yourself, "Is this my life? How the hell did I get here? And what, exactly, am I doing here?" Here I was standing in a gangway staring at my friend who was about to cut my head off with a butcher's knife for asking if he wanted a place to stay. Have you heard the parable of the frog and the scorpion? Yep.

On the other hand, it was my dumb ass that laughed at a deadly guy who was always getting shafted by life, in front of a girl he liked and all of his friends after he'd been drinking. Smooth, Eddie. *Reeeeeeeeeal* smooth. Lesson learned: Think before you laugh... or better yet, just keep your damned mouth shut... and be considerate.

So, staring at George standing there snarling through his teeth at me, breath fogging the night air, I looked a little more deeply. Is he really gonna stab me? Of course he is, you idiot. Do you see any doubt in those eyes? Nope. Fuck it. It was on. I was torn between wanting to kill him for pulling the knife and for hitting me with the beer, and feeling sorry for the little shit for the hand that life had dealt him. As soon as I thought of feeling sorry for him, I immediately pushed it out of my mind. I knew that pity would get me killed in a heartbeat. In the streets it was often your best friend that put an end to you.

And just like that I made up my mind. While I would try to diffuse this situation without hurting him, I would break him the instant he moved that knife. In the time it took all this to race through my mind, Missy, his brother J.J., and the rest of the party had come running outside and had formed a circle around us... at a safe distance. We were an island of stillness in the midst of chaos. It was like a western showdown on an open street with the sun at high noon. Or a samurai flick in the instant before the strike. One of us, or both, was an instant away from death.

My plan was this. About three feet behind George was a stone stairwell that had about a four-foot drop with sharp corners along either side. The instant I felt him tense up, take a deep breath, or fart, I was going to send him sailing backwards against one of those sharp edges and try to split his head open like a melon. If I missed the edge, then the drop would undoubtedly break something and give me time to jump full-onto his chest and try to break every bone in his ribcage before he tried to get back up. If that didn't work, stomp on his knife-hand or arm until it broke or he dropped it. If I couldn't get the knife-hand, I would go for the nuts, head, throat, knees, feet, anything. I would break everything I could until he –stopped moving. I didn't think about my friend. I didn't think about jail. I was thinking about living to see another day.

S-l-o-w-l-y I began to simultaneously peel both of his hands inward. I slowly began to twist his left hand off my collar. Millimeter-by-millimeter I began to peel his knife-wrist in towards a disarm position with his little finger towards his forehead. My motion was so slow and non-threatening that he failed to notice that the knife was now pointed towards his temple.

By this time I became aware that J.J. was standing a short distance behind my left shoulder as Missy moved up behind George. She took hold of his knife-hand and began slowly pulling it down towards her.

"George? Give me the knife, George." She gently repeated this several more times before she pried the knife from his stiff grasp. Once the knife was in her hands, I breathed a secret sigh of relief. Right behind that was a fury that almost overwhelmed me. For an instant, I was going to push him backwards down the steps and try to kill him anyway. Then I decided instead to just twist outwards and down with my left hand and break his right arm.

And then it passed. Missy was moving him back towards the house and I was thankful to be alive. John and Caesar hung out and asked, "What the fuck was that all about?!"

"Hell if I know," I replied. "Shit man, he's lost his mind."

"I've never seen him freak out like that before," J.J. said

"Wha'd you say to him?" asked another

At that point I'd had enough of the whole thing and was ready for this night to be over. Missy came back and said, "I think I'm gonna make George stay with us tonight.

"Yeah, you do that," I told her. I didn't trust that I wouldn't be tempted to murder him in his sleep or something. "Caesar, I'm leaving. Now." And I turned and left with Caesar rushing to catch up to me. He still wanted to talk about what had happened, but I was tired, bone weary of it all. All the drama. All the bullshit.

"All I know is this: If he comes at me again I'm gonna break him down and the rest be damned."

"You serious?" Caesar asked.

"Motherfucker pulled a knife on me. You think I'm gonna give him a second chance?"

"No, I guess not."

The next day J.J. came over to feel me out, to see if I was gonna go after George. I've never seen him more uncomfortable. He was torn between his brother and a friend with a place to stay for both of them, a friend whom his brother had just come close to killing. I felt bad for him. He was really upset

"What the fuck's wrong with you guys? I'm sick 'o this shit. You guys can't be runnin around stabbin' each other!" he told me

"Talk to your brother, man. I was cool until he came up with that fuckin butcher knife! Have I ever hurt him? Threatened him? Pushed him around and called him names like everyone else does?"

"...no."

"Then what the fuck is his problem?" I was pretty hurt. I felt betrayed by the whole thing. "What' he got to say for himself?"

"He was drinkin'..."

"Fuck that! This is Eddie we're talkin' about," I said.

"Well, what the fuck am I supposed to do, huh!? I mean here's my brother pullin' a knife on my best friend! You guys scared the shit outta me!"

Finally I couldn't stand it any longer. George and I were about to kill each other and there was J.J. stuck in the middle. Poor guy. I started laughing. Out loud. Then he joined in with me.

"You guys are both crazy, you know that? I though you were gonna kill him out there."

"Really?"

"Yeah, really man. I know how you are. You're a devious motherfucker."

That was high praise coming from him. J.J. and George were the two most devious dude's I'd ever met next to my stepfather. And the fact that he was worried that I was gonna kill a guy who was holding a fucking huge knife over me? I must be one baaaaad motherfucker! Damn! I wish I were me. Hah!

"Well, what's he gonna do now?" I asked him.

"I dunno what he's gonna do now? I don't even know what I'm gonna do now."

"Tell you what," I said. "You guys still got a place to stay if George promises not to pull any more fuckin' knives on me. Seriously, I got no grudges, but if it happens again, it's all over and I'll treat him like anybody else who pulls a knife on me. Understand?"

Relieved, he said, "Yeah, no problem. He feels pretty bad about it."

"Well, he damn-well should. That shit hurt my feelin's."

For a moment J.J. was quiet, looking down at his hands. Finally he looked back up at me and confessed, "You know if you had hit him, I was gonna jump you, don't you?"

For a long moment I looked back at him. I was actually touched. Here he sat in my house being more honest and forthright than anyone had been with me in my life. It spoke of the trust he put in me and of the unspoken feelings he had for me that he gave that information up to me, like an offering. It was unheard of. It was a secret you never revealed and we both knew it. Strangely, this honesty gave me a whole new level of respect for him.

"Yeah..." I told him.

"If it's okay, I'm gonna go back over to Missy's place and get George, and we're gonna get some sleep. We didn't get any sleep at all last night."

Eventually J.J. and George moved back in with their dad when he promised to clean up his act, which he did as far as hitting them went. He still drank like a fish though. Caesar soon got a place of his own.

Laying in Wait

My stepfather would incessantly ring our doorbell from the foyer. Neither Mother nor I wanted to see him, so with all the lights out, we would stay silent and wait until he would leave.

Then when someone else got tired of him ringing their buzzer, they would let him into the apartment complex and he would begin pounding on our front door, screaming at the top of his lungs and trying to kick the door open. The doorjamb would strain and crack under his repeated blows. Fortunately, it was solid oak and it never gave.

Caesar was now staying with us and we were alone in the apartment when the buzzing began, then the screaming, the threats, then the pounding, and the kicking

Caesar he was beside himself not knowing what to do. Looking to me, he asked what he should do if he got in.

"Defend yourself," I said calmly as we sat in my darkened bedroom. But when the door started to buckle on its hinges, I quietly crept into the living room and collected for us a pair of weapons. I got the pair of sharp, cast-iron, Japanese Sais that lay on a bookshelf. I handed Caesar one and directed him to one side of the hall while I squatted on the other side just inside the door, just outside of range.

And there we waited, weapons in hand. Unlike Caesar, I was strangely at peace. If my dad broke down the door only one of two things would happen: either I would kill him or he would kill me and one way or the other it would all be over.

Eventually, he tired or grew bored and left. For the first time, the ordeal had left me with a smile on my face that bewildered Caesar to no end.

Kill 'im

I was riding up the escalator at the Bryn Mawr train station on my way to Bo's house. It was one of those narrow escalators that can fit only one person at a time. Not being in a rush, I leaned on the rail while rising towards the platform. I heard footfalls approaching and they stopped some distance behind me. The two of us rode the rest of the way to the top in silence. When I neared the platform, I took the last two steps off the edge of the escalator as I heard the footsteps resume behind me, closing in. He seemed to be in a rush, so I stepped to the side as I turned to keep an eye on him. It was a white guy, a few years older, about four or five inches taller than me and about forty pounds heavier. As he passed me, we locked eyes and I saw hate.

I was amused. What would be the excuse this time? Didn't like my color? Didn't like my look? Didn't like the way I dressed? I stopped and patiently waited for what I knew was sure to come.

"Next time get outta the way, nigger," he said with contempt as he passed, then turned and spat in front of my feet and kept on walking. Looking back up at me, you could see the "what are you gonna do about it?" look on his face.

What was I gonna do? I was going to kill him.

Literally.

I took a few casual steps towards him; he saw me coming and turned. But instead of standing his ground, he continued backing away from me. In my coat pocket was a stainless steel, spring-loaded, collapsible nightstick. It was about nine inches long when closed. When it was opened, it shot out to eighteen inches with such a velocity that it could break bricks. In the next moment I had it in my left hand, away from him, hidden from view. I released the safety and now the spring-release could be opened with the slightest twitch of my finger.

As I moved forward, the fool was backing towards the edge of the platform where a four-foot drop awaited him with steel track and gravel, and an electrified third rail waited for him below. Then to make the moment perfect, I noticed out of the corner of my eye that there was a train approaching just under a hundred yards away, doing about forty. It would be here in seconds. I had *juuust* enough time.

I kept walking and enjoyed the question in his eyes when he saw my easy smile that said I had something up my sleeve. I tried not to smile a gloating smile as, out of the corner of my eye, I watched the train snaking closer and waited for my moment. I had all the time in the world.

Timing is everything. Strike too soon and he might have time to get back up and scramble out of the way. Strike too late and he would merely bounce off the side of the train relatively unharmed. Slowly, slowly.

In my mind's eye, I saw it all happening before I reached him. By the time he realized he had no place left to retreat to, I would be within two feet of him. My left hand would lazily rise to his belly. Squeezing the release, the steel baton would catch him squarely in the solar plexus if everything went absolutely perfect, the ribcage or stomach if not. It didn't matter. Doubling over he would fall back, or I would push him. Six inches is all it would take. If he covered his torso I would then have my pick of targets; nuts, knees or head, any one of which would still cause him off balance. If he reached out to grab me, I would bring my weapon down on his arm hopefully breaking it. Or a kick in the mid-section would keep him back and keep me from going over the edge with him. The train, now traveling at around forty miles per hour, would catch him right about the time he landed on the tracks.

And then I stopped. My face must have drained, because his expression changed. The lunacy of what I was about to do struck me like a brick. I had encountered many fools like this one in my life. And each one I'd dealt with in my own fashion, with either insult or injury. But I'd just planned and moved to kill another human being. Over an insult.

The ironic thing was that my friends would have loved for me to do it. He was stupid. He deserved it. The only good enemy is a dead enemy. And he had *chosen* to make himself my enemy. He had *chosen* to offend me. I wasn't my fault if he was ill-prepared to handle the consequences of that action.

On the other hand, not too long ago, there was a voice on another train platform that saved a life. Mine. The life of a stupid young man who was ill-prepared to handle the consequences of his action. Me. Though I had only started reading the bible regularly, relatively recently a quote appeared in my mind with an accompanying visual.

"*I will remove the heart of stone from your flesh and give you a heart of flesh.*" Ezekiel 32:26.

And I saw a lump of hard, dry, concrete resting in my chest unmoving and unmoved, surrounded by pink, moist flesh and organs.

Just then the man was startled when he realized he was at the edge of the platform. Turning to his left, he saw the train fast approaching and was startled again just as it whooshed past him with a gust of air. For a moment he didn't know what to do. Then he turned nervously and went off to his left, and disappeared quickly towards the far end of the platform

As he walked away I stood, still frozen, lost in thought, trying to fathom the full meaning of what just happened. And what had almost happened. My eyes followed him down the length of the platform while my mind raced within.

I had realized the final destination of the track that I was on. I realized the futility of it. I had seen "bad motherfuckers" come and go, live and die. But eventually, they all die. Is that where I really want to go? Do I continue to court and embrace and dance with death? Or do I do something else? If so, what? I had no clue, but like an addict hitting bottom, I knew that this was not where I wanted to be. Whether or not I had the ability to get someplace else in my life was irrelevant. In that moment I CHOSE.

And I chose life.

escape

 escape

Me and John's Last Fight

We were feeling pretty good. It was a sweet summer day. It was beautifully hot. One of the Chicago summers that I love so much. The kind that lets you go shirtless during the day and shirtsleeves at night.

John and I had smoked a joint and Dobbins had talked me into sharing a bowl of hash with him. At John's house under his bed he had stashed the cases of various candies we had stolen from a candy store we had broken into the night before. Now I had the munchies something fierce and those sweet, sour Love Hearts, were callin' my name. Several of us were in his living room watching TV and I said I was going to get some candy.

When he followed me up there I figured he wanted some too, but when I reached under his bed he told me, "Put that back."

"Relax, I'll just take it from my half."

"I said put 'em back!"

"Fuck you. We stole them together. Half is mine."

"The hell it is!" he shot back. I didn't know what his deal was. I'd stolen half. "We agreed to 50/50. Now I'm takin' all my shit!"

But when I brought the first box out, he viciously kicked it out of my hand. I jumped up from the floor and shoved him back from me.

"What the fuck is wrong with you!?!" I shouted.

"That's it, fucker, OUTSIDE!"

"Fuck outside!" I said and hit him.

And it was on. We started the fight right there. We bounced around the bedroom, then through the hallway, past the bathroom and into his sister's bedroom.

Fists and feet. Elbows and knees. Fast and furious. We fought like wild dogs tearing at each other. I was awesome in my fury! Terrible in my might! Unfortunately, so were the drugs in my system. Fortunately, John had smoked the first two joints with me. Unfortunately again, he hadn't had any of the hash. Comically, out of all the dozens of blows we threw, few actually landed. I was stumbling around so badly it's a wonder I didn't kick my own ass by mistake. And the effect of the drugs only got worse the harder I fought. I mean, I was tripping myself up. I was falling all over the place, tripping over everything, nothing, my own two feet, and empty air. I suppose the fluffy carpet could be blamed for some of it.

Space!

Air!

I need room. So I decided to get some. Lunging forward, I knocked him back out the door and he landed in the hall. Jumping over him, I bolted like a... stoned guy, and went for the stairs.

Skidding down the first half, I managed to keep my feet under me and took the rest three at a time. Up above I heard him coming after me. Flying through the living room and past our friends, I burst out the front door.

"Brian! Stop 'im!!" he yelled.

Brian was a big, red-headed guy who got on my nerves something fierce. He was John's neighbor and they hung together quite a bit. As Brian came off the couch and towards my path, I threw a stiff-armed hand at his face. "Outtamyway woodpecker!"

Now, on my worst day I could always outrun John or any of the guys in sprints or long-distance or short. So I bounded down the porch steps and poured on a burst of speed until I knew I has some breathing room and could turn and meet him head-on instead of getting jumped from behind. As I begin to slow for my turn, I look back and was dismayed. John! Barely four feet behind me! He was barreling down on me like a mamma grizzly on a rampage and I didn't have time to even come to a stop, much less turn and face him.

In a panic I surged ahead and began running in earnest. I was circling around the cars fighting to gain some distance. I ran full out as long as I could until my heart felt like it was about to burst, then started to turn again. Aaaaak! I hadn't gained an inch!

Just then I blew my pathetic attempt to jump a one-foot high, plastic chain fence and caught my leg on the damned thing, and went sprawling through the air like a superhero without a cape. At this point I say fuck it and decided to stop fighting it and go with the flow. Throwing myself forward, I miraculously managed to pull off a fairly decent shoulder-roll without breaking my neck.

John didn't have nearly the same problem I had with that damned fence, but seeing me roll instantly to my feet surprised him. He screeched to a halt and we both froze and stood there crouching, ready for round two.

When he didn't attack I figured it was over and turned to walk away. I'd had enough of this. The run and subsequent panic must have sobered me up enough for common sense to make some headway. I realized that this was the most serious fight we had ever been in with each other in over ten years of friendship. Sure, we'd been in plenty of fights, but the difference was, in this one we were savage, really trying to hurt each other. And it scared me.

Suddenly he began stalking after me again. And the next words that came out of his mouth I never thought I'd live to hear coming from him.

"You fucking NIGGER! Get back here and fight me like a man, you chickenshit motherfucker!"

My blood ran so cold I didn't know what to do, so I turned and started walking away.

But he just kept coming at me, walking even faster, closing the distance between us. Turning before he could reach me, I tried another tack.

"John," I said, "this is getting too serious. We need to just cool down and walk this off."

"Fuck you, you black motherfucker!" he said as he came on and I continued backing away. And I stopped.

"John, this is the last time I'm gonna say this: stop-right-there." But he continued on, ignoring my pleas. And in that instant my best friend in the world, the boy with whom I had shared women, life and near-death experiences, became my enemy.

Let... him... come.

I was going to take him out. I looked at him like a dead thing, this man that I didn't know. I stopped.

"John, this is your last chance. Stop right now," I said coolly.

His only answer was to keep coming with balled fists. I stood silently and waited as he closed the last few steps between us. When he was almost an arm's length away and raising his arms to attack, I casually, almost carelessly, snapped out a front-kick that took him squarely in the gut.

"Oooffff!" His eyes opened wide. He wretched. Doubling over, he first kneeled, placed his elbows and forehead on the pavement, then lay down and slowly curled himself into a fetal position.

Brian, who had been watching with the others from the safety of the front porch, now came running over.

"You motherfucker! What did you do to him?" Then he bent down over John.

Standing over them, I looked down into Brian's eyes with a silent invitation to pain. He shut up and backed away, leaving John where he lay.

Taking a moment to look around, I gazed at my "friends", this house I'd spent so many nights in, this neighborhood that had grown a part of me, and said goodbye. I knew that it would never again be home.

As I backed away, I captured a permanent, terrible snapshot of sorrow. I left my once, but no longer best, friend lying on his side rocking softly with Brian on his knees beside him. Turning, I left, taking the long, slow, lonely way home.

Colors

When I got to my homeroom class there was a message waiting for me.

"Oh Jiiiiiimmyyyyy…" Mr. Sachaj teased loud enough for the whole class to hear.

I gave him a low feral growl for it that just made his day. He knew I hated being called by my first name. He knew that I hated being called Jimmy even more. He also knew he was the only person I liked enough to let get away with it. The rest of the class had seen me come to blows the second time someone called me that. They didn't push it.

But Sachaj just loved to push your buttons. And somehow he managed to make it endearing to a bunch of inner-city gangstas. He would trade insults with the best of us and do the dozens like he was one of us instead of a fifty-year-old, gay, white, guy, from money. We loved him because we knew he loved us. But he wasn't a pushover. He was ferocious if you pissed him off. He was as dangerous as we were and we respected him for it. He was just bad enough not to have to prove it. He felt free to be his flaming self in front of us and nobody cared, especially during a time when "faggot" was the worst insult you could hit someone with.

"The principal wants to see you," he chimed while laughing as he waved the note in front of the class.

A chorus broke out all around me: "Aaaawwwwww-shit!", "Daaaaaaamn!!!", "You done fucked up now!", "Kiss yo' ass goodbye, Eddie!"

"Yeah, yeah, yeah. You wish you could kiss my ass," I teased back as I marched up to get the note.

"Oooooohhh! I bet he does," said Sachaj, teasing the class. "That was a good one, Jimmy."

"Gimmeethatdamnedthing!" I said and playfully snatched the note out of his hand.

"Don't let him give you any shit!" he shouted at my back as I headed out the door.

I had no idea what this could be about. I'd somehow avoided getting caught in any trouble while at Senn High School. Through my mind ran all the shit I'd gotten into recently and to my surprise, I'd been relatively low-key lately. I couldn't think of anything I'd done in recent months here at school that would qualify as the-principal's-office kind of trouble.

Arriving at Mr. Martin's door, I knocked and was invited in. He was sitting at his desk and looked up with a slight smile as he motioned to a chair in front of his desk. To my right, leaning silent and tough looking against the wall, was a detective who was assigned to our school.

"So, James…" Mr. Martin began.

"Eddie," I corrected him.

"What?"

"Eddie."

The detective, confused at this point, said tersely, "It says your name is James."

"I go by Eddie," I repeated

"Then why does it…" he began with more attitude than I was comfortable with.

"I -go -by Eddie," I said firmly, looking him steadily in the eye.

He began to say something else when Martin interjected, "Eddie… how are your classes?"

"Fine," I replied, trying to figure out where this was going.

"Nice shoe laces," he said.

Looking down at my sneakers, white with thick red and white laces woven in an intricate, diagonal, checkerboard pattern, I wondered what the hell they had to do with anything.

"You a member of a gang?" the detective asked.

"No," I said

"Then why are you wearing those colors?"

"I like them."

"Now don't be a smart-ass…!"

As I locked onto his eyes with a level stare, the principal interrupted him by calling his first name, which quieted him down.

"Eddie, do you hang out with any members?" Martin asked.

"Of course. Half this school is in one gang or another…"

The detective started to interrupt, but the principal held up his hand to him.

"…but I don't run with any one gang. I don't represent."

Silence.

"Are you aware that those laces you're wearing are gang colors?" the detective asked like I was a moron.

"No, they're not."

He stared at me flabbergasted. "Yes, they are!"

"No, the Brazers' colors are red and BLACK. There are no gangs here that fly red and WHITE as their colors."

"Well RED is still their color."

"I don't care."

"What!?!"

"I don't care."

"Well you're gonna care!"

Now this asshole was getting on my nerves. I had grown bored and tired of his shitty little attitude from the start that I'd done nothing to warrant.

Mr. Martin said firmly, "We're going to have to ask you to take them off."

"No," I replied.

"Excuse me?!"

"I said no."

Now the detective was really getting pissed. "We can make you...!" he cried as he jumped off the wall, coming towards me threateningly.

I'd had just about enough of this. "You can't make me do a damned thing! As far as I know, this school doesn't have a dress code. And unless you're prepared to ban everyone here from wearing the color red, I'm keeping my laces! And if you do ban the color red, you and you," I said pointing at each of them, "are going to have to lose those ties you're wearing, because that sure looks like red to me! And for your information, Mr. Police-man, that tie you got on is exactly Brazers' colors!"

At this they both looked unconsciously at the red and black striped tie the detective was wearing, and were momentarily taken aback.

More silence.

The principal took a deep breath while the detective readied himself to launch into another attack, one that I was more than eager to bite into now that they had my engine going.

Martin stared at me for a long moment while I met his gaze and waited for the fight to resume. I heard my breathing coming thickly through my nose. Out of the corner of my eye, I saw the detective's chest heaving with his labored breathing as I stared back at Martin.

"Eddie..." he said finally, "as a personal favor to me, could you please change your laces?"

Wow! I wasn't prepared for that. A fight, I was prepared for. A fight, I was used to. Being treated like shit, I was used to. Respect? From a white, male adult? Unheard of! I looked deeper into his eyes to see if a trick was hiding down in there somewhere. Meanwhile the detective looked absolutely pissed! He was so fuming mad that he couldn't formulate a sentence. So he just stammered.

"Sure," I said.

"What?" Martin said unbelieving.

"I said sure. If you are man enough to ask me," I said humbly, "the least I can do is agree."

The detective didn't want to let this insolent little prick off the hook, but he still couldn't put a sentence together. And before he could, Mr. Martin stood up and extended his hand across the desk to me.

Standing up, I took it.

"Thank you," he said, looking into my eyes.

"You're welcome," I said.

Looking at the detective's reddened face, it was all I could do to subdue a big, insolent, shit-eating-grin. Smiling politely, I nodded at him and said, "Gentlemen," and left.

Reflection

For the next year I was like a man on a desert island. I went though life surrounded by people, yet alone. No friends, no family, just me. I'd had enough of the lying, the cheating, the fights, the shootings, the stabbings, the stealing, the cops, everything. I'd had enough. I'd rather be alone than be surrounded with that shit.

During that hiatus I spent a lot of time watching television. I started going to school on a regular basis. I would wake up, park myself in front of the tube, eat and head out to class. At lunch I would come home, turn on the tube, eat, and head back to school. And afterwards? You guessed it: I came home to the tube.

One cold October day, I had taken my bike out for a ride along the frozen grass of the park near the lake. I tooled a couple of miles south before turning back into that cold north wind heading home.

Suddenly, out of nowhere, came this huge Rottweiler-lookin' beast bounding towards me out of the nearby bushes. Not even close to going fast enough to outrun him, I jumped off the bike and put it between him and me, and waited to meet the charge.

Did I mention he was huge? Its shoulder was as high as my hip and his head was almost at my chest. Its color was black with a few dark brown patches. Its head was blocky and square, its neck seemed as big as my waist, and its body was wrapped in corded, rippling muscle. My first impression was of a miniature, power-lifting, steroid-overdosed racehorse, and coming almost as fast.

Fortunately for me, the beast came skidding to a stop with his tongue hanging out and his little stump of a tail wagging side to side. "Damn! You scared the shit outta me dog!" I think I even said it out loud. Seeing he meant me no harm, I s-l-o-w-l-y reached over, let him sniff the back of my hand and gave him a scratch behind the ear.

When my hand came away wet, I was surprised, because it was at least thirty-five degrees outside, not to mention a lakefront wind-chill factor of about twenty. Looking around the mostly wide open grassy area, I tried to find his owner, but I was pretty much alone out there except for a lone jogger about a half a mile away and headed in the other direction. He didn't seem to be looking for his long lost dog either.

Next I tried to see if he was wearing a tag as the monster tried to lick me to death. There was no tag. Around his neck the pooch had a length of thick rope. It was knotted tight and it was as soaking wet as the dog was. The length was about two feet and the end of it had been chewed through.

I'd seen firsthand how some owners treat their unwanted pets. Shot, stabbed, dropped, kicked, burned, and drowned were among the few ways I'd seen evidence of mistreatment. This one, I guessed, had been tied to a weight and dumped in the freezing lake.

"It's a rough life ain't it pooch?" In answer, he jumped up, put his muddy, wet paws on my shoulders and started licking my face. But when that mouth first opened up, I thought he was going to swallow my whole head.

Straddling my bike, I wished him luck and started riding. Looking over my shoulder, I expected to see the mutt fading into the distance. To my surprise, he was trotting contentedly along behind me and to the right, tongue hanging out and happy as a pig in shit. What the hell was he followin' me for, I thought, and I picked up my pace. Faster and faster I went, and he didn't even begin to fall behind.

Finally I was exhausted and halfway home, and doggie was still there. "Take a hike! Fuck off! Go!" I shouted at him. But he just sat there smiling his doggie smile up at me.

Maybe he'll get tired and get lost by the time I get home, I thought.

No luck there. When I finally pulled up to my apartment, he was still there. I tried it again. "Leave! Scram! Get lost!" I yelled. Then finally, I gave up.

Well shit, I couldn't just leave him outside. He would definitely freeze to death. And there was no warm place for him to hide. The city is a cold place. No foxholes, dens, or warrens to burrow into, just cold, hard and broken concrete.

Maybe Mom would have some idea of what to do with him. I let myself in and had him stay outside while I rounded up our two cats, Onyx and Heathcliff. We'd had them since they were weaned a few years ago. Strictly housecats. I had no idea how they would react to the dog or him to them, so I temporarily put them in the bathroom and then went back into the hall and let the big guy in.

After he familiarized himself with the place, I grabbed my baseball bat, then got Onyx, the feistiest of the cats, and carried him out to meet the pooch. With him in front of me, I let them see each other and then slowly brought the cat down to his height. I moved them closer until they were nose to nose with my bat poised above Bowzer's clunky head.

To my great relief, they were extremely disinterested in each other. The dog went off into the kitchen and Onyx started to take a nap in my arms. Well, I guessed that was that, and let them both out of the bathroom.

Over the next few months, "Pooch" became family (if ya couldn't guess) and life went on as usual, which meant Eddie's temper was ready to flare to life at a moment's notice.

It was fine enough when I lost my temper at someone else, because that meant they were doing something they shouldn't, but what was also happening was that inanimate objects were also setting me off. And it would be some trivial, insignificant thing that touched it off. And for years I could never figure out why this was happening. I thought I was powerless to control these berserker rages. Still the headaches, the mindless violence, the screaming, and the tears would come, and I felt like a daemon possessed.

I would stub my toe on a piece of furniture, and I would kill it for making me mad. If I was trying to move my bed to find something under it and it wouldn't move easily enough, I would pick it up by the corner, flip it over my head, and slam it into the other side of the room. Punching holes in walls and doors was not uncommon. That already run-down apartment was dotted with holes and filling compound. My outbreaks were unpredictable and frequent.

If the cat scratched up a piece of furniture, he would get slapped and screamed at. Sure my reaction was a little more than the average person, but these cats just didn't learn too well. If the dog got into the garbage, I would punish him so he would learn not to do it again. Each time he did it, the punishment would be a little more severe in the hopes that he would get the message. Because the dog was as hardheaded as the cats, I reasoned that he needed just a little more dissuasion.

And then one day I had what was the most chilling, terrifying experience I've ever had. Nothing in my long, eventful life has ever come close to having as powerful an impact on who I am as a person as this.

Finally, he had gone and done it. This dog had really pissed me off. I came home from school one day, from an average day in my life, walked into the kitchen and found that the once full, nasty, garbage bin had been knocked over. What's more, Pooch had torn the bag apart and scattered the remnants across the entire kitchen and part of the dining room. Coffee grounds, orange rinds, potato skins, pieces of tin-foil, wax-paper, shredded milk carton pieces, and banana peel covered the floor. It stank, it was filthy and I had to clean it up.

Oh, he was gonna pay! He was going to learn! He was never EVER going to do this again. And I was going to make SURE of it!

That poor, frightened, terrorized dog was cowering in the corner before I even came after it. The pathetic beast bolted away from me, which only made my fury blindingly red. He headed for the bedroom. I cut the corner, leapt over him and he shot right and trapped himself in the bathroom. I grabbed him by the scruff of the neck before he could turn around and began smacking him on the head as the poor thing huddled into a ball on the cold marble tile.

Harder and harder, I smacked him. But I wasn't satisfied that he understood, so I curled up my fist and began punching that sad beast in the head. When my fist began to hurt, I still didn't think he had gotten the message. There was a big, wooden-handled hairbrush on the sink. That should do the trick, I thought, and I grabbed it, and began to swing.

Then, in an instant, time seemed to freeze and I saw there in front of me, not a mirror, but a reflection, and in that reflection instead of me, I saw my dad. He was beating me as I lay there screaming, curled in the fetal position on that same marble tiled floor.

The breath was sucked from my lungs and I fell back against the wall in frozen despair and terror. Horrified.

And I fell apart. I screamed as a soul in hell. An agonizing sorrow I never knew overcame me and I wept like a child. Cradling my dog in my arms, I lay on the floor with him and cried and apologized until I was numb. And still we lay there for hours.

I came to myself with that dog licking my face and there were no more tears left to cry. In that moment I made a silent promise to myself that I have never broken: that I would never raise my hand in anger to any living thing. That I would never allow myself the self-indulgent, juvenile, petty, luxury of what amounts to nothing more than a grown-up tantrum.

It wouldn't be until years later that I would understand what had been happening to me and why, that all those

bottled-up emotions would eventually force themselves out like a geyser if they went denied for too long.
  But for now I swore control, no matter what the cost to me.

Andrew M

  The phone shocked me out of a deep sleep one frosty winter's night. It was around midnight on a school night, so I was ready to chew someone's ass off.
  "Yeah?" I answered tersely into the receiver.
  On the other end I heard J.J.'s frantic voice.
  "We got Andy!"
  "Where?!" I asked. I was already up and out of bed.
  "We got 'im at the Laundromat on Petersen and Broadway."
  "Keep 'im there. I'll be there in five."
  By the time I hung up, I'd already pulled on my navy blue sweatpants, black sweatshirt and navy blue watch cap. Not sixty seconds later, I tightened up my black sneakers and hit the door a-runnin'.
  The Laundromat was just about a mile away through the Chicago ice and snow. I was flying before I hit the street.
  Andrew was a wanted man in our small circle. Last Summer I had just bought a new bike. My first. It was a competition racing bike I bought specifically for triathlons. I was in my junior year of high school. I had stopped hanging out with J.J. and the gang after a tragic series of events showed me the terminal end to my path. The shootings, the stabbings, the beatings that were our daily environment suddenly no longer seemed such a good way to go through life.
  But we would still stop by and visit each other once in a while. I began to occupy my time with actually showing up at school, and actually doing homework. Sports began to take up most of my free time and energy. I still hadn't many friends, but I had determined that I would rather have no

friends than ones who would think nothing of causing bodily harm to one another.

I don't know if it was the fistfight John and I had gotten into, where for the first time since we had met each other in second grade that he called me a nigger, or the latest knife fight John and George got into that left John with over 30 stitches. It could have been when Chris tried to split George's head open with an exhaust pipe. Or how about the time George shot Dave in the stomach? No, I know, it was that time that J.J. pointed a loaded, nickel-plated .25 semi-automatic at his brother George's head... and pulled the trigger.

God tapped me on the shoulder one day and shouted, "WhatTheHellAreYouGuysDoingToEachOTher!?!" And then I SAW it. It was insane. In-sane.

So this summer Mom was way past ready to get me away from the guys. When I told her I wanted to do triathlons, she was all for it. I only needed a bike. She went so far as to tell me that any money I saved to put towards a bike she would match, up to $100. And for us, back then, that was a LOT of money. So I saved up $100. And together with Mom's hundred, I went shopping. I found a Zebrakenko OM4, usually $290 but on sale for $180, and snapped it up with a few extras: patch kit, tool set and helmet (required for competition).

It was its maiden voyage. I took it around the neighborhood just to break it in, and found myself back in the old neighborhood. Pulling up to John's house, I saw John, George, J.J., Richie, and some new guy who was passing around a nickel-bag and a case of Budweiser.

"Dude! Where ya been?"
"Long time no see!"
"Nice bike, dude."
"Yeah! Can I try it out?" That was John. He and I had shared everything in our short lives.

"Sure," I said. He hopped on and cruised up to the end of the block and back. Then J.J. wanted a turn. Then George. Then the new guy asked.

Now I hadn't been around in a couple of months, so I figured any guy who was supplying them with drugs and booze had to be okay. But just to be sure, I looked each of my friends in the eye, looking for a silent warning or caution. No sign was given.

Then George introduced us. "Eddie, this is Andy." I figured that was the all-clear.

"Wha'sup dude?"

"How u doin'?"

I looked around the circle again just in case I'd missed something, and got nothing. "Yeah, go ahead."

WhatTheFuckWasIThinkin'?! You never trust a stranger. And you seldom trust a friend. So I don't know what act of lunacy possessed me to hand over my brand new, life-savings costing, 12-speed, bad-assed, big-red, most precious thing I owned, racing bike to this clown. But I did. He rode in a leisurely fashion up the block just like everyone else, hung a right on Clark Street and was gone.

Damn.

But as I was trying to turn over a new leaf, I decided to do something else you never do in the hood: call the police. Yeah, yeah, I know. It was a stupid, useless, waste of time. But hey, I was TRYING to do the right thing. I would quickly lose patience, however. Of course the cops treated me like I was the criminal. Even after waiting until 4:00 a.m. for them to arrive. And after the surly bastards made it plain that both of them would rather be sitting on their asses in the cruiser, staring at their dashboard. And after I showed them copies of my receipt and registration complete with model, color, and serial number. But I stuck it out. The guys even gave me Andy's address, and six months later there was still no sign that the cops had done anything other than treat my mother and I like shit.

So fuck 'em. It was time to handle it myself. I put the word out that I wanted him. Whole or in pieces. And then I waited. I could be reeeeal patient when I put my mind to it. And I was. I'd dropped by his house and the places he hung out every now and then. I asked around. And still no sign of Andy. But that was okay, I would wait.

And then I got the call. And I was GONE. About a block before the laundromat I saw J. J running down the street checking every gangway he passed. Then I knew Andy had gotten away.

"Where's he at?"

"I dunno! He got away from us! He took off through one of these gangways!"

"Keep checking the street. I'll cut through to the alley," I told him.

"Chris is on the next block!" he shouted at my back.

If Andy had heard him, it was too late to do anything about it now. Coming into the alley, I saw Chris heading my way.

"Do you see 'im?"

"No! You?"

"No. J.J.'s covering Petersen."

As we stood there in that midnight alley, we heard a gunning engine accelerating from the end of the block. The squeal of tires and flash of headlights brought a white sedan into sight just before the lights blinded us. We had both tensed up to run, not knowing if it was detectives or Andy with reinforcements Just then Chris said, with relief, "Aww, shit... it's Steve."

Steve skidded to a halt just in front of us. I said to him, "You scared the shit out of us."

"Ya see 'im?" Chris said.

"No. I went around the block twice."

"Aww-fuck it. He's gone. Let's go get J.J.

After we collected J.J. we cruised over to Hellas Gyros. We each got a gyro, a fat, greasy order of fries, and split a pitcher of beer. And then they told me the tale.

Steve had been driving that big white Buick of his (it somehow suited him). Steve was big and white himself. His street name was "Moose." He ran with the biggest, most racist street gang in Chicago. Its turf was near the lakefront on Chicago's north side. He was younger than me by about two years, but he looked much older. He stood about 5'8" and weighed almost 200 lbs. He was built like a sumo wrestler with a big gut that surrounded a LOT of muscle. At 15 the guy could bench 300 lbs. He was one bad motherfucker. Steve was the only person I knew at the time who I *didn't* want to have to find out who would come out ahead in a fight between us. My years of martial arts training notwithstanding.

He had J.J, George, and Chris with him. J.J. and George were his cousins and his complete opposites: short, skinny and soft spoken. If you pissed J.J. off, you wouldn't hear him coming. He wouldn't say a damn thing until after he had wrapped a steel pipe around your head. But he had the gift. He could talk people into doing the damnedest things. Once when he was broke (which was nearly always) we walked into a clothing store. He put on a pair of pants, shoes and a winter army coat, gave the salesman $25 and talked him into letting him walk out of there... wearing all of it!

Chris was one of those bad-boys that ALL the girls gave it up to. He had almost all of them. And I was there to witness it enough times to know. He wasn't particularly big or exceptionally handsome, but he just knew he had "IT". He had kind of that James Dean/Rebel Without a Cause thing goin' on. And the girls just ate it up. He was almost never without a female. Two other things he was never without were his leather jacket and his switchblade.

So they were toolin' down Broadway when J.J. spotted Andrew sitting at a bus stop. He quickly told Steve and Chris, who didn't know him, who Andy was and why he wanted him.

Chris got Steve to turn the corner and let him out. Chris then jumped out and told Steve to circle the block and come back for him. Chris walked over and stood behind where Andy was sitting and waited. When Chris saw Steve pull up in front of Andy, he popped open his switchblade and put it to Andy's throat.

"Get in the car," he said quietly in his ear.

J.J., now in the back seat, threw the door open. Chris got in the back seat still with the knife to Andy's throat and made him sit in between him and George. They took off.

After driving around for a while trying to figure out where to take him and what to do with him, they came across this all-night laundromat with no one in it. It had a pay phone, so they pulled into the parking lot and dragged his ass in there.

Now inside the deserted laundry they asked Andy where my bike was. When he told them he didn't have it (he probably sold it as soon as he stole it) they decided to tune him up until he came up with a more satisfactory answer.

After a few fruitless minutes of this they decided to go to plan B: call Eddie. Unfortunately, no one was delegated to keep an eye on Andy and the back door, which they ass-u-me'd was locked.. So now while the three of them were at the pay phone with me on the other end, Andy bolted out the back and ran like hell.

Now back at Hella's, after hearing their tale, I thanked the guys, admired the boldness of their kidnapping technique, and questioned, "How many guys does it take to make a phone call?"

Dropping me off back at home they said good night, but that wasn't the end of the Ballad of old Andrew.

About six months later, almost a full year from the date of the original theft, I just happened to stop by J.J.'s place. I had the decency to wait until about noon, when they usually woke up. He and George were there sitting on the front stoop.

"EDDIE!" they both shouted as soon as they saw me from their front porch. Running down to meet me, it seemed they had news.

"Dude! You should' a been here last night! We were just about to call ya!"

"What happened?" I asked.

And here is the rest of the story.

About ten o'clock last night, Andy and a friend of his were walking down Bell Street, the same street the J.J. and family lived on. Remember, George, who was on John's front porch that day, swilling beer, when Andy stole my bike, was leaving his apartment in the 3-flat that his Uncle, Steve's dad, owned. Steve, J.J. and Cousin Junior, were hanging out in their converted basement.

"Andy, what's up?" George played it cool.

"How ya been, man? Whatcha up to?"

"George, check it out man. We were thinking of stealing the stereo out of this white Buick over here. It's got a sweet system and we can get some good money for it."

"This Buick right here?" he asked, pointing to Steve's car.

"Yeah."

Poor ol" Andrew wasn't too bright, having forgotten George was there when he stole my bike, and he had the worst luck possible. And George was almost as good a liar as his brother was. Con-man all the way.

"Yeah, that sounds cool. But hey, I got some tools in my basement here that will make it a snap."

"Let's go get 'im!" reply Andy and friend.

And with that George marched them both straight into Steve's front door, lets 'em in, and locks it behind them.

"Steve, you remember Andy Mitchell, the one who stole Eddie's bike?"

"Yeah, I remember Andy from the laundromat. We're old friends."

"What's up, Andy?" That was J.J. who just happened to be in the right place at the right time.

You know I'm kinda startin' to feel sorry for the dumb fuck. Even though Andy was the sole cause of Andy's problems, some folks catch a break once in a while. Some people get the message. For example, "quit fuckin' with other people's stuff" should have become Andy's mantra by now, but no. Stealing the radio out of some random stranger's car made sense to him. I mean, he couldn't even use money as an excuse. At most he would've gotten twenty or thirty bucks for a used, stolen, torn out, car stereo. And for that he was willing to inflict three hundred dollars worth of damage to some poor schmuck's car window? Police? Retribution? These things never occurred to him. That, my friend, is what those whose philosophies come from the East would be proud of: "Existing solely in the moment."

Unfortunately, "living in the moment" doesn't work for everyone. Some people have to live with the moment after the moment, deal with consequences... repercussions... Steve.

So for the next half hour they beat the shit out of these guys just for thinking about trying to break into Steve's car. Then they turned matters to me.

"You can go," they said to the tag-along.

"You've still gotta pay for Eddie's bike." And he wasn't talking about cash. With that Steve gave him another kick in his already bloody mouth. And they laid into him some more.

Afterwards as he lay there moaning, crying, and bleeding as they went to the phone to call me. And just as J.J put the receiver to his ear, he heard George shout a warning from the back of the hall.

"Look out! He's getting away!"

Like a rabbit, Andy sprang up, shot for the only exit available to him, and was crawling out a window.

J.J. grabbed the only thing near to hand, a flat-head screwdriver, and in one motion hurled it at the scrabbling figure. His aim was true, striking him square between the shoulder blades. Unfortunately, while there was enough force to penetrate his denim jacket, there was not enough force to make it stick and it fell to the floor. By the time they all piled out the front door after him, Andy was nowhere to be found, nor was he ever seen again.

And I think that's a good thing, too. Because who knew if he would survive the next encounter. At this point I was actually starting to worry for the guy. Thinking it over, I realized he could have been killed the first time they caught him, let alone the second. And did I really want to take the man's life simply because he took a bike from me? Yeah, it was tempting to lay hands on him myself. I mean I still wanted to personally beat the living shit out of the guy. But c'mon, he'd already paid for it with an ass-kicking. Twice.

Still it was kind of funny. Here my boys didn't say word one when I handed over my bike to that knuckle-head, but then they went and committed multiple felonies to make up for it. I felt kind of honored in a strange way. It made me proud that they would go through all that, risk all that, just for me.

But enough was enough. It had taken on a life of its own. A bike just wasn't worth it. I didn't care how nice, or how expensive it is. It's not worth his life, or their freedom.

"Alright guys. You know what? I think we just need to let this one go. We got two good pieces of his ass and he won't be forgetting it anytime soon. And damned if he'll ever fuck with us again, right?"

"Yeah."

"You got that right."

I'm hoping good 'ole Andy had the good sense to leave town rather than be buried there. Even though I asked the guys to stop this thing, I don't have the greatest confidence in their powers of restraint. And after all, of all the people who have killed someone, not all of them meant to.

Good luck Andy.

Guns at Ravenswood

Walking home from the theater way up on Devon seemed to take half the night. It was only about five miles as the crow flies, but the actual trip seemed to zigzag across half the city. To get there would take a couple of busses to be there in around an hour. If we saw a late movie, the busses would have stopped running by the time it let out. Sometimes we would walk all the way back together and sometimes we would split off, one by one, each taking a different route to our respective homes like we did that night.

It was about 1:30 in the morning. It was early winter, so it was cold out but not yet freezing. Within a mile or so of home, I had already fended off some pervert's attempt to get me into his car. Thankfully, I managed to do it without having to kick the shit out of him. I was tired.

I'd been walking non-stop for well over an hour by now. Bundled up, head down, and making time, I was on the march. As I neared Ravenswood Avenue, I heard the distant rumble of some white boy's souped up hot rod. How did I know it was a white guy's car? It was Chicago. And it was the '80s.

In Chi-town in the '80s, it seemed like all the white boys drove souped up Chevelles or Novas. Loud and mean. And, like a stereotype caught in motion, each ethnic group in turn, for the most part, had their own type of vehicle. The white guys had their hot rods and the brothers had their sleek, low, tinted Cutlasses, Caddies, or Lincolns with spoke rims. The Chicanos were driving their own cultural statements, Dusters or Road Runners with fuzzy interiors, fuzzy dice, fuzzy pom-pom balls lining the windshield and Virgin Mary icons all around. Kumbia, Meringe and Mariachi were telling even the deaf where they hailed from. The Asians? They would cruise around quietly in their compact imports. None of that "Buy American" hype for them. "Asia for the Asians," shouted a small group of holdouts. Toyotas, Datsuns, Hondas, and Subarus were all done up uniquely the same, clean with a minimalist design sense and a few well-placed decals.

Sure enough, here came not one but two cars nose-to-tail on an otherwise empty Peterson Avenue. The first was the stereotypical white guy's black Chevy Nova. At the time it struck me as funny how all the racist white teenagers I'd met hated black people so much but surrounded themselves with everything else that was black; black cars, black jeans, black T-shirts and black suede shoes. The second car was a cream-colored Dad's car. A Dodge Aries. Somebody's daddy's car. They both slowed as they approached. As they passed me, I pretended not to notice as I used peripheral vision to see that there were three or four guys in each vehicle. Then the lead car floored it and they raced on to the end of the block, then hung a left behind me. They were coming back around. I knew it. I considered running, just in case. No one would blame me. I considered waiting for them. Why? Because they were bullies. One thing I hated in this world worse than ignorance was a bully, physical, mental, emotional, or verbal. Then the lunacy of that idea followed close behind the idea itself. In the end I decided to go about my business. If they came back, it would be on them. And come back they did.

A block later I had just crossed the street when up ahead I saw two guys step around the corner of the row of buildings to my right. They looked up and down the street, spotted me, then did a lousy job of pretending not to see me. They didn't want to scare their prey away. Jesus, you gotta be kidding me. How dumb can you get? Don't worry guys, you'll get your wish.

Again I briefly considered running but then anger won out. It pissed me off to no end that people couldn't just go about their business and live their lives in peace. There was always somebody like these assholes who just had to be fucking with someone. Always someone smaller, weaker or fewer in numbers. A victim, helpless. Well fine, this time it was gonna cost them something, if only their cocky confidence. I wasn't small anymore, weak, helpless, or afraid. Sure they could kick the livin' shit outta me, but damn it, they were gonna think twice next time. But... I never started fights. "Never lay a hand on someone in anger," had been a credo that I had adopted recently and if they didn't start any shit, then we would all be cool. So I did not slow as I drew near. No smart-assed remarks. No dirty looks.

They, on the other hand, turned to face me as three others joined them. Spreading out across the sidewalk in front of me, they formed a semi-circle with the tallest one directly in front of me. Then they became silent, just the five of them. And me. "Whassup punk?" the one in the middle and apparent leader said from a short distance away. Looking, up I locked eyes with him and kept on walking. Then, in turn, I look each one of them in the eye, then back to the leader. As I had looked down the street they just came from, I saw the same two cars with three more guys and a girl standing beside them. When I got to within four feet of the leader, his eyes broke away. He looked everywhere but at me. His friends each shifted or took a step back. Before he broke his gaze, I'd been determined to knock him on his ass, then use the element of surprise to pop a couple more before the rest joined in. But since he gave me a way out, I took it. I pushed right past him and the next guy, and kept on walking.

Now I was feeling pretty happy with myself. I'd managed to stare down five dudes and avoided a fight and possible ass kicking. I had actually gotten halfway up the next block and was feeling pretty cocky before they rallied.

"Hey, you!"

Damn. Turning, I saw that the five were now joined with the other three and had decided they didn't like the way things had gone down. They were running up the street behind me. Turning back around, I just kept on walking. Fuck 'em. Let 'em come.

Now, though, something was different. There was a tickle that started in my stomach. It built slowly and moved through my chest. It rolled up my throat. Then, unable to contain it, it spilled out: Laughter. I laughed! Out loud. At the sheer absurdity of the situation. Here my dumb ass was ready, willing, and possibly able, to beat the shit out of this group of ne'er-do-wells. Waiting to unleash my pent up rage, channeled and focused by years of marital arts training, sharpened by countless fights and initiated by homegrown violence perpetrated upon body and mind, I'd wanted to punish them, teach them a lesson. Protect the weak (me); defend the helpless (me)... blah, blah, blah.

The realization was this: I'm an idiot. Yeah, I know, they started it. But the fact remained that I am only responsible for my behavior. I wasn't their daddy. It was up to them, or their family, or their friends to show them the way, teach them the "Golden Rule". All I could do was walk, talk, fight, or run. And they were beyond talking, and walking wasn't workin' either. Unfortunately this wasn't the last time I would have to learn this lesson. Knowing damn well that there was nothing to gain by fighting, I ran.

A chorus broke out behind me.

"Pussy!"

"Why you runnin', faggot?"

"Spick!"
"Nigger!"
"Fuckin' NIGGER!"

It was a common mistake but, for a minute there, I thought they were gonna stop and argue about which one was right: Was I a Spick or a Nigger?

Being on the track team, and having had to run my entire life and enjoying the feel of the wind in my hair, I knew that it was a good bet that I could outrun all of 'em. All night if I had to. So I started out at a jog.

They were about fifty feet behind me and clustered in a tight knot. I led them on just fast enough to keep the same distance between us for another block when three of them broke away from the pack and began a more earnest pursuit. Increasing my stride, I pulled slightly ahead and held the distance.

At Clark Street, the Saturday night traffic thickened and the six lanes of flowing traffic that I darted between was a little much for them after being winded. Standing there, they talked to each other for a moment before turning to leave.

Once again my ego got the better of me. I wasn't going to let them off that easily. Now that I had tired them out, I wanted them to come after me just to fuck with them.

"I thought you wanted me, bitch!?" I shouted at them. "What's the matter pussies?" When they didn't take the bait, I chided, "What's the matter? All tired out? Gonna run home to Mama?" That did it. The leader couldn't take the same goading he had been dishing out and waited for the light to turn green before leaving the other guy who had continued the chase with him.

I lured him down the darkened side street before ducking behind a parked car, reversing direction and coming out behind him.

"Hey!" I said softly from two car-lengths behind him. This, aside from scaring the shit out of him, caused a most surprising reaction: he pulled a gun. It was a matte-finished, semi-automatic pistol. Needless to say, this came as some surprise to me, although it shouldn't have. I jumped right back into my hiding place and reversed direction again. As he came back to where I had emerged, I circled around the other side of the car between us and gained myself a little distance before he stepped out into the street behind me and raised the gun again. I swerved back to the sidewalk-side of the car. We repeated this process two or three more times. I was glad he wasn't a better shot than he was a leader. Back and forth we went, down the block. Cat and mouse-turned-cat-turned-mouse again. But I was talking shit all the way, hoping he would slip up. "What's the matter, bitch? Can't fight like a man? Put the gun down, punk. Ya scared I'll shove that pistol up your ass? Why don't ya cry for help, since you can't seem to handle this man-to-man?"

Then suddenly things went from bad to worse. As I was crouched there on the street side of this car, I was suddenly lit-up by headlamps from behind me. From the far end of the block I heard the gunning of a car engine. Oh, shit.

I had a moment of panic when I realized I'd let them get behind me. I imagined having to choose between being shot and run over. Then I made up my mind to go on the offensive. When in doubt, ATTACK! As the car screeched to a halt beside me, I faked away, then turned and headed right for it. My plan was a simple one. The first door that opened I would kick it shut on whatever body part that protruded from it, hand, arm, leg, head, anything. Then I would jump the hood or trunk and take out the passenger. Then I would either use him as a human shield if the shooter was too close, or gain some cover and RUN!

Nearing the car, I hesitated. It was neither of the cars they had been driving. And no one was getting out. When the driver's window rolled down, I moved forward to reach in and break anything I could.

I was surprised by a voice from the darkness.

"Are these guys fuckin' with you?"

"Kevin?"

It was Kevin, a white friend from science class. And next to him, in the passenger seat, sat Ankor, an East Indian friend from my social studies class.

"Yeah!" I told them.

"Get in." I had a flash of guilt. I didn't want these guys to get hurt in the middle of my beef.

"Watch out. He's got a gun," I told them.

"We'll just go check it out," Kevin said.

As I hopped in the back, the asshole that had been chasing me was now running full tilt back for Clark Street. Kevin burned rubber after the fleeing figure.

"We saw them chasing you at Clark so we came back around to help." By the time we reached Clark again, he was flying through traffic like there were demons on his tail. There was no way we would get through all the lanes of traffic without a stoplight. "Forget it guys, he ain't worth it."

When they asked what had happened, I told them everything that had gone on.

"Those fuckin' bastards," Ankor said.

"Man, I'm tired of these gang-bangers fuckin' with people all the time," said Kevin.

"Yeah, I know what you mean," I replied. "Hey guys, I'm just glad you stopped. Thanks."

"No problem. We gotta look out for each other."

As they dropped me off in front of my apartment, I told them, "Anything you guys need, just give me a call, or stop by."

"Thanks dude."

"Later," they said and drove off.

Every now and then we experience one of life's more affirming moments. We need to take a moment, recognize, and savor them. Standing there out in front of my apartment, that's just what I did.

Stalking Dad

This night I'd had enough. I was tired of his stealing. Stealing my life, my childhood, my sister, my mom, our freedom, safety, security, and sanity. And that night she had disappeared again. She could only be with him, like she always was when she disappeared from work on a Friday. She would remain lost to me until Monday morning when I would call her job and ask to speak with her. She would answer the phone like we had just spoken, like it was normal to leave a fourteen-year-old boy alone in a house with no money and no food, and no word or good-bye. I'll be back or go to hell.

I was going to go out and find that abusive, murderous, evil son of a bitch and reclaim all I had lost: my childhood and my mother. I dressed in all black. I was on a mission. Dark jacket, navy blue knit watch-cap and my killing knife. I'd bought it for survival, but tonight I was planning a murder. Murder with a cause.

Its blade was wide and long, about eight inches. And sharp. Very sharp. I honed it regularly on my whetstone. The handle was black plastic with a silver dragon on both sides. There was a stainless steel hand guard to keep you from slicing your hand as you thrust against resistance. There was a blood gutter so you could pull it out of the body fast, so that muscle contraction and suction wouldn't make it stick. There were notches for your fingers to grip. Its handle was thick and it fit my hand perfectly.

I would find them. I would haunt their favorite hangouts and find them both. I would say, "Mom, you're coming home." And if he made a move to stop me, if he even raised his voice in protest, I would cut his throat.

It would be one fast movement. I practiced in the mirror for all possibilities. Seeing his face, his neck, I repeated the move over and over until I could draw the knife from my jacket pocket, flick it open and slice it across his throat, moving out of the way of the gout of blood all in one smooth, lightning-quick move. I would take my mom by the hand and walk away. Not even look back. "Don't look back."

When I was ready, I left my house. It must have been around midnight. I first headed to the hotel he usually took her to on Leland, about three miles away to the south. No one inside had seen either of them. Then it was on to the Belmont

Hotel another three miles further. Neither was seen there either, so I made my way back north towards Wilson Avenue. When I could not find them in this, one of his preferred neighborhoods, I moved on to Lawrence Avenue. I scoured this neighborhood even more thoroughly than the previous one.

I was getting desperate. It was now nearing three in the morning and I had been walking for more miles than I could count. I was exhausted and no closer to "rescuing" my mom or myself. My anger, however, still glowed hot enough to keep me out and searching.

Determined, I staked out the most likely corner on Granville and Broadway, where they had been last weekend, and waited in a darkened doorway hoping, praying for him to show himself.

It was hours past curfew and I had been dodging the cops all night. But now waiting here it made me an easy target for them. If they caught me for curfew I would have to try to ditch my knife. If I was lucky, I would only be in jail until I could next reach Mom... on Monday morning three days from now.

While I watched the corner and waited, I had time to run all the possible scenarios in my head. I began by imagining my satisfaction while I watched him bleed out lying there on that cold autumn sidewalk. Hearing his moans, his screams, his cries.

Then I pictured my mother's stunned silence as I led her away. Another possibility was that, like a typical abuse victim, she could conceivably turn on me for ending her twisted relationship.

After that I saw visions of police catching me and taking me to jail. I wondered how much jail time I would get for killing the demon of my family. I even had a vision of him killing me. I watched as he stood over my body as the life drained from me and coldness enveloped me. I saw with pride that unyielding gleam of self-satisfaction in my eye in that I had finally escaped this tragic life fighting the monster, defying him. Mom could have him.

As dawn painted the distant horizon a pale shade of salmon, I emerged from my reverie and acknowledged my wasted night. I would not find him now. They would be lying in bed at some friend's place, warm and cozy, sleeping, oblivious of my Herculean effort this night, while I stood out here on a cold desolate street corner alone.

Bitter, angry, and disappointed, I pried myself from the shadows and turned my weary steps towards an empty apartment that felt even more barren than this cold and windy corner.

But perhaps that night wasn't really a waste after all. While I did not find what I was searching for, I did find something else: satisfaction. This was the first, and not the last, time I stood up to my dad. And it felt good. It felt good not to be afraid. It felt good to know that being small, weak and alone, I was still more of a man than he was, or more likely ever would be. And I did not have to kill him in order to prove it.

Mateen

I hadn't seen Mateen in ages. He was sixteen, a few years younger than me, short, stocky, muscular, and so dark he was almost blue. And Mateen, he was volatile.

We were tight, but we'd also come close to mixing it up a couple of times and while normally when someone wanted to fight me it made my mouth water with anticipation, the confrontations with him I hadn't looked forward to. He was just as crazy and unpredictable as I was. He was also very capable of doing damage. And while he was always packin' some kind of weapon, I don't think he would have used one on me. But that wasn't a bet you put money on.

I was on my way to school when I ran into him. After the usual catching up on who's doin' what and what I'd been up to, we got around to him. "Maaaaaan, I been in jail," he laughed. And this was the story he laid down for me.

His parents were prone to kicking him out of their apartment for days at a time with no food, money, or a change of clothes. I could identify with his despair at the prospect of sleeping, hungry and cold on the city's streets.

He had been running the streets alone and hungry for three days when he found himself standing in front of a restaurant window in a hunger induced daze. Oblivious to the passing pedestrians, he daydreamed about... food. Eating. Sustenance.

He had been standing there licking his chops and listening to his stomach growl for some time when he heard a voice from beside him. "Looks good, doesn't it?" Turning, he saw a well-dressed businessman with a briefcase standing next to him, looking at the same plate of food he was.

"Yeeeeeeah man. Sho do."

"You look like you're hungry, like you could use a good hot meal."

"Naw man, I'm a'ight."

"C'mon, it's on me."

And with that he walked over to the door, opened it, and held it, waiting for Mateen to enter. The smell wafting out was too much for his empty stomach to resist and together they went in.

Not wanting to take advantage, Mateen ordered a modest meal, but the man encouraged him to eat up: sirloin, baked potato, house salad, and a coke. Over the meal they talked about where they grew up, their parents, and where they'd been. It was nice, pleasant conversation.

When they walked out it was late afternoon, and the crowded street had begun to thicken with the beginnings of the rush-hour foot traffic.

"Hey man, thanks. I ain't ate a whole meal in three days. That really hit the spot."

"Sure, no problem. You sure looked hungry staring in the window like that."

"True dat, man. Well, thanks again." With a smile, a wave and a full stomach, Mateen turned to go.

"Waddayamean thanks?"

"What?" Mateen said, stopping and turning back around.

"I said what do you mean 'thanks'?"

"For the meal..." he said, confused.

"You don't just say 'thanks' and walk away from me," he said, raising his voice.

Self conscious about the passers-by, Mateen stepped closer and spoke to him confidentially.

"What's the matter with you, man?"

"You're not gonna give me any ass?" he shouted.

Now Mateen was turning red with embarrassment. But to his credit and highly out of character, he gave the man a chance to settle down. "Hey man, calm down. I didn't know it was gonna be like that. You know, I don't get down like that. But I appreciate the food. I really needed it."

"And I really need some butt! You appreciate it? You appreciate it? What the hell am I going to do with that?" he yelled as people began to slow down, gawk, and listen to this intimate extortion.

Mateen had had enough. "Hey man, I got ta go. Thanks. See ya." And he turned and began to walk away.

Catching up to him, the man grabbed Mateen by his arm, spun him around and shouted loud enough for the surrounding crowd to hear, "You don't just walk away from me! I spent money on you! Now, you need to give me something to make it worth my while."

Later Mateen would tell me, "Hey man, I really tried, but when that motherfucker grabbed me and started hollerin' like that... man, I don't know what happened."

What happened was, Mateen reached into his back pocket, whipped out a collapsible steel night-stick like the one I used to carry, only without the spring-release. He snapped it out to its full length.

The first blow broke the wrist that held him. Then he cracked him in the side of the head several times. When the man dropped his briefcase and covered his head with his arms, he kept swinging. After the man started screaming and fell to the ground, Mateen stood over him raining down blows anywhere he could land them.

When some nearby police came by to check on the disturbance, he was still beating the man into a bloody pulp. It took four grown men to eventually beat that boy off of him.

"Maaaaan, they beat the hell outta me," he said with an ironic laugh. "Shit man, I know I got outta hand, but what was I supposed to do? Let the motherfucker take me home?! I tried to leave."

"Yeah," I sympathized, "I'm just glad you didn't kill his ass. We'd have never seen yo ass again."

"Sheeeeeeeit! You got that right. They wanted to throw away the key as it was. They wouldn't believe I was sixteen. And since I didn't have no I.D. on me and my folks wouldn't pick up the phone, they threw my ass straight in jail. Judge didn't give a fuck."

I could only shake my head. Not surprising. We learned to expect the worst, because that's usually exactly what we got.

"Shit! I gotta get to class," I said noticing the time. "Drop by the house man, we'll go get the guys and we'll hit the streets."

"A'ight man, cool."

"Stay up now."

"Peace."

Sink or Swim

It was what should have been my senior year of high school. Instead, it was my second junior year.

I had been sitting around my apartment, as I did every day during that year after I left the guys, when there came a knock at the door. It was Tyrone.

He had always been on track or football or cross-country. He lived in the same ghetto I did, but he worked the system whereas I spent my time poking my finger in its eye, fighting it. Here was a black kid named Tyrone whose family was on welfare, who in high school, was studying Latin, astronomy, art, English literature, and theater. He was on the track, swimming, cross-country and football teams. He had honors and A.P. (Advanced Placement) classes for college credit all through high school. He didn't do drugs and didn't drink more than once or twice a year: his birthday and Christmas.

What Ty and I had in common was fun, art, and comics. Comic books were a complete and total escape from our miserable existences. We both drew a lot. Sure, there were other kids in school who drew cooler stuff than us, but we enjoyed it all the same. Super heroes who would do the right thing. Who were smart, and handsome, and cool. Not short, and skinny, and dumb, and shy. We would kid around, make good-humored fun of each other, wrestle around, and trade comics, and show each other our newest creations, heroes we'd invented.

The one thing that I always admired most about him was that he wasn't afraid. He hadn't had fear beaten into him. He wouldn't hesitate to talk to anyone about anything, kids or grown-ups. I, on the other hand, was afraid of everything and everybody.

We started hanging out more in high school and together we would go to comic conventions where he would grab me by the arm and go "Ooo! There's Walt Simonsen!" One of the hottest and highest paid comic book artists around. "Let's go see him!"

"Uuuuuh… what?"

"Let's go say hi! Talk to him!"

"What?" I would stammer. "What do we say? What do we ask him?"

"It don't matter! Let's go, before everybody else gets there." And if I wasn't persuaded by then, he would only say, "I'm goin!" And he'd be off. Then it was either follow or be left standing there with my thumb up my ass, doing nothing. Inevitably I would join him.

But I watched. I listened. I learned. I learned that my FEAR was only that: Fear. Nothing else. No pain, no death, nothing. Just… fear. So I went. And I eventually learned to go and to do on my own. His bravery, his fearlessness, inspired me. It amazed me how, once the chips were down, in a fight, something turned "on" inside of me. And it left no room for fear. I even enjoyed it once I got started. But the thought of going up to some famous person and just saying "Hi" was like an immovable barrier to me. Until I saw how simple it all was. Before that I would even be afraid to ask an adult what time it was. I was so used to being mistreated, cursed at, and called every name in the book, I had somewhere along the line just decided to live my life without anyone else.

When they say, "No man is an island," they're wrong. I was an island and it took a lot of years to learn how to let in and let out.

On this day, Tyrone was just makin' time.

"Wha'sup?" I asked, letting him in.

"Nutin'. I got to kill an hour before swim practice."

Surprised, I said, "I didn't know you were on the team. You must be a pretty good swimmer."

"Nope, I suck, but today's tryouts."

"Well if you suck, then why the hell are you joining the team?"

"I need something to do until track season rolls around."

In a flash I thought that it would be great to have something to do besides sit around watching boring old cartoons. Then strangely, it popped into my head that I lived only a mile away from America's largest inland body of water, Lake Michigan, and could not swim. Well shit, this just might be my chance to learn. So on to the swim team I went - couldn't swim, but what the hell.

It was winter. About four o'clock in Chicago. We were jammed into Rogelio's old '78 El Camino station wagon. It was a piece of shit, but it was our sole source of transportation. It got us there in spite of the cracked windshield, the loud muffler, and the foot-round hole that rust ate through the floorboard. Rogelio kept an old piece of carpet over it and I first discovered the hole when my foot grew mysteriously hot one day. I felt an unusual shaking and when I looked down, I saw daylight reflected off the asphalt. It was the rotating drive shaft beneath the rear floorboard that my foot was resting on that was causing the vibration, and the friction was causing the heat. Hmmm... life in the big, modern, city.

Anyway, there were about nine of us in this old thing rattling our way to our first swim meet with Roosevelt High School. Being new to the team, I was relegated to the tail section with the rest of the newbies. I didn't know any of these people. I had joined about a week earlier and the only two I knew out of the thirteen were in other vehicles. On the radio played a new song by a new group.

"This is a cool song," I said to my new teammates.

"Yeah, who sings it?" asked Marco.

"Men at Work," said Verdojeck, singing the refrain.

I said, "'Land Down Under? That the name?"

"Down Under, yeah."

"Cool."

I was 17 years old, the oldest of the group. I had a birth date that fell in such a way that I was half a year older than most kids to begin with. Then I went and flunked a year and a half of high school. It took that much for me just to determine to make up my mind that I would finish.

Arriving in the parking lot, we spilled out of the car, worked out the cramps and started looking for the pool. There was a huge crowd making their way in with us, so it was not hard to find. We would later come to see that some school's swim meets had virtually no spectators. And some schools were such virtual mazes that it would take us almost an hour of searching the deserted halls for a lost stairwell that would take us to the catacombs where the chlorinated bilge-water could be found.

This school's pool, however, was far different. It was huge, much larger than ours. And we would pay the price for it when our events came up. You get used to flipping around after a certain number of strokes or a certain amount of effort. Then unrehearsed you have to swim an extra few seconds or an extra few yards. It makes an enormous difference when you are swimming flat out. You then have to re-time your flips, the crucial part where you can gain or lose precious seconds that can mean the difference between first place and third. So by the end, that extra fifteen feet can seem like a long dark mile.

We found the locker rooms, changed, jumped in, warmed up, and then the coach called us out of the water. Once our team had formed up and taken our seats, our coach, Mr. Blakey, read the line-up. I was only half listening, distracted by the nervous newness of my first sporting event.

"This is how it's gonna be gentlemen. Thornton: fifty meter backstroke; Tang: fifty meter butterfly..."

At that point it was like some special effect in a movie: all sound slowed to taffy. My visuals took on a soft background blur as my brain struggled to digest what was happening. Backstroke? Me? It can't be. I fought back the panic that was creeping up from the pit of my stomach. You gotta' understand, I only learned how to swim a week ago. Literally. I was afraid. I mean deathly afraid. As a matter of fact, that was the only reason I joined the team: I wanted to learn how to swim.

Yeah, I know that's nuts, but look at it from this perspective: I had nearly drowned three different times in my short life. And each time I was saved not by that "sink or swim" bullshit some parents think is such a great idea.

The first time I was a baby. So young I only have memory of the terror. The second time I was saved by a sheer miracle from God. I was alone on a deserted stretch of sandy, rocky lakefront. Then I was hanging onto a slime-covered chunk of rock with the fingertips of my left hand, as the swelling waves lifted and dropped me, threatening to rip my fingers free. And the last time my embarrassment was made complete when I was saved in the deep end of a crowded swimming pool when a beautiful young woman clad in a bright orange bathing suit swam down to the bottom of the pool where I was loitering, grabbed me by my hair, and hauled me out in front of everyone.

I could see about a hundred kids staring at me from around the edges of the pool while I coughed and sputtered for breath. Had I the breath left, I would have asked her

"Couldn't you have at least waited until they all went home before you pulled me out?"

Since that miserable summer in my tenth year, I tried, and tried, tried to learn how to swim. I even took classes at the YMCA. But all that got me was a miserable version of the dog paddle, which did not work at all, when I found myself below the surface and on the verge of panic. So when one fateful day Tyrone stopped by on the way to swim tryouts, I got the crazy idea to join him, figuring that once I got there I would see something I could use. Maybe I would get to swim a few laps and try out my newfound techniques before the coach threw me out of his pool for embarrassing him.

But once we got there, the coach said that there were no tryouts.

"You come to practice, you get to compete. EVERYBODY gets to compete. Get in the pool, swim a lap, rest, swim another lap, rest. That's the way it goes, gentlemen. Lockers are in there."

And that was it. That first practice was more like a free for all. One big party. I was kind of shy, so I just kept to myself in an unoccupied corner, practicing my doggie paddle and watching the ones who looked like they knew what they were doing.

Eric impressed me. He was the captain of the team and he and I had been in art class together three years earlier. He swam like a shark. Long smooth, sleek strokes. Knifing through the water, he made hardly a splash, like a submarine skimming just beneath the surface.

Track was more like a bulldog. From Thailand, a shorter, stockier guy than Eric, he swam more like a bulldog, powering his way through the water.

Being a skinny guy, I decided streamline was the way for me to go. Reaching out, I elongated my dog paddle in what I thought was a more graceful glide.

And then I heard, "THORNTON!"

My first thought was, "Whad' I do?" but what came out of my mouth was, "SIR!"

"What are you doing, son?" Mr. Blakey said from above me in a voice filled with a self-imposed patience.

"Swimming, sir?"

Stifling a laugh, he got a hold of himself and said, "No... no, you've got to put your head in the water." Then he squatted there on his haunches and waited.

And this was it. The moment of truth. You see putting my head in the water was the whole source of my problem. Because I had no problem with water in principle. In fact, I liked water. I liked to be clean, liked to bathe, I even liked to swim, such as it was. But putting my whole entire head under the water? Well, that was where we hit a snag. I've never liked my head under the water, especially my nose. Maybe if I had a loooooong hose... never mind. Back to Mr. Blakey.

Looking up into his expectant face there above me on the edge of the pool, I had a decision to make. I could either tell him to go to hell and get out of the pool and walk my ass on home, taking the little I had learned along with me... or... I could put my head in the water like he told me to and maybe, just maybe, learn how to really swim.

One, two, three seconds ticked by with neither of us moving. Then facing my paralyzing fear, I said to myself, "Fuck it."

Putting my head into the briskly cold water, I struck out again in my own elegantly long dog paddle. When I reached the other end of the pool (with the occasional assistance of hanging onto the side gutter) I looked up in triumph just in time to see Coach Blakey smiling to himself and shaking his head as he stood up and walked back towards his poolside office.

Over the next week we'd had introductory lessons and examples of each of the four strokes: freestyle, breaststroke, butterfly and the dreaded backstroke. The backstroke, for me, was the worst. It was the worst for several reasons. See, if you take a person with a mortal fear of a particular element, dump him in an overwhelming body of it, flip him on his back where he cannot see where he is going, splash buckets of water in his face and NOSE at unpredictable intervals, and tell him to try like hell to get to the other side before everyone else... well that, my friend, is a recipe for Freudian visitations for the rest of one's natural life. Sure, butterfly was physically harder, but backstroke absolutely terrified me every time I did it. It took me years to get to be even comfortable on my back in the water.

So here we were one week later and coach was telling me that I was going to be the opening act in the one-man circus that was about to become my swimming career. I got to go out there and embarrass myself in front of hundreds of students and parents from all across the city. If I managed to keep from drowning myself, it would go down in history as the most pathetic attempt ever made to cross the length of a pool.

I launched into a protest firmly grounded in logic: I suck. And I told everybody who would listen: Coach, Eric and even Scott. In turn, each told me confidently, "You'll be fine," and walked away.

Whaddayamean 'I'll be fine'? I thought to myself. I'm gonna drown right here in front of everybody, but no one was listening. So here I was faced with a choice: Either get in the pool and swim, or figure out which bus you'll have to take back home after you tell Coach to go to hell. And I made my decision.

Steeling myself for the ordeal, I went and got my lane assignment. Lane eight. Terrific. In a swimming competition the middle two lanes are reserved for the winners, and the outside lanes for the losers. Lanes one and eight were the slowest swimmers. Lanes four and five were for the fastest and so on. On the bright side, no one really paid attention to the outside lanes, so maybe I would sink quietly to the bottom and no one would notice, until they came to clean the pool next week and by then nobody would even be able to recognize the body.

I had about five minutes to wrap my brain around the idea that this was really going to happen. I didn't even know that I was supposed to be warming up. It wouldn't have done me much good anyway. Probably just make me drown more slowly.

A whistle blew. The official announced the teams and the beginning of the first event. My event: the fifty-meter backstroke. Two laps of the pool on your back with hundreds of screaming teenagers surrounding you. Great. When we were called to the starting blocks, I took my place in lane eight at the outer edge of everyone's attention.

"Starters, take your marks!"

We were already in the water and reached up and grabbed onto the handrails.

"Set!" Came the judges command and we pulled ourselves upward and in.

The starter's pistol went off and we were suddenly launching ourselves up, out and over the water. I hit that water in a fury of survival, willing myself towards the other side in a fountain of splashing desperation. And to my credit for the first time in my life, I almost made it to the other side. I finally had to stop, exhausted and choking, about 4/5 of the way down.

When my vision cleared all I saw were seven pairs of feet all headed in the opposite direction. The first of which had already made it back to the starting point victoriously. The race was won before I'd even reached the halfway point.

I can't tell you the depths of dejection I felt at that moment. Looking in the other direction, I saw that I was still about twenty feet from the end of the pool. But now I was determined to finish or die trying. I remember wondering if anyone had ever drowned during an event before. Aw hell, I thought, somebody here's got to know CPR.

Then I put my head back in the water and struck out. It was a funny thing. Backstroke is the only race where you can't see where you're going or where you've been, only where you are. Looking up at that ceiling, I could only see where I was now, what spot or stain was directly above me.

Once I reached the wall I took several deep breaths and heard the silence that meant the last swimmer had made it back in and the race was over. I briefly thought about climbing out and calling it quits.

But then, just as quickly, I was off again swimming furiously for the other side. Exhaustion getting the better of me, I had to rest before I'd even gotten halfway. Panting and gasping, I was oblivious to the whole crowd, and everybody was watching me.

My sole concern now was survival. I'd inhaled and swallowed so much water I thought I was going to puke. I was light-headed, dizzy and weak, and had to rest twice again before I reached the finish to the scattered applause of the two or three people who were still paying attention. I took long moments to gather strength and climbed trembling from the water.

Back in the team holding area, a few of the guys patted me on the back and my best friend, Tyrone, gave me just enough shit to lighten my spirits.

Once my exhaustion began to pass, I started to feel the warm glow of a hard job accomplished. I'd finished. I hadn't quit. Hadn't drowned. Actually, I was surprised I'd done it to begin with. We then watched and cheered Track on as he took second place in the next event, which was the hundred-meter I.M.

Back in the holding area, my breathing was finally returning to normal. God, I was tired. I was ready to go home. But I thought anything had to be a piece of cake compared to that.

Then they announced, "Lllllllladies and gentlemen... our next event... the huuuunnnndred meter backstroke."

"THORNTON! You're up!"

"WHAT!?!"

"Let's go! Hit the water." And he was gone.

Turning to Scott, I said, "I can't do that!"

Trying to help, he offered, "Look at it this way: it's only two more laps than you did before!"

It didn't work.

Half laughing, I said to him, "It was only two laps that nearly killed me. And this is TWICE as much!"

But even as I was speaking, I was laughing at myself out loud, because even then I knew I was going to do it. I thought, Ain't this a bitch. Now that's irony for ya.

The thing that was different this time was that it was a more controlled effort. I paced myself. The mortal fear was gone and the more normal kind of fear was left behind. I had lane eight again and actually, for the first time in my life, made it all the way across before I stopped to rest.

Three big gulps of air and I was off again.

I made it all the way again. Now five breaths and I got halfway before resting on the gutter.

Turning around for the last lap, I paused a third of the way through, gathered my strength and determined to go the rest of the way without stopping.

At the end, few people noticed that it was a changed person who climbed tired, weak and smiling from lane eight at the end of the pool. A person with a few less things to fear in this life.

We did pretty well that meet. As a matter of fact, we did pretty well over all. At the end of the season we found that we had somehow managed to win more than we lost. I continued to get better and better. While I never did grow to love the backstroke, we found a peace together, an acceptance. Butterfly was the most fun for me, because it was the most technically challenging. I was passable at freestyle, but fastest at breaststroke. But what I excelled at was the I.M. or Individual Medley, the event that encompasses all the strokes. One lap each of butterfly, backstroke, breaststroke and freestyle. While I wasn't leaps and bounds ahead of anyone, by the end of our first season I had learned all the strokes well enough to be competent, while most of the team could do only one or two strokes at a competitive level.

At the beginning of the next season, to my shock and astonishment, Mr. Blakey named Trak and I co-captains of the team. While Trak had been on the team now for four years, it was only my second. Evidently I was the only person to be appointed to a captainship at the beginning of his second season. It was the first time I had been appointed to anything. I hardly knew what to do with myself... except get better.

By the end of my second year we concluded my last season by winning our section championships for the first time in nearly twenty years. To this day it still amazes me that it was me that did all that. It seems impossible. As a matter of fact, if I hadn't been there I probably wouldn't believe it. But I was and I did, so... there you go. When all the thinking and worrying is set aside, there's nothing to it but to do it.

Remedial

When in grammar school, I had always read well. Often the English teacher would praise my diction, pronunciation, and elocution. Listening to the other children read aloud, I sometimes wondered what was the matter with their mouths that the words came out so rough and broken. In seventh grade I was reading at a high school level. In fact, I was in an advanced English/reading class and we read the classics as well as fiction. On my own at home, aside from the usual comic books, I was an avid reader, from Ranger Rick Magazine to the Reader's Digest condensed books. "Our John Willie" was one of my favorites. My friends used to clown me about carrying around "big" books.

But I was in trouble much of the time. Either from falling asleep in class due to the stresses at home, to the hyperactivity of Attention Deficit Disorder, to fighting, lack of concentration and all the other symptoms of Post Traumatic Stress Disorder. I would not tolerate being picked on. And as I was usually one of the shortest kids around, it happened often. However, it never happened twice with the same kids. I was quite a scrapper. "Hellion" was a word I heard often when the adults thought I couldn't hear them. But I figured if some kid or kids were going to go out of their way to start trouble with me, who was I to deny them their dreams. Hey, ya gotta have goals.

So between missing class, talking back to the teachers, getting into fights with the students, getting into fights with the teachers, and getting into fights with the teachers and students at the same time... they pretty much thought I was a lost cause. After my first dozen trips to the principal, he would hardly look up from his paperwork when some teacher or security guard would escort me into his office. Noticing that it was me again, he would go back to his files and mumble, "Wha'd you do this time, Eddie?"

"Nothin'," was my usual reply.

By that time I had them all figured out. Whenever the shit went down, I would be the one sent to the principal's office. I figured it was because I was familiar with the routine or something. Anyway, in the beginning they would all give me some crap about being able to walk away from a fight. The way life was in those streets only the victor walked away. And if that was too much trouble for them to figure out, I was worn out trying to explain it to them. Trouble always found its way to my door.

When I got into high school, the guidance counselor, or whomever it was making up my curriculum, took one look at my troubled history and less than stellar marks in my classes and decided to put me into remedial classes across the board. All along what I really needed was a better home and some serious therapy. Neither would come my way for many years. So between resenting being treated like an idiot and all of the other persistent symptoms I described earlier, I just managed to fail my way through my first three years of high school. Sure, there were a couple of teachers in those first three years who really gave a flip and they sincerely tried. But they were ill-equipped to fix what was wrong with me. I remember Mr. Robert Parker, Mr. Sachaj, and Mr. Goldman among the few in my prayers to this day, and thank God for their caring and trying.

But by my senior year I was told that there was no way I could graduate on time. Further, I would not be able to graduate even if I attended a full extra, fifth year in school. I was informed that if I wanted to graduate at all, not only would I have to go to school long after my friends had gone, but I would have to take a full course load during summer school at the local community college. DAMN!

In an instant I came to a crossroads. When I was in my sophomore year there was a kid who had flunked a year and had to repeat it. I remember telling my friends that if I had flunked, I would rather drop out than spend a whole year more in school. Now here I was sitting in my councilor's office reliving that instant. In a flash I saw myself as other friends of mine who had already dropped out, working at a gas station or bagging groceries. I didn't like what I saw. I knew my longevity at such jobs would be extremely limited. I said, "Sign me up." And I prepared myself to face my peers who were going on to college or joining the workforce and tell them I would not be walking across that stage with them. Some of them seemed as crushed by the news as I felt.

So I spent that summer at Harry S. Truman Community College watching the winos, junkies, and prostitutes trawling by our window. But by now I had made the determination that if I was going to re-do all those classes I was not going to fail them the second time around. So I applied myself. I started digging into all that potential Mr. Parker and others told me I had. I got A's in my summer school classes, which I took between my swim practices, which were held twice daily. One at about 5:45 till 7:00 a.m., then again right after class from around 4:30 till 6:30 p.m.

I rode my bike each day the ten miles from home to practice, ten miles from practice to class, then straight back to practice and home again after. All together I was up at four, gone by five and on the go for fourteen and a half hours, and for forty miles a day, six days a week, including Saturday. And I started loving every minute of it.

Here's where more miracles began. All at once it seemed. In the beginning of my fourth year, which was a year before I eventually graduated, I joined the swim team, which was miracle number one that year for the kid who not only couldn't swim, but also had nearly drowned on several occasions. The second miracle was Mrs. Duddey.

I was always drawing. Since I can remember I was making art. When I started reading comic books, I started drawing them as well. Once we left my dad, the one thing I could always count on was Mom's support of my art. I always had pencils, colored pens, typing paper and carbon paper. And... a sketchbook. One day in school I was walking down the hall with an especially large sketchpad tucked under my arm when I heard a little voice.

"Hey! Whatcha got there?" Looking around, I almost missed her. There was this little woman who must have been about four feet tall.

"Just sketches of different stuff."

"Can I see?"

"Sure."

Flipping through the pad, she nodded and humphed. When she was done, she handed it back to me.

"Did you do this in art class?"

"I don't have an art class."

"How'd ya like to come visit my class?"

"I've got gym next."

"I'll write ya a note. When you put your stuff away, come see me in 237."

I had no idea who this woman was. She seemed a little eccentric. But hey, if it gave me an excuse to do something different, then why not? Arriving in Mrs. Duddey's classroom, I saw more than a few familiar faces. Tyrone's was among them. To me, it seemed like they were in the midst of a party. There was no order. People were each involved in something different. There seemed to be no class assignment. Some students were drawing, some painting, some in the darkroom and some just talking. "Hey there!" said the teacher. When she gave me the grand tour, people were doing exactly what they seemed to be doing: anything they wanted to. Mrs. Duddey explained to me that this class was A.P. art. The students each had long-term projects that they were responsible for. Each worked at their own pace and on their own terms. They had regular reviews, midterms and finals.

"So do ya wanna join?"

"Who… ME?!"

And here it was. A chance for change. I could keep doing the same old B.S. with no expectations, or I could take a chance of failure and be right back where I was now: nowhere, a real nothing, a no-matter. What the heck, I thought. Why not? She can always kick me out later if it doesn't work out.

"Sure. Sign me up."

"Great!" she said.

It was the first time I was around other creative people like myself. Only these people had been taught to put their creativity to positive use. Each had a different vision and means of expression. It was a wonderful new world of the mind and spirit. I spent the rest of that year and all of the next in A.P. art, eventually earning decent scores and college credit from Princeton University and winning a summer scholarship at the prestigious Art Institute of Chicago where I honed my hard-won opinion on abstract, non-representational art.

Miracle number three: Ms. Murtaugh. She was the remedial English teacher who had enough smarts not to trust the public school machine. In the first week of her class, she gave us a barrage of tests that lasted a few days to determine exactly where each student stood academically. Of course, we didn't know that at the time. It seemed there was always another test to take. So between filling out the answers, I joked around with Marco (who was also getting A's in physics) and other friends of mine in this class full of mostly Mexican, Eastern European, and other ESL (English as a Second Language) students, we who comprised "the dummy class". Early the second week after the test results were in, she called me up to her desk. She had my results in her hand. Uh-oh, I thought as I got up there.

"I wanted to talk to you about your test results."

Is she gonna ask me if I cheated? I wondered.

"Who told you to come to this class?"

"My guidance counselor."

"Well, I don't think you should be in here," she calmly told me.

Here we go, passed off again. "Hey, I just go where they tell me."

She must have seen my expression, because she then told me, "You're too smart to be in this class. And you certainly don't need to learn English." Handing me my test results and a note she had just written, she told me, "Give these to Mrs. Biernett. She teaches Honors English."

Friends, I cannot stress to you exactly how much that scared me. I mean it scared the shit out of me. See, all my life my dad had told me I was stupid and Mom let him, and neither ever said anything to the contrary. And while I knew I wasn't a dummy, my troubled, undisciplined, ADD, always in trouble, violent lifestyle affirmed it. Now, I was shamed by being put in the "dummy" classes and ashamed of failing them, but at least no one expected anything else of me. And believe me, it was EASY to deliver on that one, because I didn't expect anything of me. And amidst of all that shame and embarrassment was some woman telling me to go see another woman who was once again going to tell me I DIDNT BELONG!

Putting on a brave face, I made some light joke and told my friends goodbye. It was like walking the "Green Mile" on death row.

At Mrs. Biernett's door, I looked in the window. My terror only grew. There sitting in the class were ALL the top students in this huge school of nearly three thousand students. Most of them I'd only seen at a distance, heard stories about. The nerds and geeks and the brainiacs. Then I thought, fuck 'em, took a deep breath and opened the door. I walked that long mile from the door to the teacher's desk and waited for her attention.

"What can I do for you?"

Handing her the test results and the note, I told her, "Mrs. Murtaugh told me I didn't belong in her class and sent me up here, but I don't think I belong here either."

"Well, you're right..." she told me, as she looked over my scores. Removing her spectacles, she looked up at me. "You belong in A.P."

I knew it. "What's that?"

"Never mind. Tell me, where have you been all these years?"

"I just go where they tell me," was my response.

"Well! We'll just take care of that right now!"

Digging under her desk, she pulled out a big box of books. Studying the volumes, she pulled specific items and added them to the growing stack on her desk. The only name I recognized was Shakespeare. When she had a stack about as high as my chest, she handed them over to me. Sternly, she said to me, "I'll expect you to have these all read by the end of the month. I'll see you here tomorrow at two for class."

"Are you in this class too?" Tyrone asked me.

"I guess..." Stepping out into the hall I stopped to let it sink in.

I can't begin to put into words how I felt entering this class. The fear was almost paralyzing. At the same time, I wanted to run.

From that day on, for the next several years and into college, I ALWAYS felt like I was skating on thin ice. I felt like I was sneaking into the theater and any minute now some big ushers were going to grab me by the collar and say, "What are you doing here?! You don't belong here!" and hustle me out the back and it would be as if I'd never been there at all. But it never happened. To my great surprise, we got along great! Here were the kids from the "other side of the tracks" and all different cultures and "classes" and they all had one thing in common: brains. So, what the hell was I doin' here? There must be some mistake. But in the meantime, I'll learn SOMETHING before they "find me out" and kick me out.

I devoured those books and everything else she threw at me. It was quite a culture shock though. Everyone in that class except Ty thought and acted so differently from me it was hard to accept where they were coming from, hard to accept their point of view. My knee-jerk response was that they were bourgeois, and superficial; totally lacking in common sense and street smarts. Well I was right for the most part, but the interesting thing was that I found out they had other merits, other virtues. So for the first time in my life I began to stop thinking that everyone else should be more like me, and started thinking about what it was they were doing that was working for them. Then I looked at how I could apply that in my life. Walk, talk, dress, and think, like anyone, any group of people who had something I needed, wanted or was curious about. Instead of being locked inside my own narrow head and body, I could be anything I wanted in this world. The only question was: Was it going to serve me? Would it further my life? Family? Happiness? Career? Finances?

What comes to mind here is a line in the movie "White Men Can't Jump" where Woody Harrelson tells Wesley Snipes something like, "The trouble with you is you would rather look cool than be good. Whereas I am perfectly willing to look like a fool if it will get me closer to winning and the money." I started looking at myself, my mind and my body like a tool. I could use them rather than taking them for granted. Before I'd always thought I'd been "keeping it real" by my ghetto walk, talk, dress and so forth. I wore it like a weapon that told the word that, since you reject me, I reject you, and as loudly as possible. Then I started thinking about, what if someone offered you a thousand dollars to dress, walk, talk, think, and act like a crack-head, prostitute, homosexual, child, White, or Asian? Hell, actors do it and get paid.

If, by adopting some of the things that makes them successful, some of their ways of thinking or doing business, why not? Because, Lord knows, mine certainly hadn't gotten me any farther ahead in life. I didn't have to like it or even use it, but damn it I wanted options, options, options. And if, after all was said and done, I still wanted to hang in the hood and smoke weed all day, then at least it would by choice, not by accident. Sure, my way won me survival in the hood, in the streets, but I was starting to see that there were other things out there, other places to go, other things to be than me right now. I was like Luke Skywalker gazing at the stars saying, "I wanna go there!" For the first time, I started thinking about getting there.

So for the next year I absorbed everything I could in that class. The way I saw it, it was a short course on the world at large and I had to soak it all in. I read so much, my eyes started going out on me. I was getting blurry vision and constant migraine headaches. Mom figured out what it was and took me to the eye doctor. He gave me a prescription for reading glasses and tinted lenses, and I was all good. Blasting through that year I had lots of fun, made new friends, and gained a whole new respect for both those who were different from me as well as myself. By the end of the year I had stopped feeling like a "dummy" and had even more college credits from Princeton to boot. Sweeeet.

Just a year before, I was mentally living in the streets. Before I was through Mrs. Biernett's A.P. English class I was aiming for college and beyond, but I scarcely dared hope I would be able to go. It had been a tossup between majoring in Art or English. I'd had my eye on Oberland College where I could double-major before Tyrone and I stopped in to visit the American Academy of Art. In those magnificent hallways we found home. The artwork that hung upon those walls took our breath away. There were illustrations in the tradition of Frank Frazetta. There were designs worthy of Syd Meade. There were paintings more beautiful than some of Monet's. This was what I wanted to do. This was magic and I wanted to make it! And when, just a few days before the Academy's entrance deadline, Mom said I would be able to attend, I thought I had died and gone to heaven.

"Teacher"

There was this teacher that took over the classroom after my Intro to Data Processing lab class was over. It was in my junior year of high school; the second time I was doing great. I had made great strides academically: getting all A's, and personally: going to school, being more responsible and less... criminal. I was now on the teams, swimming, track, and cross-country. Like a reverse pole on a magnet, I had turned my life around and was beginning, for the first time in my life, to feel good about myself.

My lab had ended and next came my lunch period. The next teacher and his students began to file into the now empty-except-for-me room. But this day I wasn't going home for lunch like I usually did, since for some reason we no longer qualified for subsidized lunches and we couldn't afford the few extra dollars each day for the crappy cafeteria food. No, today I was doing something unusual: I was applying myself. Trying to fulfill my potential. Today I was doing something called EXTRA CREDIT. Yep, me. Eddie Thornton was not only going to class, and doing homework, but today he was actually going to do some extra school... on his own!

It took me about an hour and a half of wrestling with the problem before I whipped it and was ready to go. So, with problem solved, I was ready to go home, wolf down a "sammich" and be back in time for my next class.

However, due to the security guards that patrolled the halls and the recent policy of a "closed campus," I now needed a note to go anywhere, since classes were now in session. It was really Orwellian. The halls were absolutely desolate between classes. And that was quite impressive when you remember that my high school was four stories tall, encompassed an entire city block, and housed nearly three thousand students.

Now back in the day, I wouldn't have been there in the first place. But on the few occasions I actually showed up for a class and split early, I didn't need no stinkin' pass. I just left. And didn't stop for any security guard. Hell, let 'em catch me if they could. And they didn't. Not once. Nobody told me where to go, where not to go, or when I could. Fuck them and fuck their rules.

But this was a new me. A law-abiding me. I, for once, was gonna follow the rules. So, after finishing my paper, I quietly wrote a note to hand to the teacher who was in the back of the classroom, and was now ignoring his students. I approached him with the small request.

"Excuse me... Sir?

"Mmm."

"My name's Eddie Thornton. I had Ms. Klassen in the last class in here. Well, I was in here now finishing up an extra credit project and now I have to go home for lunch. I was wondering if you could sign this note for me to get home?"

He looked up at me with a sour-assed expression like I had pissed on his leg or something. "Why do you have to go home for lunch?" he said, looking back to the same papers he'd been looking at since he got there.

My first impulse was, "What the fuck business is it of yours what I do for lunch? Just sign the goddamn note, motherfucker." But instead I swallowed that and answered him politely, "Because I always go home for lunch."

Then he spared another look in my direction before turning right back to those goddamned papers and saying, "No."

I didn't understand. I was leaving. Going home. Why would he not want me to go home? What possible reason could he have for not wanting me to go? By his shitty attitude, I knew for a fact he didn't want me to stay in his classroom. What was I supposed to do? Roam the halls until security picked me up and suspended me from school? What the fuck was his problem?

In desperation, I tried one last bit of sanity. Holding the two-sentence note that I had written in front of him, I said, "I've already written the note. It just says that I'm going to go home. If you could just sign it..."

"I said no!" he interrupted me.

I wanted to smash that bad cracker stereotype motherfucker right in the face. Split those black plastic glasses in two with his neon-plaid-pants-wearin' ass. Pocket-protector wearing motherfucker.

But once again, I swallowed it. The satisfaction of smashing his smug, arrogant face in was not worth the price of getting kicked out of school. Especially when I'd only just started to turn it all around. And getting arrested would really screw the pooch. Yep, I'd be fucked but good. So I swallowed.

Balling up the note in front of him, I shot it past him and into his garbage bucket for a nice three-pointer. "Thanks for nothin'," I told him sourly, and turned and left. Fuck 'em. If security came, let 'em come.

I had gotten halfway down the looooooooong corridor when I heard a voice call out from behind me, "Hey." Turning I saw that goofy fucker standing outside his open doorway. "Come here," he said.

I thought he had changed his mind, so I turned and walked all the way back to him while he stood there patiently waiting for me. When I got to where he was, all that son of a bitch had to say to me was, "Go that way."

What?! He must be crazy! Shaking my head, I didn't even respond. I just turned right around and went back the way I came.

Do you know that motherfucker ran around and got in front of me and put his hand on my shoulder, like he was gonna stop me from going on my way? I stood there face to face with him thinking, this can't be happening to me. Does he not know that he can get his ass kicked? "Motherfucker, you better take your hands off me," I said, my voice rising.

Taking my backpack off my shoulder, I stepped up to him. I was going to knock him on his ass, step over him, and be on my way.

But something stopped me. Don't ask me what it was, 'cause I don't know. And I had time to think, is kicking his ass worth a lifetime of minimum-wage jobs and a few weeks in jail? Close, but no. So for the first time in my life, I backed down. I turned away. And it took EVERYTHING I had. And frankly, I didn't think it was possible for me to be pushed that far without losing it. I was quite surprised actually. But when the asshole ran around and got in my face AGAIN, it was too much.

They say that before you die your life flashes before your eyes. That's bullshit. I've been nearly killed and thought I was dead at least half a dozen times in my life, and my life *never* flashed before my eyes. Usually I was too busy trying to survive. But that day, in that moment, my life flashed before my eyes.

It happened just before the punch landed. One second I was standing there smelling that sour breath and looking at the crumbs stuck in his greasy, dark brown beard, and the next I was watching my left fist flying through the air like it was someone else's, towards the right side of his face. I swear to this day I can still hear the sound of it hissing through the air.

And that's when it happened. I saw my life flash before my eyes, or my future more precisely. I saw me then, in school having fun, getting good grades. And I saw me getting arrested, spending time in jail, fighting in jail. And then I saw me getting out and trying to find work with my other friends that had no high school diploma, no college and no job prospects other than stacking boxes at the Collin's Brothers Warehouse, or pumping regular or high-octane at the Chevron on the corner of Ridge and Broadway.

And I panicked. Leaning back, I pulled back with all my might. At the same instant, thank God, he flinched backwards and my fist thankfully missed the tip of his nose and I started to rejoice as my fist sailed right past him... and slammed full-on, squarely into the locker that he had been standing next to, leaving a fist-sized dent that remained in it long after I graduated.

Then the reality hit him. You could see it on his face and in his eyes: he could get his ass kicked right here in this hallway. Right... NOW. His mouth dropped open as if to scream for help and he stepped back once, twice. And before he could find his voice, I shoved past him and down the hall towards the nearest exit.

It was only then that I noticed the faces. There were heads and faces staring out of a dozen opened doorways that were previously closed. They had heard our exchange and came out to see where the action was just in time to see the fireworks. If that punch had landed, there would have been a couple dozen witnesses to send me off to jail on assault charges.

Even though it was about forty degrees outside, I didn't even bother going to my locker. I was so mad I had to get away from everybody before I snapped. From the nearest exit it was the equivalent of a three-block walk to my place. When I got inside, I was still so mad I couldn't sit down. As I paced back and forth, the cold started to wear off. That's when I noticed my hand.

It had swollen to about twice its normal size and was beginning to throb violently. And something about it was satisfying.

When I went back after my lunch break, I took my hand to see Coach Mr. Blakey. After examining it, he said, "You got yourself a hairline fracture there, Mr. Thornton. You better go see the doctor," which I didn't of course, because we had no money for x-rays, or casts, or medication, or even office visits.

I took it easy on the hand for a couple of weeks and eventually the tenderness and swelling went away. But what didn't go away was the fear. The realization of what I'd almost done scared the shit out of me. I'd almost thrown it all away. All my hard work and my future right along with it. It was the only time in my life I had been glad that I'd missed. But it wouldn't be the last time.

Dads End

By my third year of high school, "Dad" was still calling and coming around. I had grown in size and now stood about six feet tall and weighed about 140 pounds. I was still skinny and looked emaciated, but when I began participating in track, cross-country, swim team, and the martial arts, I began, for the first time in my life, to look and feel healthy, though still thin.

I had begun to hang around with a whole, new type of people. The friends I now had did not regularly visit Chicago's penal system. They were positive and helpful instead of destructive and self-destructive. I began to see, for the first time in my life, positive relationships. These were the first people I ever hugged. Not my mother, father, or sister, but my teammates. I still remember it like a milestone. It occurred to me that here my friends and I hugged each other on a regular basis, but at eighteen years of age, I had no memory of ever hugging or being hugged by my immediate family.

I still remember how hard it was for me to hug my mother for the first time. Getting beyond all the hidden anger, resentments and just hugging was difficult. She took it like a wooden board the first time, but dammit I was determined to be a human being and hugging my mother would be a part of my life. I did love her, as she loved me, though we were both extremely flawed in our love. Fortunately, she warmed up to it over time and today we can share laughs and hugs freely. But it was hard to get there.

It wasn't until my fourth year of high school that I started dating. While I'd had sex for the first time just after my 12th birthday, it took me until six years later to ask my first girl out on a date. It was for my senior prom... well... my first one. It was also the first time I ever danced.

In college I attended a local school, the American Academy of Art, which was downtown. I continued to grow spiritually, socially and personally. My stepfather had become a more infrequent visitor, but one day, one of the last times I would ever see him, I was showering when I heard a pounding on the door. It actually never even occurred to me that it would be him. So I wrapped a towel around my still-wet form and answered the door.

He was angry and quickly launched into his usual bullshit. "I want to see your mama!"

"No."

"Don't make me come in there."

I think what surprised him was my calmness when I said, invitingly from the middle of the doorway, "C'mon in."

The funny thing was, I didn't care one way or another. The samurai have a philosophy that calls for "resolute acceptance of death." It meant that a warrior could not be a true warrior at all if he was concerned with living or dying. He must only accept life and death as they come in their turn and in their own moment. Prefer neither, accept both. And in that moment that is the closest thing to describing what I felt. I was done fearing him; I was done hating him. I accepted what would come.

"Oh, so that's the way it's gonna be?"

I nodded slowly.

"Stop playin' around and tell me where your mother's at."

"I said 'no' the first time you asked me. What makes you think the answer's gonna change?"

"Don't fuck with me, now's not the time."

"I'm sorry you're having such a hard time. I hope your day gets better." Then I moved to close the door.

"This is the last goddamned time I'm gonna tell you this. You better open that motherfuckin' door. I know she's in there!"

Here I finally began to run out of patience. "I'm not concerned with what you think you know. What I am concerned with is that I've got better things to do than stand here talking with you all day. You can come or you can go. You can fight or you can leave, but you need to do it now."

Stepping back, he looked at my dripping wet form from head to toe and back again. Shaking his head, he began to turn and walk away. Over his shoulder, he said, "Nah. You ain't dressed for it."

Stepping out into the hall, I looked into his eyes and invited him. "Naked or clothed doesn't matter. When you want to do it, let's do it. Anytime you're ready." Stopping, he looked back at me again. After long moments he just lowered his eyes and left. I stood there watching him go. I felt no anger or disappointment about it, just indifference.

It was much later that I began to fully appreciate that landmark moment in my life. It's not many people who are fortunate enough to have the opportunity to face down their demons, outer and inner.

It wasn't until my senior year in college that I saw him again, for the last time. This time he came not with threats, but an invitation. Knocking on our door, he politely asked for Mom. I was cold as I told him no, but then he asked if I wanted to come out and have a drink with him. I was just as cold when I refused his offer. But as he turned to leave, I saw that the lion had no fangs and knew he was old and beaten. In my mind it was like he, once proud and now old, was slinking off to die. He had become emaciated from the heroin or AIDS, and his front teeth had been knocked out. I couldn't help thinking this was the last time I would see him.

"Wait, let me get my coat."

We walked down to Broadway and Bryn Mawr to a diner where we had coffee and told each other stories, and it was nice to share a moment without the fear or hatred that had filled so much of my life. Looking across at his once-handsome face, his once-strong figure, I couldn't help being saddened. This man had managed to fuck up and chase away everyone that had ever cared about him. How much must a man hate and loathe himself to do that? And afterwards?

Then we went across the street to a bar where he ordered bourbon and I ordered a Kamikaze.

"Banzai."

Here he turned to talk of Mom and the future, and the old bullshit returned.

"You know your mother and I are talking about getting back together, don't you?"

Laughing, I told him to knock it off.

Feigning hurt, he said, "What, you don't think we are?"

"I wouldn't let it happen even if you were."

"What do you mean?"

"What I mean is, you had your chance and you blew it. Time and time again. It's time to move on."

"What do you mean, I blew it?"

"I mean all of it. The mind-games, the name-calling, the beatings, all of it."

"I never laid a hand on you," he lied, looking into his bourbon.

For a moment I looked at him with death in my eyes. How dare you? I could reach across this table right now and kill you with my bare hands for daring to trivialize, to deny what you did to my mother, my sister, to me! For creating the beast that now dwells in my belly fighting to escape and urging me to end-your-life-right-now. And he wasn't even man enough to look me in the eye while doing it.

"Okay," is all I said.

Nothing I said would have broken through his fortress of lies, deception and denial. Nothing but violence. And that I would not lower myself to. I had worked for years to destroy that part of him that was in me. I wasn't about to bring it back again. Then I realized that I needed to leave, because I was longing to more and more.

But I didn't want to leave without giving him my forgiveness. Even if he didn't want it.

"That's okay," I said again, "you did the best you could."

He didn't understand what I meant, so he changed the subject. In the wrong direction.

"So how's Pamela..." he began, but I cut him off.

"Let's not talk about Pamela."

"What?"

"I mean the subject of Pamela is off limits. Don't talk about her."

"Is she married? Kids?"

That nearly sent me over the edge. I thought, 'Do you realize how many of you I would destroy to keep my sister safe?'

"I'm sorry. Perhaps I didn't explain myself clearly." Locking eyes with him, I said, "If you ever come near Pamela, I will kill you." I let that soak in as we stared at each other.

"And if you persist in talking about her, I can't promise what will happen next."

After long moments locked in each other's eyes, he broke the silence. "What the hell's wrong with you? You crazy?"

Laughing self-consciously, I said, "Congratulations, you do good work." I then laughed again. I could see I was starting to worry him too, so I got a hold of myself and patted him on the shoulder. "That's all right. I forgive you. Now I just gotta work on forgiving me." I slid a bill onto the table and got up. For some reason seeing him sitting there still confused saddened me. I think a part of me wanted him to confess his sins and claim redemption, to grow and find the freedom I was finally beginning to have. But hearing him spouting the same old line of bullshit... and then the denial? It said to me he would do it all over again. Although I forgive him, I would never let him damage anybody else if I could help it.

I no longer hate him. I have forgiven him many times over. I even understand him having become what he had become. I desire him no harm and only good. My mother chose him again and again. I forgive her also. And I could take anything he could dish out. But I wasn't lying. If he ever came near my sister or her children, or anyone else I loved, if it came right down to it and nothing else worked, I wouldn't hesitate to kill him. I would bury him deep, and then pray for forgiveness.

Truman Gang-fight

I was on the bus, Wilson Avenue, and I was on my way home. It was my second year of mandatory summer school and it was just beginning here at Harry S. Truman Community College. I had just taken my seat on the Wilson Ave. bus when the light turned red. As I sat there gazing at the group of rowdy teenagers hanging out in front of the school, the smell of grilled onions, wonderful, greasy French fries, and juicy sausages came wafting through the window.

The sounds of the city surrounded me: conversations on the bus, shouting outside, street traffic, radios from windows thrown open wide as the curtains billowed out in the breeze. I took it all in as I watched what developed outside my window.

I could always tell when a fight was going to break out. It was like I could smell it in the air and I was glad to be leaving. You never knew when you would get caught-up in some nonsense. It was easy to wind up dead or in the hospital if you didn't keep your eyes open.

The school and the neighborhood was a mix of all races, but there was a rowdy bunch of Puerto Ricans hanging around out front looking for victims. They were loud and obnoxious, pushing each other and talking bad. It was only a matter of time before they tried it on someone they didn't know. And then you would have to deal with all of them.

Now they were shouting and talking shit to some outnumbered black cats. This was not unusual for this neck of the woods. As a matter of fact, it was the norm. Uptown was made up of almost every divergent ethnic group. Add in a full cup of poverty, half a cup of misery and a heaping tablespoon full of heatwave and you're in shit soup.

Suddenly one of the black guys had had enough and he stood up, faced off with the loudmouth of the bunch who was wearing a gold baseball cap, and started swinging. The look of surprise on the loudmouth's face told me that this was the last thing he expected to happen. After ducking, he backpedaled to get some breathing room. And there they stood facing each other, both of them breathing hard. Looking around him, he found that his backup had backed up also.

Looking desperately both ways for help or a way out, he found it. A short distance to his left was another Puerto Rican dude just standing there minding his own business, cool as a cucumber. They were both about the same age and size. Now the first guy saw the umbrella he was holding and figured it would make the perfect weapon. Running over to him, he grabbed it by both hands and attempted to run back to where the black guy was still waiting for him. Only to his surprise, the owner was hanging onto it as well. Indignant, he turned back to the owner and said, "Give it up, motherfucker!"

"Fuck you nigga'," was the reply.

"Either let it go or I kick yo' ass!" And with that the owner let it go... and started wailing on him. He had hit him two or three times before he knew he had been hit. Getting over his surprise, he then dropped the umbrella, the weapon he had originally wanted to use on the other guy, and started throwing punches back.

Now here is the interesting thing. For a few moments they stood there, those two gladiators, toe to toe, trading punch for punch. Each one landed punches in the mouth, eye, nose, and jaw. And each one took them, absorbing and dishing out equal doses of punishment. Then the curious thing happened. The instigator of this whole mess just... gave up. Just like that. He covered himself up and for a moment just crouched there with his arms over his head getting beat on. Then he broke, turned and ran a few steps away. The other guy then calmly picked up his umbrella and this guy's gold baseball cap, which he had knocked off in his initial assault, put it on backwards and went back to doing what he had been doing before: standing there waiting for his ride.

Now the knucklehead who had lost his cap was pissed. He stormed around several times in a circle looking at the crowd. His friends were quietly at a distance. Others were laughing and several were just oblivious. He was so mad he didn't know what to do. Spotting a big chunk of broken cement weighing about five pounds and as big as a softball, he grabbed it up and started back towards the waiting man.

Upon seeing him coming, the waiting man turned to face him, took a step towards him and extended an invitation: "C'mon punk." That made him stop. Thinking better of it, he dropped the chunk and started cursing. It was clear that he had been beaten... twice. It was also clear that he was going to do nothing. And as my bus finally pulled away, the waiting man went back to waiting.

I think I learned more from watching that fight than from any other I've ever witnessed. All things being equal, winning is a choice. So is losing. So it's the one who wants it the most, the one who is prepared to suffer more, endure more, and give up more to achieve his goal. The waiting man was fully prepared to take as good as he gave. He didn't care about the pain, only the giving. The other punk wasn't prepared to take anything. He didn't even want to fight the first guy, the one he had started harassing in the first place. He had to run and find a weapon. And then he wasn't even willing to put up a real fight for the weapon. Finally, he decided he'd had enough and had run.

Now I'm not against running. To the contrary, I'm all for it. I've had to do it many times in my life. Dennis Cormier, an incredible instructor, had a three-step process for any physical confrontation: 1) Walk your way out; 2) Talk your way out; and then if both of those failed you were forced to 3) Fight your way out. The time to run is before you end up in a bad situation. This asshole had created not one but several bad situations. And he couldn't even do that well, because each time he had come up short.

Golden Waffle

One summer, just before my last year in high school, I asked Mom if some friends could drive down with us and spend the week in Georgia on my grandparent's farm. And to her credit, she said yes... to all four of them... in one tiny rental car... for ten hours of driving. YEAH, MOM! Way to go and thanks. That really made our summer.

Gregg, Sam, Jeff and Ramona all spent the night before at our place so we could get an early start. But first there are a couple of things I should tell ya. We, the four of them and me, we were all dark. Starting from Jeff who was as black as coal, then Sam who was Columbian and Puerto Rican with the rich African blood that they carry. Ramona was Cuban and I am like coffee with a lot of crème from my multi-ethnic heritage: Madagascan, Irish, and Cherokee Indian among others. The other thing is that my grandparents lived deep in the Appalachian Mountains. Yep, I'm talkin' banjos and moonshine.

The drive down wasn't as bad as I'd anticipated. I had prepared them for the worst: sitting for long hours in a cramped car with everyone getting on your nerves and nothing but hundreds of miles of the Midwest cornfields to look at. But we all actually had a good time. Even Mom was amused by our antics. We were natural clowns when we were all together.

We had left Chicago and driven through the night. It was now late morning and the guys started getting hungry. From a distance down the highway, we could see a big golden sign that implied food. We all decided to stop wherever it was to eat. As we drew closer, I had second thoughts.

"Oh, maybe we should eat someplace else. It was a Golden Waffle and we were in the Kentucky hills. Back woods. Rebel country.

"Naw man, we're hungry now."

"Yeah, really hungry."

"I'm tellin' you guys, you don't wanna eat there."

"Aw c'mon! Let's just eat."

"Yeah, we've been driving for hours."

"And I gotta take a leak."

Mom was driving, so she decided to round out the democratic vote and pull off the highway.

If I was concerned before, I knew for sure that it was a bad idea even as we pulled into view of the crowded parking lot. There were mainly two types of vehicles that populated that gravel lot: Harleys and pickup trucks. And even before we pulled in, I could see the stars and bars of the rebel flag hanging defiantly in the rear windshield of at least two pickup trucks. The license plates of several other sported the same secessionist design. Shotgun racks and rifles decorated others. Some of the choppers had Nazi motifs and spiked German helmets hung from handlebars.

I was reluctant to get out of the car, while everyone else was chatting away outside, glad to be free of the cramped quarters. "Don't worry," I said to myself, "any minute now they will notice where we are… that or a welcome committee will notice us and come out to… welcome us."

"Whattareyou gonna have!?"

"I can't decide if I want breakfast food or lunch food."

"I'm gonna have me some waffles!" they all said as we filtered in the door and I realized that we really were gonna do this. Holding the door open for the last one, I took a deep breath and plunged in.

I walked in just in time for us to be noticed. It was like a vacuum sucked all of the sound out of the place at once and left only frozen silence. Every head was turned in our direction. All eating had stopped. All breathing had stopped.

"Boy, it sure is quiet in here," Ramona said, oblivious.

Steeling myself, I headed to the front of our group and led the way to the counter where we waited for the frozen waitress to snap out of it. I waited to see whether she would kick us out or seat us.

That poor child was so mad, she didn't know what to do. Finally breaking her incredulous trance, she snatched up five menus and went stomping off to the table farthest away from everyone else. Amused, I turned around. "I guess we're supposed to follow her." Again I let everyone else go first as I slowly turned and made slow deliberate eye-contact with everyone who was still staring at us from their little clan convention. The greasy cooks that probably would put a little something extra in our food. The bikers with the ZZ Top beards viewing us with disinterested coldness. The toothless old men and the toothless young women with disapproving sneers. The skinhead punks with SS tattoos on the sides of their heads throwing intimidating looks my way. I was used to it all. And the fact that I looked each of them in the eye, they knew we were not afraid and would not be bullied. In those few seconds, one by one, most of the eyes looked away. All except the bikers. I looked at them just long enough to let them see me, but not long enough for them to feel like it was a challenge that they had to answer. Then I followed the rest to our table.

There in the South where ice water is a given at every table, we had to ask twice before we finally got it in dirty glasses with no ice. Looking around, I saw that the glasses at all the tables were dirty, so I decided not to push that issue. The waitress with the faded blue eyes, and white, well, it used to be white, uniform and unkempt gray hair, was hard to hate. She was just so... worn out. And hating us seemed to give her something to live for.

Slowly, one by one conversation resumed in muted whispers at the other tables. Glances fell our way at regular intervals like they expected one of us to burst into flames at any moment. The rest of our service was as silent as a funeral, which was fine with us. I had grits, scrambled eggs, and burnt bacon. There was toast with my favorite strawberry jelly. A large orange juice balanced it out. While I pecked reluctantly at my food, I did little conversing and hardly noticed what everyone else had to eat as my eyes and ears were constantly scanning the crowd for signs of brewing trouble.

"I wonder if these are real eggs or just Egg Beaters?" Sam said as he pushed the yellowish, runny mess around his plate.

"They're real," I said.

"How do you know?" Ramona asked.

"Cause I just bit into an eggshell."

Then came the part I was dreading: Jeff. We love him to death, but he loved to complain. And this was neither the time, nor the place for it. "My bacon is burnt!"

Trying to put it into perspective for him, I said, "Mine is too."

"No it's not, Jeff. I love my bacon like that," Ramona said, trying to help keep him chilled.

"Fine, then you can have it," he said, handing his over to her. "This coffee sucks," Jeff said a few moments later.

"Mmm, mmm, good," Mom said, joining Ramona and me.

Then, just as I was bringing a forkful of grits to my mouth, I saw a dark speck that was just a bit larger than the pepper I'd put on it. Bringing it closer, I saw that it was a gnat. My eyes quickly flicked up and around our table to see if anyone else had seen it. As none had, I put my fork back down and thought about it. If I made an issue of it, Jeff was likely to pipe up again and get us all lynched. Tapping it off on the side of my plate, I gave it a quiet burial in a watery grave and continued eating like nothing had happened.

Then Jeff piped up again anyway. "These waffles are greasy."

Exasperated, I looked down at his plate and saw the soaking, soggy waffles. They held a dark, liquid substance in the tiny cells, which had run onto the plate.

"You put too much butter on them," Ramona told him.

"I didn't put any butter on them."

"Syrup?" I asked hopefully.

Clearly out of patience, he said, "I didn't put any syrup on them!" And with that, he picked up a double wedge of waffle in his fist and while he looked me in the eye, he squeezed. The dark, runny, oily grease slowly oozed through his fingers, down his hand and onto the plate.

The waitress noticed this and looked angrily over like she was going to complain about how he handled his food.

Fed up, I looked her in the eye. "Yes?"

Then she shot me a dirty look and left. I half wondered if she were going for Bubba or the shotgun.

Taking a deep breath, I put my orange juice down and addressed the group. "I'm sorry, guys. It sucks here and they don't like us, and I don't give a shit. It's a greasy spoon diner at best. What did you expect? Look at where we are. Look around us. Do you think it's going to get any better? Why do you think I didn't want to eat here? It sucks! Now either let's finish eating or let's get the hell outtathere, but we're not gonna sit here and bitch about it."

Looking slowly around us, they digested my little speech and reluctantly went back to their food.

After the waitress slapped the bill down on our table, we got up, left no tip, paid the cashier, and made our way out of there. We got just as many stares as we headed back out to the parking lot, but they were short-lived. Holding the door open for the last of us, I gave a last look around the staring faces, wiped the grease off my feet and we hit the road.

Kung Fu

Whereas my dad had introduced me to the pugilistic arts at a very young age, it wasn't until Jr. High School that I discovered the Eastern martial arts. When I was in 6th grade I had a friend, Gordon, who was taking karate lessons in the neighborhood. I had been hearing of various martial arts ever since Bruce Lee became a household name. I made Gordon show me everything he'd learned *and* explain it to me. I would ply him with questions. We would try out the techniques and I would come up with the "what-if's." We would spend all day asking, "if he does this differently, then what will I have to change," and so on. I would practice on my own at home, alone, and with friends.

By the age of seventeen I had taken classes in Aikido, and taken seminars in Ninjutsu, Kali, Fencing, Tae Kwon Do and Karate. I had dabbled in about a dozen other marital arts and read dozens of books on various self-defense systems. In a quest that paralleled my later quest for spirituality, I had investigated just about every variation of martial art I could find. And I narrowed it down to a few well-chosen arts for my purposes of street survival. Unfortunately, none of those systems had schools that I could get to regularly.

I had been shot at, stabbed at, been chased and beaten up by gangs, and been in more street fights than I could count. Eventually I started coming out on top, consistently. I would go into a rage, an almost demonic frenzy, a berserker state where I just stopped caring, and started trying to destroy instead of fight. But then the aftermath was that at the end of it, I was screaming like a maniac, crying like a lunatic, and was left with a migraine that was worse than any ass-kicking and it would last for hours afterwards.

I hated it. Eventually I decided that there had to be a better way. When a Wing Chun school opened up just a mile away from my house, I was down there the next day. Mom was to the point where she would try anything to keep me out of trouble, even if it was only for a few hours a day. It was well worth the price. I would spend six days a week and about four hours a day there training, sparring, fighting, learning, and growing. And I loved every minute of it.

Different from track, swimming or biking, martial arts had something I could use in every day life. Something practical, something applicable.

Wing Chun, as taught by the instructor, was a no-nonsense means of dispatching an opponent. It's not pretty. It's not flashy. It just works. And as a byproduct? Full-time martial arts training gave me an outlet for all my pent up fury and repressed anger. And as all the studies would suggest, the more I vented in class, the less I vented on the streets.

Another unforeseen gain from the marital arts is awareness. I began to focus on seeing trouble forming, so that instead of inviting it or walking right for it, I learned to avoid it or head it off at the pass, nip it in the bud. And that is worth more than all the fighting skills in the world. It has served me well year after year, decade after decade.

Unlike other people who were studying martial arts at the time, I wasn't about belonging or discipline, or sport or doing high kicks or fancy moves. For me it was like learning math. If two and two come out to five, it's back to the drawing board until it worked right. I was all about, "Yeah, that's cool and everything, but does it work?" And if it didn't, I had no time for it. I was very pragmatic about the whole thing. By the time I was in 5th grade I had already seen my share of street fights. I knew just what would happen if you tried to get fancy. You got iced. Death comes suddenly on the streets. You don't get to *plan* on it. You don't get to *prepare* for it. I'd seen blood and broken bones. I'd seen kids kicked and stomped into unconsciousness by all the present friends of the person who was winning, both male and female. So over the years "Does It Work?" became my mantra for just about everything. I would use just about anything as a punching bag to practice hitting something without breaking wrist or knuckles.

A couple of years later when we left my dad and moved north, there was an Aikido school and a "Ninjutsu" school nearby. This was just after Chuck Norris brought Ninjas to public attention with his movie "The Octagon." When I told Mom I wanted to take martial arts, as the forward-thinking woman she was, she jumped at the chance to get some self-discipline in my life. So she and I first paid a visit to the "Ninjutsu" school near the intersection of Broadway and Petersen. The instructor, to my dismay, was fat and had a huge, bulbous, whiskey-nose. He had an arrogance that I immediately disliked. I wanted to leave almost as soon as I walked in, but I was secretly hoping that there would be some redeeming quality. Then he told us that he had accidentally broken a student's nose and he blamed it on the student. "He wasn't supposed to move." That was enough for me. I was outtathere.

The Aikido school, in contrast, was orderly, well disciplined and respectful of everyone involved. I signed up on the spot. It wasn't what I wanted, punching and blocking, where I was heading, but it was better than nothing. I figured I would learn something valuable in the meantime. And I did. Even though I was there only about a year, it's been well over twenty-five years since and I still use those basics I learned there in life as well as in fighting. Falling, rolling, reversals and the Circle are invaluable to me today.

After interviewing every instructor and advanced student there, I found that for Aikido to be useful in winning a street fight, or a fight with multiple opponents as is more common in street fighting, I would have to study it for about a decade and hold off on all fighting until then. I don't think the gangs in my neighborhood could be convinced to wait for me. I stopped going to the Aikido school when I found the Degerberg Academy. It was like a martial arts clearinghouse. They held seminars and classes in all manner of martial arts by world renowned instructors.

Over the next few years I sought out every type of martial arts I could experience that the world had to offer in terms of fighting arts, starting with fencing and boxing and moving on through such arts as Savate, Kendo, Krabi Krabong, Muy Thai, Jeet Kuen Do, Kali, Ninjutsu, and so on. I would visit schools, invite practitioners to work out with me, and read voraciously. Martial arts books and magazines I read by the dozens. No matter how remote, unlikely or obscure the art form, each one was given its proper time and consideration.

From all this investigation, I narrowed my personal search for the "ultimate" street martial art to these: Ninjutsu/Hwa Rang Do, Kali, Wing Chun, Muy Thai. Each of these arts has at their heart, a PRACTICAL purpose, something I call "Survival Through Victory." Each martial art has its own merit, but for my purposes "Survival Through Victory" would help keep me alive and healthy on the mean streets of Chicago. Then, through a sheer act of God, in my junior year of high school, when all those miracles were coming together in my life, a Wing Chun kung fu school opened up just a mile from my house. My friend Gregg and I paid the instructor a visit and checked out his school. We were suitably impressed. He was a street-oriented fighter who had previously risen to some notoriety as a ring fighter before he "saw the light". There at his academy, I was surrounded by like-minded folks who wanted nothing more than realism in training. We were fed up with the "Martial Mess", with hollow forms and useless drills of predetermined patterns.

Over the years at the Wing Chun Academy I rose from being a mediocre fighter among other older experienced fighters, to being an instructor. I was the youngest student-instructor in a school with over three hundred students on the books. Also I was still skinny. So it goes to say that I got my ass kicked on a daily basis, even though I kicked a little ass of my own. But there is one unmistakable lesson I learned during those early years taking those hits: I never learned more than when I was being beaten. When I was winning, I wasn't learning nearly as much, I was merely beating. But when I was losing, I was *learning*. How did he get through my defense? My defense was too extended. How did she overcome my superior strength? Superior strategy. How did he overcome my speed? Planning ahead. This guy is twice as strong as I am. How can I overcome his strength? Improve my tactics. And so on. Learn, learn, learn. Grow, grow, grow.

Eventually, I rose in skill to near the top of the school in level. I always chose partners to train with who could either beat me or who were at least my equal and willing to grow and share in equal portions as I was. Whenever a student had prior martial arts or military training, I would pick his brain about that skill no matter what the art.

This was when I began to encounter the tactics of the military's Special Forces. Wing Chun, like Kali and Jeet Kuen Do, was one of the arts that special warfare operatives sought out to supplement their combat training. Over the years I had the opportunity to teach and exchange techniques and tactics with many Navy SEALs, Army Rangers, and Green Berets. Also there were police, FBI, and CIA officers and operatives that trained with us. Some of this I only found out after I became their official instructor, due obviously to necessary confidentiality, others only after we had become friends. As an instructor it is absolutely imperative to know who you are teaching and why they are there. I refuse to teach certain techniques to just anyone. It is not only dangerous, it is also irresponsible. It's like giving a loaded gun to some schmuck off the street. A SEAL or CIA op has different training needs than a cop. One has both license and need to kill on occasion, such as sentry removal (SEAL), and one does not kill except in self-defense (Police officers). And the average citizen needs only the skills to temporarily disable one or more opponents in order to safely escape alone or with a loved one.

In the course of years, I acquired many invaluable skills from this cross-training. To my knowledge, I was the only one to absorb this kind of training besides Dave and Mark, until we formed the Chicago Wing Chun Association.

Bert, a good friend of mine, had joined the Army just after graduation from high school. He eventually joined Special Forces and we trained together from time to time. When he got out, he came over and had a talk with me. He was interested in a Ninjutsu instructor named Ali and since I was an experienced instructor, he wanted me to come with him to check the guy out.

By this time it seemed that every other martial arts school in Chicago had jumped on the "Ninjutsu" bandwagon and was teaching some made up bull concocted from several martial arts thrown together and calling themselves "Ninja". So we paid a visit to Ali at his house one Saturday morning. Ali was a serious Ninjutsu instructor and had been for years. I had read just about every book on the subject, both real and fake. Ali was the only other person outside of Stephen K. Hays whom I had met, that both knew more than me on the subject, but also had a good, clean, consistent technique. Because, believe me, I tested him. I know I got on his nerves with my endless questions and demand for demonstration of technique, but I wasn't going to leave until both Bert and I were satisfied legit. And after grilling him a couple more hours, we were. Ali was the real deal. He had been teaching Ninjutsu since Jesus was a baby and could back up the knowledge with working, realistic technique.

Once Bert began studying under Ali, our training together began to go to an even higher level. Eventually he became an instructor and opened up his own school under Grandmaster Hatsumi's banner of Bujinkan. By that time I was head instructor for the Chicago Wing Chun Association, and we were both in hog heaven. Bert and I had the best of two worlds. I had unlimited access to his training and knowledge, as did he of me. And between the two of us we had trained with dozens of other selfless, sharing, learning martial artists from a hundred different styles of martial arts. There are over three hundred different martial arts that have been documented.

Two of my other favorite martial arts: Kali the Filipino stick, knife and sword arts, and Hwa Rang Do, (the Korean version of Ninjutsu) had students in my Wing Chun School supplementing their training as well. Both of these arts, in addition to Ninjutsu, gave me huge amounts of skills that no single art possesses to such a balanced degree. Kali is almost unparalleled for knife fighting and stick fighting, and the machete. And in Chicago I have had knives pulled on me almost as often as I've been shot at. Ninjutsu and Hwa Rang Do delve more deeply into psychological and spiritual aspects of fighting than most other formal arts out there. Also, they deal with more practical weapons as well, such as you find on the street: knives, short stick, length of chain/rope/wire, throwing implements, firearms and such.

People ask me all the time, "Have you ever had to use your martial arts?" And I answer, "All the time." Only it's not the way they think. In my own narrow little view of the world if I ever find myself having to lay hands on a person in violence, it means in that instant I've failed. It means that my mind has not found sufficient, suitable alternatives to physical force. And believe me, there are almost ALWAYS alternatives to violence. Until that first blow falls and often even after, there are dozens of words, steps, techniques, and strategies that can be employed to obtain your objective.

You see, in most fights it's not that one person or group wants to see another "beaten up", there are other things at stake. And if you ever forget that, you may as well hang it up right there, because it will all have been for nothing. All the blood and pain and death one can inflict will leave you in, at BEST, the exact same position as you were before. Only now you have to worry about Dads, brothers, cousins, friends and police coming after you for vindication. No matter whom, or how many you beat up, you will ALWAYS be wrong in the eyes of them and their loved ones. And everybody's got 'em. Oh, and the law frowns upon it also.

It took me a while to figure out that kicking everybody's ass wouldn't get me very far in the world, in the game of life. If you think being a good fighter makes you strong, or powerful, just ask Bill Gates or Donald Trump. Ever see or hear of them kicking the shit out of five guys? Three guys? One? The president? The judge who will lock your ass up after you get caught? Your boss at work? No, if you want power, study yourself. Sun Tzu says: To know your enemy, know yourself. And if you know yourself, you will know your enemy.

So it's up to you where and what you spend your time, energy, and money on. Personally, I'd rather be good than cool. Cool doesn't buy my car or pay the rent, or put food on the table. It doesn't grow your business or multiply your money. Being *good* at something almost *always* pays. You just have to figure out how to make it work. I know it's a challenge. A lot of folks don't want to deal. They would rather sit around drinking beers, talking about "wanna's and gonna's", as in all the things they *wanna* do, that they're *gonna* do.

This is the biggest lesson people fail to learn: If you cannot control yourself, focus, or be disciplined, you will never be able to really control anything else. And I mean that like a boss controls his business or a good businessman controls a negotiation. Or when you go in to buy a car and pay what you want to pay for it and not what the salesman can get out of you. Because hey, let's face it, that's his job. No hard feelings. But if you let yourself be CONTROLED by your urges or emotions, your fears or your desires, you are lost.

Drive

Ken was a fellow student at the Wing Chun Kung Fu School I was attending in Chicago around 1984. While I was nearing twenty and a beginning student, he was in his fifties and at the intermediate level. With graying hair and an enormous handlebar moustache, he was in fair shape with a little gut left over. He was a really cool, down to earth, open-minded guy. We had many a discussion on martial arts, philosophy, and life.

His daughter attended with him. She was about twelve years old and just as cool a person as her dad was. Tall, trim and beautiful, she had long, straight blonde hair.

They were both tough without the attitude that usually accompanies it. He had half a lung. Years before he had worked in a chlorine plant when there was an explosion. He made it out alive, but not before the chorine got into his lungs. The gas had destroyed all of one lung and half of the remaining one.

We used to trade stories. I would tell him tales of gangsters and fights I had been in, and brushes with death. He told me stories of growing up in the depression and having to scavenge food from garbage cans for his family to survive.

At the school we used to have inter-school tournaments about every six months or so. I hadn't been there long enough to participate, so instead I watched eagerly on the sidelines, cheering on whichever underdog was up.

Then our Sifu called on Ambrose to enter the fighting arena. Yeah, Ambrose was a tall, lean, wiry, and muscular Asian dude with that bad-ass Bruce Lee presence. He was a cool guy, but one you did not want to fuck with.

I'd worked out with him on a few occasions where he schooled me in my technique and answered my many questions and what-if's. Having been there a couple of years before me, he was much more advanced. I was really looking forward to seeing him fight.

Then Sifu called Ken into the ring. Ooooooh-shit. "Well Ken, put up a good one. I'll be rootin' for ya."

Having both fighters face each other, salute, then square off, they were a study in opposites. On the one hand there was Ambrose: cool, calm, resolute. And then there was Ken: antsy, fidgety, distracted. One might say, worried.

And then with a mighty "HAI!" from our teacher, it started. And boy did it start. And it wasn't pretty. Fists were flying in a blur, feet shuffling madly and forward, forward, forward he went. A barrage of hands flew before him driving, driving, driving his opponent back, back, back.

When Sifu called a halt, it was because the fighters had run out of space. Ken had chased an astounded, astonished Ambrose entirely out of the ring.

He didn't know *what* the hell had happened. Both fighters were called back into the center of the ring for the second of three rounds. And we were dumbfounded. What the heck just happened? How did he do that? Well, Ambrose will be ready for him this time, we thought with our jaws still hanging open.

Ambrose marshaled his resolve and his "face" and they squared off again, with Ken much like he was the first time.

When it began again, it began almost exactly the same. Ambrose managed to interrupt Ken's punches to his face and chest with a few punches and kicks of his own, but to no avail. The taller, faster, more experienced Ambrose was chased right back out of the ring. Ambrose was pissed and we were cheering. We had never seen *anything* like it. It was an incredible, beautiful sight. In the center for the third and final round, Ambrose looked determined and Ken was... just Ken. We were silent, hopeful, expectant.

This one lasted longer than the last one. To his credit, Ambrose did even better this time. He put up a better offense and even got to mount an embryonic defense. But still, it was over with a *quick*ness. Ken blasted right through Ambrose's attempted defenses, offenses, and just kept going.

There had never been a more spectacular fight. Never had there been more on the line. And only Ken knew it. The comeback of George Foreman was the only thing in my mind that rivaled what I saw with my own eyes that day.

When it was over, I asked Ken how he had done it. "I had to," was his reply. "I knew that with only a fourth of a lung to breathe on, I didn't have the wind to mess around. I only had about three good minutes in me. If I didn't get it all out by then, I was screwed." It was as simple as that.

Now twenty years later, I still carry that lesson with me. The drive, the determination, the motivation Ken showed that day combined with the element of surprise helped cement in my mind that determination can surmount any obstacle. What you don't have in experience, skill, talent, ability, and knowledge, you can make up for with sheer guts and will.

Mom's Love

While Mom was emotionally unavailable and uninvolved in our lives, one thing is certain. Somehow I always knew she loved me. Don't ask me how I knew, because aside from minimal food, clothing, and shelter, she didn't give us much or do much for us. Hell, we rarely even saw her. After we left Dad, when I was around 13, she began to occasionally spend the money he usually stole from her on me. But by then my childhood was over. I didn't care. Heck, sometimes I think I accepted those gifts just to punish her for all the things she was not. But I give her credit. She tried, for what it was worth. Not to minimize it. It was what it was. Things. But some things are better than no things. And one thing I always appreciated was art supplies.

Mom made sure I had everything I needed where art was concerned. As I had some small measure of talent and a high level of ambition, she supported it. From work she brought me black, red, blue, and green ink pens, typing paper, carbon paper, pencils, erasers, and liquid paper. And I loved it. I filled up miles and miles of paper escaping into fantasy worlds. Drawing superheroes from comic books, novels, and magazines, I lost myself for hours at a time. I suppose Mom was just happy I wasn't out fighting, breaking into places, doing drugs, or getting arrested.

Later when I went to art school, she would always manage to supply me with what I needed to get by. Just barely. We were still broke as hell. I still remember having to cut open other people's discarded tubes of paint and scraping just a few more drops onto my palette. Sometimes my oil paintings looked more like watercolors, because I had to scrub one drop of alizarin crimson and two daubs of olive green across the entire canvass. Here's a tip: Use lots of mineral spirits. But supplies and books were, thankfully, always at hand.

Growing up, all my toys were second-hand hand-me-downs that some neighbor or other gave me. Sometimes the church would donate a few toys to us. Usually they were half-broken with missing pieces and paint. But when we left Dad, I finally started getting some cool stuff: a Shogun warrior, Micronauts, comic books, and Matchbox cars. She also began to support my martial arts habit. Occasional seminars, classes, books, martial-arts magazines, and practice weapons were usually on hand.

Whereas Mom used to cook all the time, when we left Dad she stopped cooking altogether and kept very little food in the house. While I enjoyed her terrific cooking, I also enjoyed eating out, which I don't ever remember doing before. I got used to it, and then began to enjoy trying out new places and cultures and foods. It became something I looked forward to every couple of weeks or so.

Movies were something else we now got to enjoy. And now I actually got a vote! My dad had been in the habit of dragging my five-year-old butt out to see a midnight movie at the drop of a hat. And it was usually some type of horror, death and destruction flick of some sort. I remember him taking us to see Damien, The Omen, Towering Inferno, and The Poseidon Adventure. I still remember being carried, half-asleep, from the car, underneath the brightly lit theater marquee, and into the darkened interior, only to fall asleep about five minutes into the show. I would wake up occasionally, just long enough to be thoroughly confused by someone killing, someone dying, or someone having sex. When I would ask what was happening all he would say was, "You'll understand when you're older." Then why the hell am I here now? I would think just before drifting off into a troubled, dream-filled, frustrated sleep.

But now I got to go see movies that I had an interest in. One of the coolest memories was Pamela telling us she wanted to go see some new type of movie I was unfamiliar with. It was called "Science Fiction." Her excitement was contagious and I can remember standing in the longest line I'd ever seen before or since, when a movie called "Star Wars" opened at the Esquire Theater. The lines actually wrapped around the entire block. The movie was unlike anything I'd ever imagined. I was officially hooked. Heavy Metal, the live animation version of Lord of the Rings, the Warriors, Beat Street, Breakin', Crush Groove, all drove me forward. The Oriental and the Mc Vickers Theaters downtown always played triple-features. For a buck you could see, The Five Deadly Venoms, The Chinese Connection, and The Street Fighter. I would go in the morning and when I got out, night had fallen.

Years later, after the first time I hugged my mother, I would start to figure out that she was capable of showing the type of love and affection that I'd seen on TV. I had to learn to offer what I could, and accept what she had.

headed east

 headed east

D.C.

I was far too old to be starting over. When I graduated from the American Academy of Art, I was twenty-three, had two degrees and no job. A year later, after much job hunting, hustling odd jobs, and scraping to get by, the situation hadn't changed one bit. Hell, it wasn't even looking like it was gonna change. There was a glut of artists already in the market and no one was hiring in the art and design field. I had spent the last six months being told that I was obsolete. My Associates Degrees were in Fine Art and Commercial Art. I was an artist and a painter, but everyone was looking for computer artists. I hadn't learned anything about computers in school, and the only thing I could do was data entry.

After banging my head against the wall unsuccessfully, I started calling around the country trying to find a region, state, or city that was in need of traditional commercial artists. Finally after more frustration, I found out that the Washington D.C. area seemed to be the only place where work was to be had. So like a white-collared migrant worker, I laid my migration plans.

After a brief visit to the homestead in Georgia, with a one-year layover to build a car, I headed east, contrary to Horace

Greeley's advice. I had only four things in my possession: a newly rebuilt 1964 Mercury Comet that friends had nicknamed the Batmobile, two Hefty bags full of my clothes, my art supplies, and, after gas, $60 dollars in cash.

Fortunately Tyrone, my best friend, was scheduled to be re-certified at an aerobics convention in D.C. at the same time I was planning on arriving there. And so, on a crisp fall day, I threw my two bags in the back, checked my money and my pocketknife (don't leave home without it), kissed my mom goodbye, scooped up Ty, and we left. Ghost, gone, fumes, out like a tan at a Klan rally.

My family and friends didn't know what to think and I didn't know what to tell them. I didn't spend four years of my life, ten hours a day, six days a week, busting my ass just to flip burgers at Mickey-D's. Been there, done that. Far too many times. I wasn't gonna pay back tens of thousands of dollars' worth of student loans that way. I had to do better. I couldn't afford not to. Not to mention I wasn't mentally or emotionally suited to working at a fast-food joint. Yeah, I can see it now, "Now for the 11:00 news: fast-food worker Eddie Thornton was involved in a high-speed chase with the police after going ballistic and beating the shit out of a customer who was complaining that his coffee was too hot." I've never been good at putting up with bullshit. No unfulfilled job dissatisfaction, slow-suicide from resentment-driven alcoholism for me.

When we hit D.C. after driving all night, it was a chilly, foggy morning. It was a Sunday, I think, and it soon turned into a warm, wonderful, sunny afternoon. Tyrone would fly back home after his meeting, so I dropped him off at his hotel and got to work. Let's see, I had no friends, no family, no job, no money, and no place to stay. Nooooo problem. I had lots of work to do. My first priority was a place to stay, for free, or as close to that as I could get.

I checked the homeless shelters, which were unusually full to capacity, fire departments, and churches. I scoped out some abandoned buildings to sleep in later, in case I could find nothing else. I would have to find some places that were on darkened streets and with access that was out of plain sight so that I wouldn't be discovered (and evicted or arrested). They had to be fairly inaccessible so that no one but me could figure how to get into them.

Then, after stopping at several churches that were unable to help, I found one that could. The lovely lady at the door suggested I try the Youth Hostel. What the heck was that? A cheap stay apparently. I was skeptical because, due to the high real estate values in the area, even the freakin' YMCA cost as much as a hotel. Sooooo off to the phones I went. I had found that the wonderful, beautiful, exciting Union Station had up-to-date and well-maintained phone books. And there it was, the address and phone number: The Washington International Youth Hostel. Always pinching my pennies, I drove. At a dollar a gallon, it was cheaper than a phone call.

It turned out that the hostel was even cheaper than the "Y". Much cheaper. But even at $13 dollars a night, I still couldn't afford to both stay and eat for long. But at least I would get one good night's sleep, and a shower and shave, to start the job hunt off right. I had already picked out an abandoned building for me to crash in, with gas stations and fast-food places for my sponge-baths nearby. This was when the first blessing came my way.

Just after I had paid and gotten my room number, I was about leave the counter when I overheard the assistant manager telling one of the other hostel guests that he could pay for his stay by working a few hours. I turned on my heel, held my breath and dove right in.

"What do I have to do to sign up?"

"Be here at six a.m. First come, first served."

Oh my God, I thought. I couldn't believe it. It was too good to be true. The first thing I did when I got to my room was dig out my alarm clock and set it for five. Then I set the alarm on my watch for the same time just in case the clock went out. Having secured lodgings for the night, I moved on to my next priority: work.

About a year and a half before, I had spent some time in Frederick, Maryland where my sister and brother-in-law had gone to bear their second child via midwife. While there, I attended a tent service the Seventh Day Adventist Church was having. I also met an art director and freelance graphic designer named Howard. I had exchanged cards with him and while in Georgia, I had called him to find out how the workflow was in the D.C. area. He had said that work was good and that if I ever got out that way, I should look him up.

Now, dropping my twenty cents in the pay phone, I hoped he still felt the same way.

"Howard!" I said, "it's Eddie Thornton, from Chicago. Howzitgoin?"

"Hey, Eddie! How are you?"

"I'm in D.C.," I told him.

And that's when the next miracle hit me. Straight outta the blue, he says to me, "Hey, I'm glad you're here. I could use some help. I got some work for you if you're free. Do you feel like doing an illustration for me? It pays $350 cash."

Was he kidding? "Suuuure, no problem." And just like that, I was in business. I met him later that same day and after giving me the pertinent materials, he paid me in advance, in CA$H!!

Thank you Jesus!

Every now and then, just often enough to remember, God drops miracles like this in my lap. Despite all the things that were stacked against me, all the obstacles, something told me I was going to be okay.

Sam

The last time I had to reach out and touch someone, it was my mom's boyfriend. His name was Sam and I hated him the instant I laid eyes on him.

Mom had had a couple of men interested in her over the years after she left my stepfather, but she never seemed to be interested. Some I'd met were some really nice guys. One was even a pastor. So when she told me she'd met someone, I was happy for her. She needed to get out, get a life.

After the year I spent in Georgia building my "Batmobile", a 1964 Mercury Comet, white with red top and gold rims... sweeet, I returned to Chicago in order to earn some cash for my trip to D.C. Once back, I was in for some extremely unpleasant surprises.

She didn't tell me he'd moved in with her - into our apartment. She didn't tell me the guy was my age... exactly my age. He was a young, black, street-hustler. Are you sensing a pattern here? From my father, to my dad, to... Sam. I smiled, shook his hand, and out of respect for my mom, said, "Glad to meet you." Sure, he put on that Mr. Innocent act that all hustlers can put on, but it doesn't work with me. Ya see, since a hustler raised me, I have a bullshit-detector that is in tip-top shape, and I could smell it on him. We had dinner and passed conversation, and when it was over, they said goodnight and crawled into the rollaway bed together... right in front of me... right in the living room.

I was so mad, I didn't know what to do. I was so angry, I went into the room Mom had kept for me and paced the floor. I –was furious! In my entire life, no matter how angry or out of control I got, I never even came close to hurting my mom or sister. But now... I wanted to kill her. I wanted to go stomping right into that living room, drag them both out of bed, and beat them –to death! And the longer I waited, the more my anger went from a simmer to a boil. It was only a matter of time before it erupted beyond all control.

Putting my coat back on, I burst out of that place like it was on fire. Outside, the cold night air did nothing to cool my fury. As I walked the desolate streets, I thought about it and the more I thought about it, the more I wanted to go back and beat the shit out of both of them. And the worst part was... I didn't even know how to express why I was so angry. Betrayal? Disrespect? Lack of consideration? Poor judgment? I couldn't begin to tell you. So I walked. I walked up and down those streets until I got tired of thinking about it. I woke Jeff up out of a sound sleep and he let me spend the night over at his apartment. "Damn bro!" he said when I told him what happened. Then he just gave me a hug and left me alone.

The next day I confronted her about it and she seemed to have no clue as to why I was angry... at all. Further, after I'd explained exactly what type of guy he was, she accused me of being jealous! If she wasn't even going to try to understand what I was going through, then fuck it. I was determined to sever my relationship with my mother. It was just too emotionally volatile, painful, and destructive to endure. I decided to get out and had little to say to her. She wasn't listening anyway.

It's funny how miracles come, not when you want them, but when you need them. Sam had a female friend who was pregnant, who coincidentally moved into the same apartment building as ours. He was to move out and into his "sister's" apartment a few days later. And the miracle was this: About a week after he'd moved, I picked up our phone to make a call, and I heard Sam's voice on the line. How the heck did that happen?

"Sam? Sam. SAM!"

No matter how I shouted, he just kept up his conversation. Then it occurred to me that he was talking to a woman. So, I admit it, I eavesdropped.

"Yeah baby, I missed you so much. And when I se'ent you last night, I just wanted to jump over duh counter and just hug you to me, baby! Squeeze you! Feel those lips on me. I miss layin' with you, baby. So, can I see you tonight?"

"I dunno."

"Baby! It's been a week! I got ta see you. I got ta hold you."

"Okay."

"That's good baby, 'cause I got ta have some."

The funny thing is, I wasn't even angry. I knew exactly what kind of slime he was all along. Here was just proof of it. I also knew that Mom knew what type of guy he was in spite of her denials. He had to be exactly the type of guy she was looking, waiting for. I knew no matter how much proof I brought to her, she would just explain it away, excuse it, justify it, or just deny it.

Eventually I heard him "cheating" with several other women, selling cocaine and marijuana, threatening someone's life, and just being an asshole in general. The funny thing was, I wasn't even trying to listen after that first time. Again, I knew what kind of guy he was. I didn't need more proof. But every time I went to make a phone call, there his voice would be talking shit... every time. I couldn't get away from him.

I would meet his thug-buddies going up and down the stairs. Even my friends would call me up. "Hey Eddie, I just saw that nigga' Sam hanging out on the corner drinkin' whisky over on Kenmore, talking plenty o' shit. Is your mom still seein' that fool? Don't he have a job to go to or something?!"

Hard-core, gangsta-thug, wannabe. I once even found a note he'd dropped on the floor of our apartment that was a "love-note". It went into graphic detail about he and some other chick's latest sexual escapade, complete with blindfold and ropes.

Of course, I told my mom all of my discoveries after I overheard the first couple of calls. I even told her my suspicion that his "sister" was really his girlfriend and "her" baby was really hers and his. She listened to all this with an air of patient forbearance, then promptly dismissed it. All of it.

Okay, it's not my life. I'm out. I never again told her of anything I uncovered about the guy. It was all a waste of time, breath, and energy.

But it wasn't that easy. I got angrier and angrier at him for his pure ignorance. I wanted to slap the shit out of him each time I laid eyes on him. But! It was my mother's choice who and what type of person she spent herself on.

It was a sad, strange irony to see our roles reversed so. It had only been about four or fiver years prior that she was trying to tell me to quit hanging out with my old gang. How's that for the shoe being on the other foot?

Eventually my anger grew toward her as well. I hated her stupidity at allowing herself to be fooled by this thug. It got to be so that every time I talked to her, I wanted to grab her and shake the shit out of her, hoping to shake some sense loose.

It was getting harder and harder to keep my temper in check. I even considered just catching him on the way home from one of his "hoe's" houses, dragging his ass into a dark alley, and then just breaking him into little tiny pieces. I wouldn't kill him. Just put him in the hospital long enough to "see the light". I briefly thought that a couple of weeks eating through a tube would actually change things. Then, thank God, I came to my senses.

I realized that no matter what I did to him, my mom would blame me and be chased right back into his arms with all the comforting sympathy she never gave me. A lose/lose situation.

Finally, my irrational thinking told me that I needed to just divorce myself from both of them lest I explode and do some irreparable harm to all three of our lives, let alone our relationship.

Then, one day I was over at Tyrone's apartment and his mom, Vera, and I got to talking. I told her of my plans to sever my relationship with my mother and she managed to talk a little bit of sense into me.

"Eddie," she said to me, "don't let some silly little nigga' come between you and your mother. This fool can get killed by someone he did wrong, tomorrow. But your mother? She's forever your mother. Can you imagine how you would feel if, God forbid, something happened to her today? You will never forgive yourself if you let this no-account break up your relationship with the woman who done raised you, for good or for bad, for the last twenty-some years."

I had to smile. She was ab-so-lutely right. Thank you. I went back to Mom and told her that if she wanted to accept Sam for what he was, or if she wanted to deny it, that she was an adult and could do whatever she wanted to. I would accept it.

"Just don't sit there and try to tell me his shit don't stink. I'm not havin' it. You do your thing, but if you love him, don't you ever let him lay a hand on you, because I'll kill him and bury the body deep."

"Honey, you don't mean that," she laughed.

"Mom, don't fuck with me. Because you see, you being with him is like you being with my stepfather all over again. It's like you telling me that Pamela and I would have to go through all that hell, all over again. I won't have it. I hate that motherfucker and would snap his neck like a chicken bone, but you like him and that's your business. I love you, but whatever you do, don't let him put a finger on you."

Time passed.

I moved out, worked, made money. Got laid off. Used money to eat. Had a falling out with one of my closest friends in the world and then moved to Washington D.C. in search of more gainful employment.

Sam moved back in with Mom and there was a constant parade of his friends, male and female, in and out of the apartment.

One Friday night about a year later, I was working the front desk of the Washington International Youth Hostel when I got a call from Pamela.

"Eddie, when was the last time you talked to Mom?"

"Couple, three weeks ago. Why?"

"She didn't tell you..." she said to herself. And with tears in her voice she told me, "That figures. You'd better sit down for this.

"Mom's sick. She's got pneumonia. She's been sleeping in the cold, wet basement of the church for the last two weeks. Mom finally figured out that the baby upstairs was Sam's, then it all started to sink in. She put two and two together and figured out that he's been sleeping with that Mexican lady that doesn't speak much English, who is living with them.

"Well, Mom confronted her one night and told her that if Sam was her boyfriend then they both had to move out. The lady must have called Sam, because he came home pissed-off.

"After Mom had fallen asleep, he came in, woke her up and started screaming and yelling at her. Things like, "Who are you to tell me what to do in my house?" and "I run this shit around here! Don't you ever talk to her! And so on.

"Then he grabbed hold of an old liquid fire extinguisher and, while she was still in bed in her nightgown, sprayed her from face to feet, soaking wet.

"Mom got up out of bed, grabbed shoes and a coat, and fled.

"Outside there was a foot of ice and another foot of snow on the streets. It was around twenty degrees Fahrenheit outside and exactly four point seven miles to the church. She walked the whole fucking way. Wet hair, wet nightgown, wet feet. Then, after the caretaker let her in, she slept in that cold, empty church in her wet clothes.

"I don't know what to do," she said.

When Pamela had finished, I was deadly calm.

"When Mom calls you again tonight, tell her to make a list of only the things she absolutely needs that she can carry in her hands, and I will be there tomorrow."

After hanging up, I picked up the phonebook and called half a dozen car rental agencies before I found one that I could afford. I reserved a Chevy Corsica for ten p.m. when I got off. It was now eight.

Hanging up the phone, I went into the back office and knelt down. "O' Lord," I prayed, "I know he doesn't deserve to be on this planet, but that's not for me to judge. But I'm gonna kill him Lord, unless you help me. I don't want to be that person. And I don't want to go to prison, because she'll just find another one exactly like him and then I won't be able to help anyone. So please, have mercy on me, on him, on us. Thank you Lord. Amen."

At ten I packed an overnight bag and ran to the rental agency. I paid them all the money I had in the bank and hit the road.

I drove a hundred-and-ten miles per hour, as fast as the car would go, until the car started to overheat. Then I figured I wouldn't help anybody if I didn't get there at all, so I slowed down to one hundred for the rest of the seven-hundred-mile trip. Like the Red Sea before Moses, the fast lane cleared out. I never even had to change lanes. Not once. The whole way there, I had one thought in mind:

"O' Lord, please don't let me kill him."

It became my mantra.

Stopping at a rest stop, I dozed a few hours at about four a.m. and arrived in Chicago just in time for the Saturday morning service at the church. I took that time to recite my mantra and afterwards we had hugs all around, and then headed for the apartment. On the way there, I told her to make a list of the things we could carry in one trip that she could not live without. We were gonna grab those things, and never set foot in that apartment again. I couldn't afford to stay there protecting her from herself.

Taking the keys from Mom, I told her to wait outside the door. The first thing I did when I opened the door was to go through the apartment and make sure nobody was hiding in the closets or under the beds. Then I let Mom in. The place was a dump. There was stuff everywhere.

"Get your stuff," I told her, mad that she had even put me in this position. Then I went through the place again and collected the many weapons that he had stashed and available. I found three machetes, a hatchet, a sword, and several assorted knives lying in various corners and under mattresses, and on top of the fridge. There were also a variety of sticks and softball bats lying around. All of these I hid deep and high amongst my mother's clothes closet.

I happened to be walking past the front door when I heard someone entering the lobby. Several people had arrived and departed in the hour we had been there, but this time I froze. It was him! I don't know how I knew it, but I knew it. It was that little voice that hadn't failed me yet.

Positioning myself squarely in front of the door, I waited. Then, about thirty seconds later, I heard it, the key in our door. I could taste the satisfaction already. This was going to be fun. I was going to savor his pain.

When the door opened, he had been looking down, not expecting anyone else to be there. Needless to say, I was the last person he wanted to see. But I gotta give him credit, he covered it well.

"Oh, hey Eddie," was all he said.

"Hey Sam!" I smiled winningly at him and moved as if to allow him to pass. Closing the door, he went to pass me on my right. I was momentarily blinded by an instant rage at the sight of him. Raising my right fist, it shot forward of its own accord. Then the hole I was visualizing in the middle of his face never materialized. Instead, my hand was thankfully around his neck. He was about my height, but a little thinner. Stepping forward, I pinned him, head and shoulders, against the door, up on his toes, and whispered in his ear, "Pack your shit and get out."

For a moment we just stood there in surprise, and then he decided he didn't like that and began to struggle against my hand. With both hands, he tried to pry it from his neck while he cursed and fumed at me with hoarse grunts and croaks. Then, giving that up on that, he started to swing at me.

I backed up, dragging him with me. When he swung with his left hand, I swung him by the neck in that same direction, neutralizing the power of his swing while I slammed him against the wall. Then when he swung with his right, I would repeat the process, keeping him off-balance and struggling. I must've bounced his head against the walls eight times or more. And each time he fell down, I would drag him back up and hit him with the other wall. In this fashion, we made our way down the hallway.

When we got to the bathroom, which was on my right, since the door was open, he found himself inside with me still holding him by the throat. He was out of breath and disoriented.

"Are you finished?" I asked him coolly. His mouth began to work, but no sound came out.

"What was that? I can't hear you," I said. Then I realized I had begun to squeeze tighter. Laughter tried to bubble up from the back of my throat. I sobered myself and reluctantly eased my grip.

When I saw the inviting bathtub behind him, I decided to give him one way out, because if I didn't, he would wind up in bloody pieces in that tub and I'd be looking for hefty bags.

"I'll say this one-more-time. Pack your shit and get out." Then he made a mistake that almost cost him. Mom had come up and was standing over my shoulder. And he looked at her. Then he started to say something to her. Clamping my hand tighter, I said "Noooo… you don't wanna do that. You don't look at her. You don't talk to her. Do you understand me? I'm afraid you don't understand me." Raising my left hand in front of his face, I moved him further towards the tub. My left hand shook as I held it out, inches away from his face. As he watched it, I said, "Do yo see that? That is how bad I want to do you. Right here. Right now. Now I'm gonna let go of you and you got a choice to make. You gotta decide if you want to leave here alive or if you want me to go to jail." Dropping my left hand and releasing his neck, I stepped back and waited.

To my disappointment, he lowered his eyes and slunk past me.

"Don't turn your back on him," my mother whispered when he had gone into the dining room.

I let him think I was going to wait there for him. Then I silently followed behind him and waited until he began to dig in under a pile of magazines and then look in the kitchen. As he rooted through the footlocker I'd just cleared of weapons, I snuck up and scared the shit out of him.

"Looking for something?" I whispered inches from his ear.

"Whaaa!!!" he shouted. Then he recovered and dashed to the closet and began to quickly collect his clothes and holding them in a heap. All the while I stayed close and kept an eye on his hands. As I followed him out, I stopped at the front door. Halfway down the stairs, at what he thought was a safe distance, he began talking shit.

"You DEAD, man! You motherfuckin' DEAD!!" and he ran down the stairs.

"You wanna come back and talk about it?" I said invitingly.

"I'm a come back with my boys and you dead!!"

"You can come back alone and get the rest of your shit, but if anyone else comes through that door with you, I'm takin' you all out." And then I closed the door.

When he had gone, Mom said, "Should I call the police? There's a warrant out on him."

"Hell yeah!" I told her. After trying the phone, she got no dial tone.

"The phone's not working," she told me.

"There's a pay phone on the corner. I'll use that one."

By now I was at the living room window watching Sam. He had gone out the front gate with his armful of clothes.

"Wait," I said to her.

He stood there looking right then left for a moment before turning left and running up Glenwood in the opposite direction from the pay phone.

"Okay," I said.

I wanted to stay inside the apartment in case Sam had a bout of courage and decided to come back up. It wouldn't do for him to lay in wait and get the jump on us if we both left. So I watched from above as Mom turned right out of the gate and headed for the corner.

Then moments later, here came Sam again. I wondered what he'd forgotten. He was on the opposite side of the street and heading in the same direction Mom had taken, but luckily he had not seen her. And just as he came to the font of the building, he stopped, turned around, and turned around again. Apparently he had forgotten where he had parked his car.

Spotting it across from my window, he opened the passenger side door and tossed his clothes inside. Closing the door again, he stood up and looked up and down the street while I held my breath. While trying to figure out what he should do next, he looked idly around. Then it happened.

He spotted Mom at the corner. When he moved, I moved. Like lightning. From the open window I heard him shout at her as I hit the door, "You dead!"

Fuck it. That's it. It's over. I tried, Lord. I really did.

As I spun out of the gate, I tried to decide whether I would flee or throw myself on the mercy of the judge.

My first priority was to keep Mom safe, not to kill Sam. So I raced past him and got to Mom before he was even aware of me from across the street.

"Mom! Watch out, he's coming."

With Mom having been warned, I was now free to turn my full attention to Sam. He finally noticed me after I passed him across the street. The instant he saw me, he spun around and began to run back towards his car. Whether for a weapon or escape I didn't know, and frankly it didn't matter. Either way my strategy and goal were one in the same: destroy him. Break him in as many pieces as I could. Consequences be damned. Whether I would leave him alive or not, I had not decided. Either way, I had to get to where he was. If he was fleeing, I wanted to chase him down and beat him like the dog he was. If he was going for a weapon, fine. It would give me an excuse to end him. But I had a better chance of protecting us if I could disarm him, and I had to be up close to do that. If he was running, I didn't want him to be able to threaten my mom and then just walk away. I didn't want him to get away that easily.

It was a short race and a close one. He was almost half a block ahead of me when I began to chase him down. When he got in his car and started it, I was about fifty feet away. As I reached for the passenger door, he threw the car in drive and rammed the car parked in front of him. Throwing it into reverse he then rammed the car parked behind him and knocked out one of its headlight on the driver's side and his own taillight. Slamming his car into drive again, he clipped the corner of the car in front of him a second time and flew out of his parking space. He shot out of the space so fast that his momentum carried him wide to the opposite side of the street where he then side-swiped a car that was parked there, putting a three-foot long gash in its driver's side fender and door. Flooring it, he high-tailed it up Glenwood Avenue and screeched around the corner and was gone.

I stood there listening to his gunning engine and my racing heart, and tried to decide whether I was happier that I hadn't gotten my hands on him, or angry that I hadn't.

Taking a deep breath, I had time to think and in retrospect, I was glad he'd gotten away. In the end, I don't think I would have killed him, even in the heat of fury. But you never know. I have no desire to live my life as a fugitive. And the judge, I'm sure, wouldn't have seen things exactly as I had at the time. Facing it, even if I'd just kicked the shit out of him, legally and morally I wouldn't have been justified. Sure, everyone tells me that he deserved it. And the police and people who knew him wish I had put a hurtin' on him. But I wouldn't have felt good afterwards, because no matter how many pats on the back, no matter how many "attaboy's" I got, I would have regretted it. I would have been cheapened for it. And I can't even claim credit for self-control. I was released from the final decision by Sam's speedy departure. And for that, I'm thankful. Thankful to God for answering my prayers.

After Mom had filled out her police report, Tyrone and I made a couple of trips to the apartment to get more valuables. We dropped them off where Mom was staying, said goodbye, and took a loooong, slow drive back to D.C.

"Freeze!"

I had been in D.C. nearly a year when I took a job in College Park, MD. with false hopes and weak promises of better pay and benefits besides. Dave, the owner of a picture framing shop, hired me when my job as a night clerk at the hostel was being phased out. I'd had a month to find a new job and a new place to live.

The ad stated that he needed an assistant to help him with the shop. But what he really wanted was, for $6 an hour, without benefits, someone to run the place for him. Desperate, I took the job and before long it became Dave's habit to disappear about an hour after my arrival and then return just before my lunch break, which he tried to make me take in the shop. Fuck that. When I'd return, he would wait about half an hour pretending to work, then say, "Ed, I gotta run to the house and get something to eat. I'm starvin'." And that's the last I'd see of him until I was closing the shop for the night.

At this time I was using my bicycle as my sole source of transportation as I was not making enough for bus fare and could not afford to keep my Batmobile. It was a long ride there and a long, cold ride back. Ten miles each way in heavy traffic, and in the dark on the way back. Yep, it sucked to be me back then.

Late one Friday evening, after saying goodbye to Dave, I was on my way out the back door. Having donned my summer cycling outfit, I wore white, cleated cycling shoes, my blue cycling shorts, and a bright red tank top, and always safety conscious, my cycling helmet with reflective tape. Throwing my big-ass backpack and grabbing by BIG RED, bicycle, I headed, clackety, clackety, clackety, up the back basement steps after jangle, jangle, jangle, locking the back door.

Just as I took my BIG RED bicycle off my shoulder and sat it down in the crunch, crunch, crunch of gravel, I heard a screaming voice cracking at the top of his lungs, "FREEZE! DON"T MOVE!"

And I did. Being that we were in a dark alley and that the screaming voice was trying its best to be commanding, I felt reasonably certain that it was a cop that was doing the shouting. S-l-o-w-l-y I turned my head to the left, and what I saw there scared the shit out of me.

I should tell you right now that, as a dark-skinned child spending summers in the Deep South, I'd been shot at in those North Georgia mountains. Growing up in Chicago, I've been shot at by cops and criminals. Here in D.C., I'd been shot at and around. Over the years I'd had more guns pointed at me than I care to remember, but this was the first time that I was worried.

Right there, on my left, hidden between the darkened corner of the next building and a telephone pole thirty feet away, was a metallic gleam coming off the muzzle of a trembling pistol. Inch by slow inch, there emerged the parody of a police officer, a strange stereotype out of a Saturday morning kid's show. The man was young, no more than 22 or 23. He was in full-crouch, squared forward, both arms fully extended, both hands on the handle. And when I said trembling, I was just being general. What I really meant was he was shaking. I mean really shaking. I mean like rickets. What I mean is, he was shaking so badly I thought he was gonna fuckin' shoot me by accident! Damn!

So now I was standing there having visions of this man poppin' one in me, then saying "Oops." I'm telling you that I was in such fear for my safety that I considered running for it just to keep from being shot. I figured my odds were better running than trusting him not to twitch that finger that was wrapped so tightly around that trigger.

Then I realized that while my left hand was in his line of sight holding my bike, my right hand was hidden from him down by my right side. I just knew that he had to be thinking that I could be hiding a gun in that hand. So, hoping to ease his paranoia, I began to s-l-o-w-l-y raise my right hand out in the open where he could see it.

Then he began one of the slowest, most excruciating exercises I have ever been the victim of. He would s-l-o-w-l-y crane his head first right, then s-l-o-w-l-y left. He would lower both arms, do a sort of crab-like shuffle to his left, then raise his arms again pointing the gun at me. Crane, dip, crab, point. Crane, dip, crap, point. For an eternity. Actually, I was grateful that he was so painstaking. The fact that he lowered the gun before he moved at least eliminated my worries that he would trip and shoot me in the falling.

Looking in his eyes, I saw, not anger or hatred, rage or disgust, or any of those things a black man sees in the eyes of a cop stopping him because he "fit the description". Instead, what I saw was fear. Weather it was fear of me or fear of him shooting me, I couldn't tell. I just knew that it was a level of fear I had seen before. It was fear on the verge of panic, the worst kind. The kind to be avoided at all cost. At this point I would rather have seen rage. That, at least, was predictable.

After he had made his way to the other side of the shop and checked around the corner to see if anyone was hiding there, he reversed his direction and crabbed himself back to his original position. From there he leaned back and looked down the alley from which he came. S-l-o-w-l-y I turned my head to follow his gaze. I was surprised to see what in all this time I had failed to notice. There was another cop sitting in a squad car down at the end of the darkened alley with the lights out. Shouting down to him, the frightened voice he called out, "Joe, is this him?" Then with some relief, I saw a black police officer, wearing wire-frame glasses, emerge from the driver's side with the microphone in his hand, while he leaned forward and squinted into the night at me.

I found myself wondering if his prescription was current and if they were reading glasses or not.

"No," was his reply, whereupon he got back into the cruiser and started speaking into the mike.

However, my attention was immediately re-focused on the first officer when I heard him shouting. Turning, I saw another first in this bizarre evening. This young man was jumping up and down, waving his gun, stomping around, cursing at the top of his lungs. "SHIT!" "FUCK, FUCK, FUCK!" "God Dammit!" He was so upset I thought he was going to throw his gun down. At that point I gave up all hope of trying to predict anything that would happen this night.

"I'm sorry, man," he said to me. "Man, I am so sorry." He looked like he was going to cry at any moment.

"Hey man," I replied, "I'm just glad you didn't shoot me."

The next thought that went through my head was one of ironic surprise. That apology was the first I had ever gotten from an officer for mistakenly drawing his gun on me. It's pathetic that a civil officer had to almost blow my damned head off before I got an apology.

So now I was standing there trying to decide between conflicting emotions: relief, anger, sympathy, insanity. He was still freaking out and stomping around in circles. And in the next instant we are both interrupted by a racing figure that came zooming past the other end of the alley.

It was a short, dark-skinned man sporting a natural, covered with a dark blue baseball cap. He wore a navy blue windbreaker and had a stocky frame.

I, on the other hand, I am about a foot taller than that guy, weigh half as much and am an albino by comparison. I've got hair down to my shoulders and let's not mention the ridiculous outfit I was wearing or the big-ass, bright red bike I was carrying when he stopped me.

How do I know all this? Because immediately afterwards we all watched as half of the College Park Police Department came down on this guy. Two of them tackled him into the bushes about forty feet from where we stood. Another seven guys immediately surrounded them and three more squad cars pulled up at the same instant with sirens and lights all around. Then the cop in front of me, and his partner in the car, took off to join the party, leaving me standing there.

Apparently that was the guy whose description I seemed to fit. Suuure, I see it now. When you look at him from a certain angle... FUCK YOU! Every time a cop points his gun at me it's because I "fit the description". It's amazing how many different people I look like.

Having had enough of this nonsense, I decided to go before anything else crazy happened. "Stop the insanity!" would be my new mantra. I had just thrown my leg over my bike when I heard a soft, mousy voice coming from the back of the frame shop.

"Hey Ed. What's goin' on?" Turning, I saw Dave's face poking out from the partially closed back door. "What's goin' on?" Seeing the alley clear, he was bold enough to come out of his shelter all casual like. But I realized that he had been careful to make no sound as he unlocked, then cracked open the door.

Walking up to me, he said, "I heard the cops yell 'Freeze' but I couldn't hear what you guys were sayin'.'"

Son-of-a-bitch. You mean to tell me this motherfucker had heard the cop that was just about to shoot me, mistaking me for some type of deadly bicycle-riding, spandex-wearing criminal, right outside of his place of business and he didn't even come out to try and stop 'em?! To see if they were going to haul my ass off to jail!?!

"Officer, there must be some mistake. Eddie's been running my shop for me for the past ten hours." Motherfucker! Right now I could either be dead or in jail and he would've just let it happen. He heard that police car drive off and figured it was all over. "Coast is clear! Let me go see if they shot him in the head or the chest."

I wanted to smack the shit out of him. Instead, I got on my bike and left him there. I never looked at him the same after that night. It was bad enough that he was getting cheap slave-labor out of me with no benefits and no insurance. Then he would add insult to injury by lying and saying, "Maybe after you've been here a while I can start offering you some medical benefits." I had been there over a year! He had owned that fucking shop for over ten years. I found out he hadn't paid benefits to his last "assistant", who had been there over three years and was a better craftsman than I was. But now he sits safe inside and doesn't even have the balls, the manhood, the honor, or the common decency to, at least, vouch for my whereabouts with the police?

Eddie, truly you are alone in the world. Don't believe the hype. When the chips are down most people will cut bait and run. I've seen and experienced it time and time again. Outside of a few rare individuals in my life that I call friends, there are those that when the shit hits the wind, so do they. Thanks for nothin'.

Rescue

The next year I was working as a private investigator. Serving summons, and hunting down deadbeat dads were the usual de jour. Following cheating wives and husbands, criminals and victims alike, was what made up my day. It was not as glamorous as on the TV shows.

This particular evening was warm for a D.C. October. It must've been about nine, ten o'clock at night. I found myself stopped about three cars back from a red light on Rhode Island Avenue, the not-so-nice part of town. I was thinking about how I wanted to peel off this itchy, charcoal gray, wool "F.B.I. suit" as my partner called it. Having been lost in thought, it was curiosity, which quickly moved into self-preservation that brought me back to reality.

The sound I heard had begun as a curious whining. It slowly began to rise in volume until I recognized it. It was the screeching of tires. Oh shit! Not wanting to be rear-ended or side-swiped, I quickly scanned front, right, left, then my rearview mirrors in a vain attempt to determine the direction from which the squealing sound was coming from. An instant later, it occurred to me that it was a long time for a car to be in a skid.

Then I saw it. From the right side of the cross-street there came a flash of fire. In an instant, it seemed like a comet was streaking across my path at about twice the legal speed limit. Then like a snapshot, my brain took it all in. It was an old nineteen eighty something Datsun or Honda wagon. It was a weather-beaten gray car and it was out of control. The sound and flames came from a single source, the driver's side rear wheel. As the car streaked across my field of view from right to left, the rear wheel, which had been bent under the body of the car and was burning rubber and grinding metal against cement caused a shower of sparks and flame to pour from underneath.

In the driver's compartment I saw even further confusion. The driver, a young man, a teenager, with short hair and a white sweatshirt, had his arms fully extended in front of him on the steering wheel. His body was pressed back tight into the seat. The passenger was young as well, and he also had his arms locked out, hands on the wheel. I was confused as to whether he was helping him or fighting him. On their faces were expressions of pure panic.

As the car cleared the intersection, it struck the curb on the opposite side of the street with both front, then both back wheels. Thus becoming airborne, the car sailed about ten feet through the air before heading right for a tiny little walnut tree that stood planted squarely in its path. Woe for that little tree. It was only about six inches through the trunk and that old car was made of pure steel. When the car met that little tree all it did was give a little shudder. The car, on the other hand, came to a complete and total stop. In mid-air.

After its pause at four feet in height, the car, which had partially embraced the little tree with its bumper tilted to the right, rotated about 90 degrees and slipped back to the ground and lay peacefully on its passenger side.

When the car stopped, the rest of us became unfrozen. The spell broken, cars started to inch forward then stopped again as they rubbernecked. Gridlock. Snapping myself out of it, it occurred to me that those boys would need immediate medical attention, but I could not go forwards or backwards either. Finally looking across to the wreck, I saw flames and smoke spout up from the uppermost part of the wrinkled hood. No time to fuck around now, I thought.

Heading into oncoming traffic, I drove my "Cream-sickle" beige, piece o' shit, Mustang II through and around several vehicles, up and onto the curb and into the vacant lot of the Domino's Pizza building where the burning car lay. Bolting out of my car, I was amazed to find that the wreck was already surrounded not by rubber-neckers, but by the homeless and drug addicts and winos who populated the vacant lots and alleys nearby. There were about eight of them trying to figure out what to do next. Running up next to the car, I found out why they were hesitant. Aside from the smoke and flames, the car was balanced precariously, threatening to topple over onto us with the next stiff breeze. Putting my hand on the rear bumper, I shouted for those nearby to look out. With a gentle rocking motion I found that the car would only rock so far before it stabilized again.

From the rear of the vehicle, I heard something thump, thump, thumping. Going around towards the sound, I found one wino trying desperately to kick in the back windshield. Putting my hand on his shoulder, I asked him to go around and stabilize the car while I gave it a try. Once he and four or five others had braced both sides of the car, I took another look at the flames. By now they were rising about a foot above the uppermost side of the hood, but were not growing or spreading too rapidly. Stepping back, I executed the most perfect sidekick I have ever delivered in my nearly thirty years of martial arts. Thank you Sensei Dennis Cormier! Releasing, I drove my black, sixty-dollar, wingtip, size eleven dress shoe straight through the rear windshield shattering it into a million pieces.

The glow from the rising flames combined with the smoke made it hard to see into the black shadows within the car, and a shadow crossed my soul before I forced myself to crawl into that cramped, dark, suffocating, hot, burning car. And even as I was moving, one of the wino's emaciated figures scrambled past me and dove into the rear seat. There wasn't room for the two of us, but I was right behind him. He reached down into the shadows and came up with an armful of fifteen-year-old boy. While I was waiting my turn to go smoke diving, I was surprised by the homeless man as he handed me the boy and turned to dive back into the smoke for another.

I was moved by his courage. I turned to take away my charge and was met with a sea of open arms reaching out to take the boy to safety.

Relinquishing him, I turned to plunge in again and was handed a second figure. We then formed a firemen's brigade handing off the second and then the third unconscious child.

Then I noticed the flames. They were rising with a vengeance and making up for lost time. I began to worry. I knew the driver and co-pilot were still inside the burning wreck, but I didn't know if we would have time to retrieve them before the flames fully engulfed us all and took the gas tank up with us. I had to stop those flames from reaching the boys inside. Stepping out, I looked around, casting about for salvation. We needed a miracle.

At the Domino's, I found it. I knew that as a commercial foodservice establishment they would be required by law to have a fire extinguisher, fully charged at all times. Let's just hope they obeyed the law, because there was nowhere else to get one nearby and a bucket of water just wasn't going to cut it.

"I'm going for a fire extinguisher!" I shouted, pointing to the pizza joint, and took off in a flash.

Crashing through the front doors, I encountered another teenager behind thick, burned, scarred bullet-proof plastic. He had a broom and dustpan in hand and looked up at my sudden, unexpected arrival.

"I need your fire extinguisher!" I shouted at him.

"Huh?"

"FIRE EXTINGUISHER!"

"Uhhh... I can't..."

Pointing out the front door to the burning car, I unleashed a torrent of profanity. "THERE'S KIDS IN THAT BURNING CAR IN YOUR GODDAMN PARKING LOT AND IF YOU DON'T GIVE ME THAT FIRE EXTINGUISHER RIGHT GODDAMN NOW I'M GONNA KICK THAT DAMN DOOR DOWN AND DRAG YOU OUT THERE WITH ME!!!"

Thank God that worked! There's no way in hell I could've kicked down that solid-steel, double-bolted, bullet-proof door. But he thought I could, so I went with it.

Rushing to the back, I figured he was either calling the cops or getting his gun, or finding that fire extinguisher. Thankfully it was the latter. Rushing back to the front and hurrying to unlock the multiple locks, he opened the door, thrust out the fire extinguisher, then slammed it shut re-doing all the locks.

Extinguisher in hand, I plunged back out into the night. Although I had only been gone for a minute or two, the flames had already engulfed the entire engine compartment and were licking the windshield, the roof, the driver's side door and filling the wheel-well. I checked the pressure level, praying it was full.

Arriving at the front of the car, I took a deep breath and shoved the nozzle right down into the engine compartment and triggered it full-blast. There was a burst of smoke and chemicals while the flame flared briefly. After a few, long moments of struggle, it began to subside and only smoke came gushing forth.

Back at the front of the car there came another thump, thump, thumping. So I handed off the extinguisher to somebody standing next to me and told 'em to keep an eye on the smoke. "If it starts to glow, hit it again and don't stop until it runs out!" I shouted over the swirling chaos. Then I headed back around to the front of the car.

Looking down to the windshield, I saw the driver lying with his upper body against the glass while his bottom half was "sitting" on the passenger side door, which was on the ground. His co-pilot was lying just behind him. The thumping came from another druggie trying vainly to shatter the upper half of the windshield. Touching the man on his emaciated shoulder I smoothly told him to step aside. Can you believe that? Maybe I should have said something like, "This is a job for Superman!" or something equally ridiculous.

I thought if I could strike the windshield about a foot above his head, I could shatter it completely without harming him with the shards. Picking my target, I stepped back and chambered my, by now, world-famous sidekick and unleashed!

There was a very anticlimactic "crack" that left my foot sticking halfway through the PLASTIC safety lining of the windshield. Shit. How ignoble the hero. I wonder if anybody saw that?

Pulling my foot free, I struck out again. And again. And again, until finally I had drawn a line of cracks down the center of the glass. Stepping back, I then began to turn around to look for something to cut the plastic with when of the winos thrust a broken-off stop sign in my hands.

"Here! Try this!" This is phe-nominal! I thought. Who would have thought...? Turning back, I thrust the sharp end of the long, heavy sign into the uppermost part of the plastic and began to rip down the center. Nearing the center, I had to slow so as not to split the boy's head open along with the glass. Finally, carefully, I had split the entire windshield.

Before I could even withdraw the jagged steel, something happened that nearly brought tears to my eyes. I watched a mob of hands, naked hands, broken degraded, diseased, disregarded, skeletal hands reach in, bare, and take hold of each side of the windshield, jagged with slivers of shattered glass, and pull them apart. I saw the blood well up from between homeless, addicted fingers and I despaired for the humanity that had discarded them.

As they held the glass apart, I climbed in. The frantic sounds of the frantically discharging fire extinguisher lent me speed. I carefully grabbed a hold of the (Unconscious? Dead? Broken?) body of the driver and pulled him forth from that burning, jagged womb.

Turning, meeting receiving arms, I gave up my charge before going in for the last remaining body. When I finally emerged, I was standing alone with the boy in my arms. Everyone else seemed to have withdrawn some distance. I carried the boy a good distance away from the smoking wreckage before lying him down in the half-dead grass and dirt of that untended lot.

After ascertaining that he was breathing freely, I began to gently check his body for other injuries besides the bleeding mouth and ear. Both of these injuries worried me. Both could be from potentially fatal internal, unseen injuries.

Before I'd finished checking him over, however, he began to revive. Slowly at first, then he started with a panic. Jumping up suddenly, he startled me with his immediate recovery. Shock? Drugs? How was he even moving? He spun around like a cornered felon before I took him by the shoulders and calmly said to him, "You've been injured. You're bleeding. You need to see a paramedic." He struggled to fight me off, but I was determined to get him to calm down before he hurt himself further. But the more I held on, the harder he struggled. And the more he struggled, the more I worried about causing him further injury by holding him down.

And then it hit me: sirens! It's not me he's trying to get away from, it's the cops.

"HEY!!" In that instant, as I turned to the source of the shout, he snatched his arms free and tore off the ground and down the alley like an escaped prisoner. Shit, I wasn't going to chase him. Upon turning, I was greeted by a trio of steely-eyed, hardcore gangsters. They were about thirteen years old and about half my size. The one in the center and slightly forward of the two flanking him must be the leader. He followed up his shout with an angry, "What chu doin' to my friend?!" as they stalked towards me. As he said this, they were about ten feet away and closing. Before the words were even out of his mouth, he had lifted up his jailhouse denim jacket and began to reach for the rubber-handled, chrome-plated revolver that was stuck in his waistband.

In an instant, I made my decision. There was nowhere to run to but the open lot. There was nothing to hide behind closer than a dumpster at the end of the alley. He would have time to empty his entire ammo supply into my back before I got halfway there. And that was probably what they were used to. So my only other options involved attack.

An attack of the physical variety would probably only serve to get my ass shot off. Or it would get me beaten up for punching out a bunch of "kids" by everybody who didn't see him with a gun in his hand. So what I was left with was an attack of the mental variety.

Stepping rapidly forward, I closed the distance in three, quick steps bringing me belly to belly with the leader before he knew what had happened. My left hand shot down and trapped his right, gun-hand and his gun, which hadn't yet cleared his waistband against his stomach. Surprised, he stepped back trying to get away and I went back right along with him.

"Is that your friend?" I asked, further confusing them.

"Huh?"

"I said, 'Is that your friend?'"

"Uhhh..." Finding his courage in front of his rattled homeboys, "YEAH! Yeah, that's my friend!" he said, recovering himself and his bravado.

"Well if you want him to live, you'd better get him to a hospital." The re-direction worked.

"What?"

"He's bleeding from his ear and mouth. He could be dying right now from internal injuries. If he's your friend and you want him to live, you need to go after him and make him see a doctor."

Then I waited. If they didn't go for the bait, I would have no choice but to cut them down before shots started firing. 'Cause I sure as hell wasn't just going to just stand there and let them pop me. I don't care who it is. If I'm goin' down, I'm not goin' down without a fight. Not without a damned good reason.

I breathed a sigh of relief when he said, "Yeah... okay," and they all took off down the alley.

Turning, I took a look at the surreal scene that had occupied my night. The three baby-faced gangsters that were about to shoot me were running away down the alley. Across the alley one boy sat in a doorway, legs unmoving, talking with a paramedic who had just arrived. To my left, several yards away, another boy was sitting against a tree still trying to get his brain and body to respond to his wishes, while a wino and a couple of prostitutes ministered to him.

By now, after the danger had passed, a scattered crowd of about sixty or so was spreading throughout the block talking animatedly and pointing from the kids to the burnt vehicle. The wreck of the car still sent a column of now white smoke heavenward towards the night sky.

More sirens were converging on us from several blocks away. From the rising and falling tone, I noted that these, unlike the others, were police sirens, not fire trucks or paramedics.

At that point I had decided I'd had enough. Had enough of the craziness. Had enough of pushing my luck. Once the police got here they would want a description of the boy who got away. "Which way did he go? What did he say? What was he wearing? Who are you? We're gonna need you to come downtown to fill out a statement. You should get home in time to change for work. Breakfast? We'll give ya a cup of stale, tarry coffee. Ya like doughnuts?" Thanks guys, but I've had enough. It's been a loooong night.

Quarter

The Washington International Youth Hostel at 11th and K Street, where I was working again part-time, was in a pretty rough neighborhood. Prostitutes of both genders worked opposing sides of 11th between K and Massachusetts Avenue. The funny thing is, both sexes were... kind of... girls. The women hookers worked the east side of the street while the transvestite/transgender hookers worked the west side of the street. We used to wonder how many tourists took home the wrong kind. The hookers and pimps populated it by night and the businessmen held sway during the day.

I worked the closing shift at the Hostel store. There I sold food and touristy stuff to the hostellers. Between customers I would sometimes watch the hookers and their pimps argue and fight out front. I could hear the jibes and catcalls through the open window as they were thrown across the street from one group to another. This was a Sunday night, however, and all was quiet when I stepped into the warm, dark night. Eleventh Street was deserted when I moved to the curb under the lone streetlight to look for my bus. If none was coming, I would walk the two miles to my home.

As I gazed down the block, I got the distinct impression I was being watched. I pretended to still be looking for the bus as I used my peripheral vision to find where the sensation came from. From the shadows at the end of the block and across the street, I found myself being watched, and as soon as I noticed them, they moved.

Making a b-line straight for me came two of the predators that populated the area after dark. Briefly I considered going back inside before realizing that after I walked back up the steps and rang the bell, Randy would have to come all the way from the back office to find out who it was before he would buzz me in. They were quickly closing in, so I decided to play the unsuspecting tourist just to see what their move would be.

As they drew near me, I noticed that the leader, slightly in front and facing me, was shorter and stockier than I. He was about 5'10" and a very muscular 220 pounds. While I'm 6'2", my weight is about 165 lbs. on average. He wore a dark blue shirt and black jeans that blended into the night. His partner was about 6' and maybe 170, wearing blue jeans and a blue windbreaker. Notice a pattern here? They wore clothes designed to blend into the night. Stalkers. When the leader came within about six feet of me, he squared off with me, took a wide, ready stance, and said, "Gimmee a quarter," while his friend circled around to my left. Simultaneously, I circled to my right in order to keep them both in sight and not be caught between them. Taking a moment to let him see me looking him and his partner up and down, I said, "No."

His friend then got nervous seeing that I was not threatened by them, and started to fidget. "C'mon man, let's get outta here."

"I said, give me a quarter!" the first man demanded.

"I said no," came my calm response. This made the friend even more nervous. He started to move and I shot him a look ready to strike. Startled by my look, he stopped and then backed around to his left until he was behind his buddy, tugging at his elbow. "Le's go man!"

"NO, man hol' up!" he replied. Then he took a step closer and I was ready to go.

In an instant, my mind flashed through half a dozen possible physical scenarios. Picking the most direct one, I began... then stopped again before the impulse reached my body. What the hell are you doing? I asked myself. You're standing out here alone facing these two clowns who may have who knows what for weapons. I'm about to attack them in front of my place of business. And with my luck, the police would roll around the corner just when I threw my first strike and lock my ass up. Then instead of acting, I thought, What am I fighting for? What do I stand to win? What do I stand to lose? And, more importantly, is it worth it? My answer was... no.

Was it just a quarter? The "Principle"? Or was it something else? This guy had pissed me off. He was a bully. And he was trying to hurt me, or humiliate me or... what? Was he being successful? No. He would, however, be successful if he caused me to do something stupid, to compromise myself. I had a brief vision of myself beating the shit out of these two guys and then... what? For... what? No, I would not get locked up or fired for a... quarter.

Then I reached in my pocket and looking him in the eye, I fished out a quarter. He held out his hand expectantly, almost triumphantly. Still looking at him, I reached over him and held the quarter out to his friend. He reached for it and I quickly lifted it just out of reach. I handed it to his partner who reluctantly opened up his hand while I dropped it into his palm.

My conscience was now clear. Come what may, jail or injury or being fired, I would not be moved. If I had to take both of these clowns out and stand trial for it, so be it. The next step would be theirs. I had done all I could do.

The three of us stood there for a few beats while the muscular guy tried to figure out what had just happened. Was my act of compliant defiance a victory or a loss? "C'mon man... let's get outta here," his friend said, tugging insistently at his sleeve. "Let's go."

Angry in his frustration, his reply was, "Maaaaaan, fuck this shit."

I gave him my ironic little smile as he let himself be led away. It was ironic to me, because he was the one who started this shit. You figure he would be happy he got his quarter. But no, it wasn't the quarter he wanted. He wanted a victim. The quarter thing was just a probe to search for openings. At the first sign of weakness, they would have been on me like jackals on a carcass. But I gave them nothing, no fear, no anger, nothing. The great Chinese military strategist Sun Tzu says: "Never show the enemy your face." That is something they weren't used to. They didn't know how to react or where to go with it.

There are many people like that in the world around us every day. They don't just lurk on dark streets. We work with them, go to school with them, have relationships with them, marry them. They are us. Have you ever worked hard to achieve a result and been confused about how you felt about it when you got it? I have. That only happens when I'm not clear about why I want it. What's my motivation?

Yep, it sucks to be them.

Thanksgiving in Southeast D.C.

One step above homeless. That was how I described my condition. I was renting a room in a house. A group-house as they are called. It was a three-story row house near 13th and U. Street N.W. in Washington D.C. There were seven bedrooms, each rented to a different individual. I was only paying two-hundred a month, but my temp job washing dishes for the Senate of these here U-nited States of A-merica was paying me only about six bucks an hour. I still had the "Cream-sickle" of a car left over from my private investigator work, and was driving it to and from the Capitol Hill Seventh Day Adventist Church.

Rick was a friend of mine from church and he had been homeless himself. He was raised on the streets like me and was in the process of moving his life forward as I was. It was the night before Thanksgiving and most of my friends were going out of town for the holiday, and I was faced with a big, empty house for my own Thanksgiving. It was one of the thankfully rare occasions when no one had invited me over. So I got the idea into my head that I would host a Thanksgiving dinner for the "orphans" among us with no place to go or no one to be with.

I had invited about eight people before I remembered Keith. Keith was a homeless man I met in front of the church when he accosted me looking for drug money. After I gave him the opportunity to get some things off his chest, he asked me what he should do next. Inviting him into the church, I told him I didn't know where his path lay, but there were pastors inside who could help him choose his next steps. Eventually, Keith would go on to be free from drugs and find gainful employment as a construction worker and a home of his own.

But on this night he was staying at a homeless shelter on the city's southeast side. While at a Wednesday night prayer meeting, I invited Rick and told him I was looking for Keith, who was not present. Rick told me that Keith had been staying at a particular shelter that he had previously stayed at. He then offered to show me where it was, as I had no idea how to get there. So we hopped into my Cream-sickle and were on our way to do a good deed.

We managed to find the shelter, which was in a notorious area of town near the deadly public housing project called Berry Farms. But after asking the workers and residents, no one had seen Keith for the past couple of days. After checking with several other shelters in the area, we finally decided to call it a night.

It was around ten p.m. Traffic was heavy and we had just turned around. We were headed back north on Martin Luther King Jr. Avenue. Rick and I were making plans for tomorrow as we passed through a crowded intersection. Then out of the night sky there came a "Pop..." I cocked my head to the side like a dog catching a scent, and said, "Was that..." Pop! Pop!

Pop! came the confirmation. "Duck!" I yelled and put my head down.

Now here comes the amazing thing. As I sat there, cruising along at thirty miles per hour with my head sunken between my shoulders as far as it would go, I got this three hundred and sixty degree snapshot that appeared in my head. No kidding! It was like I had a panoramic photograph in my lap and all the time in the world to study it. I saw everything.

In my mind I could see where I was in the right lane going through the intersection. I could see the source of the shots, which were two men on my right on the side street. They were standing on either side of a car that was parked facing us on the wrong side of the street. The streetlight was out so, they and the car only appeared as silhouettes. The man on the street-side had the gun in his outstretched right hand, which was also pointed in our direction.

I could also see their target. It was a brown Monte Carlo full of about five gangsters wearing all of their up-to-no-good attire. Their car was on our left and slightly forward of us by half a car-length. When the shots went off, they started shouting wildly. There was an old lady directly in front of us driving an old blue Impala. She had hit her brakes when the shooting started and was nearly at a standstill just five feet from us... leaving us right in the middle of the intersection. I could see the headlights in both lanes behind us, so there was no backing up. The cross street to our left had headlights then taillights in all four lanes. And the two lanes of oncoming traffic left us nowhere to go.

All of this information appeared in my head all at once. And in the next instant I turned my head, looking over my right shoulder, over Rick's doubled-over form, and right out the window. An ironic laugh ticked the back of my throat. The Mustang II that I was driving had low doors and low, low windows. So low, in fact, that poor Rick, sitting there with his face between his knees, was entirely unprotected from head to hips. Unfortunately, this meant that I was equally unprotected. I couldn't believe it. Ain't this a bitch?

In a moment of desperation, I considered ramming the old lady in the Impala sitting there in front of us in order to drive her simple ass, and us, out of the line of fire. Then in the next instant I looked over at the target of all the shooting and they had swerved into oncoming traffic, in turn causing them to swerve, and veer, and stop before they came into the intersection. As bullets ricocheted off the rear undercarriage of my car, I turned and like a running back following a guard, I followed in the wake the gang-bangers had created.

We swerved through traffic for about half a block using both sides of traffic before they bore a hard left. Again cutting off traffic, they swung up onto the curb and into a vacant lot. I had just enough time to see them make a hard left at the alley and figured that they hadn't had enough.

Once they had turned away, the shooting stopped. In all, about ten shots had rung out. To be honest, after the first three I only heard the two ricochets that hit us. Laughter bubbled forth from my throat. That made it official. I'd now been shot at in every place that I had ever lived. I was beginning to wonder if it was me. "Just another day in paradise," I said out loud.

I noticed Rick with his head in his hands shaking his head, and thought he shared my sense of irony. But the cry that escaped his lips quieted my laughter. "I'm sick of this shit, man!" he cried, "I can't stand it anymore! I gotta get outta here!" His outburst worried me. There was something not normal about it. I had seen people freak out before, but there was something about it that gave me the creepy feeling that he was about to lose it permanently.

"Rick," I called to him gently, "it's over, man. They're gone. We're okay."

"It's not over, man! These niggas are crazy! They're always shootin'" he retorted.

"Rick, when's the last time YOU were shot at?"

"Well, it has been a while," he said.

And then he smiled. And then we both laughed. Sometimes that's all you can do.

back to chi-town

 back to chi-town

Fuse

I was desperately trying to finish my Bachelor's degree at the American Academy of Art in Chicago. I was close, but I still had a long way to go. After this there would be just two more semesters to go. In just about a year from now I would have my Bachelor's degree... if, that is, I survived. Ya see, I was thirty-three years old and starting life over.

Two years after my college graduation, I'd already become obsolete. A fossil in the professional world, I felt as useless as a broken pinky toe. As a commercial artist, I was no longer necessary, as the advent of the Macintosh computer revolutionized the graphic design field. They were in demand and everyone was expected to use them. When I graduated, the Mac had just been introduced to the curriculum and I had no opening for the class. Not if I still wanted to graduate with my second Associate's degree in anything like the near future, and without filing bankruptcy, that is.

So fast-forward. I had almost ten years of traveling around the country trying to find enough work to survive in the post Desert Storm economy, years of being rejected for jobs, because I didn't know the PC, or the Mac, or because I didn't have a Bachelor's degree, or because of just plain ol' subtle, creepy racism.

Ten years of taking any job I could, in between freelance illustrations and painting portraits. Everything from night jobs, day labor jobs, babysitting jobs, management jobs, blue-collar jobs and white-collar jobs. None of them fulfilling. And in none of them did I fit in.

In the ten years of hustling for a dime, not once was I able to find a job that paid enough for me to afford to get my own apartment or buy my own car, by far, most of the jobs I had paid either minimum wage or a little above it. And I'm not a spender. I don't waste my money on things like cigarettes, alcohol, iced lattes or cappuccinos. The only extravagances I would allow myself were the occasional matinee every few months or so, video rental once a week or so, or a bag of Famous Amos chocolate chip cookies with pecans.

So when, at the ripe -old age of thirty, I made the decision to go back to school after almost a decade of just getting by, I did it with a vengeance. I wasn't screwing around. I wasn't going to become obsolete again. So after a short couple of years at the University of Tennessee at Chattanooga, I found myself in a good relationship gone bad (with both school and my now ex-fiancé), and I found out that my old school was now offering Bachelor's degrees.

Upon moving back to Chicago and enrolling at the American Academy of Art, I worked like a madman. I was there to work, not play. Fun did not enter the equation. Things like recreation, fun, love, sex were all extraneous distractions that would be there when I was back on the job track again and had the money to play with. I had become like some hermit or monk with his eye fixed on the Holy Grail. Nothing would stand in my way. The complex hardship of work/money/school was just like any other enemy. You just had to find the weakness and exploit it. Attack! Like a bull. Just put your head down and keep charging. When there was no more resistance, I would then take the time to look up, stop, and smell the roses.

The only problem was that all of that hard charging came at a price. It was a subtle price. It was slowly creeping up on me and then one day it suddenly caught me completely unaware.

And that is where the real story begins...

See the problem is that I was working a full time job and going to school full time. I was getting no sleep, I had no social life and hadn't gotten laid since I don't know when, not even a date. I hadn't had a real workout in over six months. If I was lucky, I would get in a few push-ups, sit-ups, or a short run on the odd Sunday. During the day I was a habilitation aide at Misericordia Homes on Chicago's North Side. It's a physically and emotionally demanding job... and it started at 5:30 in the morning. It was about a half hour bus ride in the cold dark of morning.

Once I was there, I got to wake up, feed, bathe and entertain about a dozen adults with the minds of adolescents. And they would most likely be that way until the day they died. They all suffering from developmental disorders from birth or from brain trauma, like drowning or concussive head injuries. While they had the brains and emotions of little children, they still had the bodies of adults. You ever try getting a 200 lb. grown man to eat or put his clothes on while he threw a temper-tantrum? It makes for a good workout. If all went well, I was finished and off by 3:00 p.m.

Then it was straight to the Howard train station and an hour-long journey downtown to school. I usually ate dinner on the train. Then I would read or something to keep myself from falling asleep and missing my stop, and getting mugged or my pockets picked.

Arriving at school, I was usually just in time to hustle straight into my first class which began at 4:00. The last class the school held let out at 9:00 p.m. Usually I would be outta there and on my way home by 9:30.

It was usually about 10:30 by the time I walked in my door. A late dinner and homework would keep me up until around midnight. Then I would hit the sack and in the blink of an eye, I would be up again and it would start all over.

Fortunately, there were no classes on the weekends. Unfortunately, I still had to work. Usually, it was just Saturday, and on Sunday I would find myself in a kind of coma. I would manage to get a little more homework done, then I would just collapse behind a good book from the library, which was about two blocks away or veg in front of the TV.

Family? Sure, I had 'em. Mom was in Georgia living on the ol'' homestead. Pamela, my sister, was with her family in Ooltewah, Tennessee, just outside Chattanooga. Friends? Yeah, I had them, too. I just never got to see 'em. Even the ones I lived with. Jane and I had some friends in common, Sam, and Carlos, and Hollis, and when they came over on an occasional Sunday, they would take one look at me, shake their heads and plop down on the couch around me and sympathize.

To their credit, they tried not to have too much fun while I was within earshot. They didn't want this poor slob to feel even worse knowing just how much fun I was missing.

"Hey babe, we're going out to Ann Sather's for breakfast," Jane would say as she, Sam, Carlos and Hollis headed for the door. Being that Ann Sather's was my favorite restaurant in all my travels surpassing only Ronnie's Steakhouse for their barbecue, it would bring silent tears brimming to my eyes as I smelled the aroma of cinnamon rolls and the world's best French toast... or is that "American" toast now... still... I'm sorry, I need a time-out here. I'm overcome!

Okay, I'm back now. Sorry about that. So, where was I... oh, yes... Anyway, while they had long ago given up on inviting me out, they still held out hope that I would someday come to my senses and join them, so they would always let me know where they were going.

Now don't get me wrong. I'm not complaining. I have always considered myself very fortunate to be able to go to school and for what I wanted to, no less. Having a job is a privilege, not a right. If it was, God would dole jobs out while He was handing out the hands and feet. But he doesn't. So if ya have a job, you are lucky. Very lucky. And if you are earning enough to keep a roof over your head and food in your belly, that is a blessing. No, I'm not complaining... I'm tired. For various reasons, I have always had to work harder than most folks just to keep ALIVE. Forget about things like "vacations" and such.

I was getting so little sleep that I was a walking zombie. My brain wasn't functioning. And my body had run out of steam. I was living in lethargy. But the way I had it figured, there would be time enough to sleep when I die. So for now it was work and school. Problem was that I was so tired, I was in danger of sleeping right through all my classes and my job. Getting fired would be unacceptable and failing even one class was unacceptable also. But the tiredness had gotten to a point where I could no longer be sure of anything.

I would be in class listening to the instructor lecture about 3D computer animation and then he would be talking about the Georgian forest. And I would blink and realize he had been talking 3D all along but my imaginations had become so vivid, I worried that they would soon become hallucinations.

One evening I came -to only to find myself standing inside my walk-in closet completely naked. Being that it was winter and very cold, I wondered what had happened to my clothes. Then I looked up, saw the light chain swinging and watched that for a while.

All of a sudden, it dawned on me that it wasn't evening at all. It was 4:00 a.m. and I was supposed to be getting dressed for work. That scared the shit out of me. What if I missed class because I fell asleep on the train and wound up in Wisconsin or something? Keep it together, baby. You can hang.

Then I caught a lucky break. I got a date! Becky happened to catch me in a brief moment of semi-lucidity and asked me if I wanted to go to a movie. Her treat. That really brightened my day. The movie started in about an hour at 4:00. Perfect! That gave me enough time to grab a quick shower and drive north 30 minutes to get to the theater.

After showering, I remembered I had a video that was due. So I figured I would drop it off first. There was only one slight problem. The video store was a 20-minute drive in the opposite direction. But do you know what? That little detail didn't even enter my consciousness. Why? Because it was NOT WORKING!

So at 3:30 I hopped in my car and hit the road in heavy traffic. At about 3:50 cruising down Clark Street, some kind of alarm bell went off in my head. I was only about half a mile from the video store when I suddenly realized that I now had ten minutes to be at the theater. The only problem was, I was now 40 minutes away in the OTHER direction! Aaaarrrrgggg!!!

As soon as I saw a break in traffic, I cut the steering wheel to the left, yanked up on the emergency break and on that rain-slick asphalt I pulled the most hair-raising u-turn possible. Gunning the engine, I got about two blocks before I was caught up in the gridlock again. It was stop-and-go for the next mile with me steaming behind the wheel.

I wanted to scream! I wanted to get out and run! It probably would have gotten me there faster if I had been in better shape. Another mile and still it was no better. Making another left turn, I decided to try side streets. It would be about eight miles to the theater and it was five minutes till four. Now I was fantasizing about traveling eight miles in five minutes if I hit no traffic and every green light and...

It was a Sunday. A rainy, cold, overcast, winter and I was going on little sleep and no brainpower, driving like a maniac. Coming up to Ashland Avenue, I had to get across. I came to a stop sign and awaited my turn through the intersection. The vehicle in front of me just cleared the intersection before he came to a stop due to the gridlock, and I began rolling forward to take my turn through when the truck behind him merely slowed at his stop sign and then gunned his engine and jumped my turn! Ashland was jammed solid with traffic and this asshole stopped square in front of me, completely blocking my way through. The driver and his passenger just sit there glaring at me, trying to mad-dog me like some kind of punk. They were supposed to be some bad-assed gang bangers and I was supposed to be scared of them.

Time-lapse.

And then it was like I awoke from some weird dream. Now I was soaking wet and didn't know how I got this way. All of a sudden, I was standing outside my car in the middle of the street.

I heard someone screaming like a mad-man. And then I realized it was me! I was SCREAMING at the top of my lungs to the two gangsters who had just deliberately blocked me in. I was calling 'em every name in the book, shouting like a maniac.

"You stupid motherfuckers! What the FUCK is the wrong with you, blocking the goddamned intersection like that? Now I can't get through! What are you, some kind of fucking IDIOT?! Ain't you got no goddamned sense?! Move outta the fucking way!!! What's the matter with you?!! Huh!?!

And in that instant, standing there in the rain like a lunatic and breathing hard, I came to a sudden realization: Eddie you have lost your fucking mind.

Okay now, just caaaaaalm down," I told myself, "and get back in the car." But I didn't. I was just standing there in the pouring rain. Breathing hard, chest heaving, growling through bared teeth.

Fortunately for me, those two gangsters were just kind of... frozen. Paralyzed, I guess, trying to figure out exactly which mental institution I had just escaped from.

Then a curious thing happened. Was it an earthquake? No, Chicago doesn't have earthquakes. Then why was that truck rocking like that? Those guys hardly seemed to notice. Then my eyes scanned towards the back of the truck with the tinted windows. And I saw shadows moving around in the back.

Oh... my... God. There had to be at least 1... 2... 3... 4 more guys in the back of the truck. As I peered into the dim interior, I could just barely make out the four figures moving and gesticulating wildly.

It went through my head just what they were gesticulating about: me, and what to do about me. Kick my ass, most likely.

So now I was thinking, I'm screwed. It was now a lose/lose situation. If I backed down now, they would think I was scared and be all over me. And there was nowhere for me to go. Other cars were now blocking the street behind any possible escape and me. There was no choice but for me to follow through.

Raising my hands out to embrace them all, I shouted at the top of my lungs, "COME-ONNNNNN!!!"

And all the while I was praying that they didn't.

One thing you need to know about me right about here is that I've been doing martial arts and self-defense since I was about knee-high to a grasshopper, and have been teaching since just outta high school. I'm pretty good. I've faced real opponents with numbers, baseball bats, knives and even guns. But I'll also tell you this: no matter how good you get, you can always get your ass kicked! It doesn't take a master, just one good shot. So I quickly went over the possibilities. One: they have guns and they shoot me dead - not good. Two: they just beat the shit out of me - also not good. Three: I kick the shit out of all six of them (Hey, I'm an optimist) then I get arrested and go to jail. I got no money for bail. That's not so good either.

And miraculously before all my fears could be realized there it was: the traffic on Ashland started to flow forward again. And as I stood there with my arms raised and dripping wet, the wild gesticulating in the back slowly died down. The rocking slowly subsided, and first the driver, then the passenger, slowly, reluctantly broke eye contact. And then they slowly drove away.

I stood there a moment or two to make sure they were not coming back. Then I got back in my car, closed the door and breathed a silent thank you to God. My entire body was shaking from the adrenaline and I had to take a deep breath before putting my car into first and driving through the intersection, slowly and calmly.

I couldn't believe what had just happened! I almost made one of the biggest mistake of my life. I just lost complete control of all of my faculties. That hadn't happened to me in a looooong time. Since I was a kid. But now I was in my thirties. When I was young, I had a terminal temper problem. But with the help of God, therapy, and a lot of discipline and will power, I have been able to overcome what once was an insurmountable problem. But this? This was something completely different. This wasn't a temper problem, it was an insanity issue. And it couldn't be allowed to happen again.

So for the rest of my long s-l-o-w trip to the theater, I ran every option that I could think of. I was going to do everything within my power to ensure that I would never again put the safety of myself, or others, at risk simply because I was overworked and under rested. And by the time I met Becky, I had my plan of attack. First: calm down. I would start meditating again, three times a day, seven days a week. I would start out with five minute at a time and work up from there. (I learned long ago that if I start out making huge plans they will quickly become too time or energy consuming to continue. Start with baby steps. Little increments.) Second: get my aggressions out in a proper fashion. I would find some way to get a workout in at least three days a week. Again, at five-minute minimums. Third: get a life! I would make absolutely sure that I got to go out and socialize no less than two days a week, even if it meant just having a cup of tea at a coffee shop with a buddy. And a date would be even better. Nothing huge. Just get out of the house.

I was already praying and reading the bible like always. And I started doing all of those things. Becky and I missed our movie, so we just hung out and talked, and it was nice. That night when I got home, I sat myself down and started meditating. I continued to do so.

At 4:30 the next morning (Monday), instead of standing and waiting in the snow for my bus to arrive, I got there ten minutes earlier in the dark of morning and I started power walking. I got to walk a good, intense, vigorous mile before my bus arrived. I had gotten a good sweat going and I was tired. I actually felt refreshed and more energized when I arrived at work.

I would squeeze in 50 push-ups, sit-ups or a little martial arts here and there. And I started going out with Tyrone, Romel, Jane, Sam, Hollis, and Carlos here and there. Again, nothing big, just getting out of the house.

Eventually, I even found myself on a couple of dates here and there. All in all I didn't miss the little extra sleep. So the next week was gone before I knew it. I didn't immediately detect any changes for the better or worse.

The very next Saturday night found Romel and me cruising the crowded parking lot at Heavenly Bodies looking for a parking space. We had gone around and around without finding any vacant spots. Then we saw a man exiting, so we followed him to his car and waited.

He sat there in the cold for a long time going through some papers before we saw his brake lights finally come on. We had our headlights on, so we knew he saw us, but we were patient.

Finally his reverse lights came on and Romel put his turn signal on while we watched him back sloooooowly out.

Just as soon as he cleared the spot, a car full of young punk gang-bangers came spinning around the corner, around us, around him, and into the spot we were waiting for.

Both the guy pulling out, and Romel and I, were dumbfounded. There was no way those assholes didn't see him coming out or us starting to turn in. Those BASTARDS!

"What the fuck!" Romel shouted.

"Motherfucker," I murmured.

Four of the five guys that were in the car jumped out quickly and had started towards the club loud, laughing and talking shit.

For a minute I considered letting it go. "Is this worth a fight?" I asked myself. No, but... Then a little voice in my head said, "No. Those guys were wrong and you need to let them know that. Never let bad behavior go unaddressed."

As I got out of the car, Romel got out with me. I smiled to myself, proud of my friend. He had no martial arts training at all, he wasn't big, nor was he a bad-ass. But here he was about to follow me into the thick of things with a group of thugs that outnumbered us. My man Romel.

Turning to him, I said, "Wait here" And as an afterthought, I added, "...and keep the engine running."

While I told myself I was not going to start any trouble, I knew that trouble didn't always wait for an invitation.

Walking up to the driver, who was still in the car putting the club on his steering wheel, I calmly and gently knocked on his window. He pretended he did not hear me as he continued to struggle with the club. The other guys saw me standing at his window and came running back. The laughter had stopped but the shit-talking had not.

"Wassup!?" one said.

"Yeah niggah, let's go!" someone else shouted as they approached the car.

I turned and stopped them with a gaze that gave them fair warning. It said, "You sure you wanna do this?" They slowed and came to a stop near the rear of the vehicle. I knocked again, more insistently this time, and he looked up at me. Making a circular motion with my finger, I asked him to roll his window down. With his friends around, he apparently felt confident enough to roll his window down about a quarter of an inch. I repeated my motion again and he gave another inch.

I waited until I had his attention, and calmly said, "This is our spot."

"Huh?"

"You heard me. I said, this is our spot."

Turning to make sure his friends hadn't abandoned him, he said, "I dunno man... these guys are waiting on me."

Stepping closer, I blocked his door so he could not get out. "I'm not talking to them, I'm talkin' to you."

"Uuuh, I dunno..."

"I'll tell ya what I know. I know that you saw us sittin' there waiting for that man to pull out. You saw that it was our spot and you took it anyway." I glanced at his friends again and back at him. "You know you were wrong and you know this is our spot."

Sensing movement off to my right, I turned and stepped forward to meet the threat.

"Be cool man," the guy I was now face-to-face with said.

Now I was beginning to lose patience. "Be cool? We've been sittin' in this damn parking lot for fifteen minutes!"

"Dude, you can find another spot."

"There are no more spots. This is our spot," I said with my voice raising.

"Look! There's another one!" another guy shouted from the other side of the car.

Wary of a trap, I stepped back from his buddy and followed his pointing finger. And there clear across the huge parking lot was a lone vehicle pulling out of a space.

"Yeah," I replied, "and by the time we drive over there, somebody else will pull in before us." What, did these guys think I was, stupid?

"Naw man, we'll hold it for you!" another one said.

Dubious, I said, "You mean you guys are gonna go over there and hold that space until we get there?"

"Yeah, bro!" And with that all four of them took off running to the other side of the parking lot leaving me slack-jawed staring after them.

I couldn't believe it. These gangsters just went from gangstering an unearned parking spot to running across a snowy lot just to save a spot for us. Most guys would've just gotten into a beef that probably would not have even made the papers. I couldn't believe it. The driver had gotten out and followed his buddies over there. Left all alone, I said to myself, "Well okay," and headed back to the car.

Romel was still standing outside his opened door with the most puzzled look on his face.

"What the hell is going on?"

He had been just out of earshot and missed most of what was said. Shaking my own head, I didn't know if I believed it.

When both of us were back in the car, I said, "They're gonna hold a spot for us."

We stared silently at each other for a long moment then he said, "You're kidding."

"Nope."

We stared at each other some more with bemused expressions before he put the car in gear and, shaking his head, made his way around to the other side of the parking lot.

Just as we pulled into the end of the row where the guys were standing in a semicircle around the vacant spot, another car had entered the lot and tried to pull in. They tightened the circle and waved him off shaking their heads. Pissed, that driver decided to move on.

When Romel wheeled up to them, they parted like the Red Sea. Rolling down my window, I stuck out a solidarity fist and said to them, "Thanks guys."

"Allright bro."

"You got it, man."

And they headed off towards the club. After rolling my window back up, I turned to Romel. "They steal our spot and I thank them for getting us another one. Kind of ironic, huh?"

"Yeah. That's pretty weird."

And that was that.

As we headed across the parking lot towards the entrance, I took a moment to reflect. It was incredible that it was exactly one week ago that I had lost my mind in the middle of that rainy street with no control whatsoever. Now here I was, able to reasonably and rationally negotiate my way out of a hostile takeover without violence or the threat of violence. It seemed that my new way of living was paying off in dividends. While I would not gloat, I was actually pretty proud of myself. I had remained cool and in control of my faculties at all times, even when my patience and temper were taxed.

It seemed my brain had started functioning again, my energy was returning, and my nerves settled down. And life was getting livable again. I still didn't miss the few extra minutes of sleep I was sacrificing for my morning walks. I was no more tired for exercising or going out with my friends. Those precious few minutes of sleep that I had been working so hard for were, it turns out, entirely extraneous. The vast improvement of my quality of life more than made up for anything I might have been missing sleepwise or restwise.

That week in my life taught me an invaluable lesson, that "Surviving" is no replacement for "Living". And how you are living is almost as important as the fact that you are living.

Sometimes we think we are doing the right thing by giving something up. "Sacrifice" we call it. But just because you can live without something, doesn't always mean you should. So I still work out, meditate, and share time and money with my friends. I don't always have a lot to share, but I always try to.

Sometimes it's just as important to them as it is to me. We need our friends. They need us. If they are positive, supportive and loving, as all my true friends are, then you cannot truly live without them. And I've learned that I cannot hide from myself. I always end up back at... me.

Violent Notes

By the time I had reached my middle teens, I had figured out that to survive you had to be tough. And I was going to be the baddest guy on the street. Being the toughest meant being the most ruthless, the cruelest, the one who cared the least, and felt the least. So, as my dad had taught me, I had a head start on the cruelty part. And as a result of his torture, I had already learned not to feel. Good. I was on the right track. Just one last thing to bring that train into the station: don't give a fuck. Not about anything. Not myself, not my family, not my friends. And certainly not some asshole victim on the street.

From childhood, my friends and I had been groomed for death. A jail cell or the grave were the two things we were guaranteed in between the long line of pain that was our lives.

We learned to abuse each other as our way of life. We called each other names. We lied to each other. We cheated each other. We stole from each other. We cheated with each other's girlfriends. And we fought with each other. Nothing was sacred. Sure, there was some sense of honor among thieves. A twisted kind of honor. When we fought, we beat each other with fists, feet, sticks, pipes, bricks, mace, knives, and shot each other with guns. But we never gave each other up. Never ratted out. It just wasn't done. Never happened.

I remember the one time my mother tried to give me counsel. After one of the many times I had been arrested for being with the guys when they decided to get into something stupid and I happened to be along with them because they were my boys, she suggested that maybe I should find a different group of guys to hang out with. I became incensed. I told her she didn't know what she was talking about and to mind her own business. Who did she think she was? All that? Here she was runnin' the streets with... him.

At that time I had no desire to change friends. They were my friends. It took a lot of time and a lot of bad things to happen to me, and those around me, until I began to really see what was happening and WHY.

For the Boys
For the ones who ain't here

I count every day as a gift, but for that voice on the train tracks on that cold, cold night I would surely be dead. As a gift, free and unconditional gift, I have been given over two decades' worth of todays. An even bigger gift is that I've managed to come this far without becoming a statistic like so many of my friends. Every single one of the boys I used to hang out with have one or both of these things in common: jail or the grave.

Dave managed to survive gangs, police and women, last I heard. But he was one of my personal inspirations for leaving the chaos of my friends and street family when he almost didn't survive his friends.

One day J.J. had stolen a new semi-automatic pistol and wanted to be a smart-ass and show it off while they were at Dave's apartment. So the way he went about doing this was to come up behind his brother George, put the muzzle up to the back of his head, and pull the trigger. It was the "Klick" of the hammer dropping that scared the shit out of George.

"Woah! You motherfucker!!"

"Relax, George, it's not loaded."

Snatching the gun from his brother's hand, he held it in front of him and pulled the slide back to check the chamber. Well, when he'd gotten the slide about halfway back, it slipped from his fingers and snapped back. Much to George and J.J.'s surprise, when the chamber closed the gun went off.

They were even more surprised when Dave, who was sitting on the couch in front of them, suddenly fell over.

By the time he got out of surgery, Dave weighed about half a liver less.

And I wasn't gonna wait around to be the next casualty in our own personal little war upon us.

Punkin' was one of the youngest in our group. Rambunctious, precarious, gregarious, loud or obnoxious in turns. He was our friend, none the less.

After years of being chased by the Chicago Police Department for killing a man by throwing a man off a hotel rooftop, he finally met his end. Not by the Chicago P.D., or a gang-banger, but by his wife. He slapped her around one time too many. She finally got tired of it and she stabbed him to death. "Right in the ticker."

Caesar, who was a strong man, but thought he was stronger than everyone else in or out of jail, had two babies. And in one tragic night they were burned to death in an electrical fire.

Caesar fell apart. He was never the same man after that. I can't imagine how a parent doesn't die of grief on the spot when something that horrible and unthinkable happens.

It's been years since I've heard anything about J.J. He'd already been in and out of Juvie a few times by the time I met him in my early teens. As he continued his criminal career, he continued his familiarity with the system as he graduated through various penal systems of Chicago, Cook County, and the State of Illinois.

One night J.J. called me at my grandmother's to inform me that his father, Johnny, was in the hospital. His voice was shaky as he recounted the story. A fire had broken out in the same basement apartment where Steve had beaten Andrew. He had been burned over 70% of his body.

I could hear the tears hiding just behind his words as he described his father's screams as the doctors peeled the scabs free of his burned tissue. He could hear them echoing throughout the hospital corridors so that he could not escape the sound of them.

"George is going crazy. He's drinkin' a lot and doin' all kinds of coke and I don't know what to do!"

I fought my own tears as I searched in vain for something worth saying that wouldn't sound... useless.

I had secretly hoped that J.J. would use this as an excuse to get himself clean and sober and go straight, but that hope was in vain as well.

George was a lot like me. Only he didn't make it. He was impetuous, impulsive, quick to act and slow to think. Most of the guys, his family included, always called him stupid. It used to bother me, but he defended himself with his usual "fuuuuck youuu." Sometimes it really pissed him off, but he always gave the same response. I knew that of all the problems that George had, being stupid wasn't one of them. Yeah, he was kind of dense sometimes and kind of slow. And yes, he was missing some social skills, and he definitely had trouble controlling his anger. But that boy could solve problems. Sometimes his problem was that he would out-think himself.

He was always getting into trouble for shooting his mouth off, and I mean everywhere: on the street, in school (the few times he did attend), at home, and even with the police. He just didn't know when to shut up. And once you got him going, there was no stopping him. It was time for damage control. And definitely forget about it once he got a beer in him. It was over. What made it even worse was that he was the type of guy who would get drunk just by looking at the label. It was ALL downhill from there.

Trouble was guaranteed to follow him around. You could count on it like clockwork. George, like his brother J.J., was short, skinny and just a little goofy looking. So you would think that would make him more cautious. Nope, it only put an even bigger chip on his shoulder.

Yeah, George was definitely NOT stupid. That boy was a notorious thief, and a damned good one. Out of the many I knew, he was the best. He and J.J. were both professional burglars and thieves by the age of 13. They had to be just to survive.

Their dad was an alcoholic and woke up just in time to be at the bar before the doors opened, and shut the place down every night.

I mean, they would usually have to rip off a grocery store just to get breakfast. Then they would steal something to sell for dinner money. They even had to steal clothes to wear.

But of the two, George was the best. Sheer genius. I mean there wasn't an apartment that he saw that he couldn't break into. He could probably figure out ten ways into Fort Knox. I'm not kidding. We would be sitting around watching TV and he would say something like: "All you would need to break into that office building would be a screwdriver, a hammer and a beer can. Oh, oh, a knife too, 'cause you would have to cut the beer can..." Then he would break it all down for us. Once in a while someone would try to trip him up. "What about the burglar alarms, stupid?" "That's what the beer can's for asshole!" He would go on to tell us about rotating guard shifts and security camera sweeps.

He could even forge his own documents. I've seen him get fake ID's with a forged birth certificate and forged social security card. The kid had more alias's than even he could remember. The guy was so notorious, I knew him by his reputation a year before I met him. He must have robbed half the apartments on the North side. He was that bad. We finally met when he was about 14 and I, 16 or so. And then I couldn't

home

home

 home

The Difference

Somewhere along the line, I learned to tell the difference. The difference between being tough and being strong.

The streets were full of tough guys. Nursing homes are full of once-tough, old guys. But I found there were very few strong guys. The tough guys could walk tough, talk tough, and beat up lots of lesser fighters. But when the shit comes down the pipe, they fold up like a house of cards. They couldn't take hardship. They couldn't take pain. You see them crying like babies and throwing tantrums when things don't go their way. When they can't get what they want, they threaten, bully, and intimidate. These are the guys who fall apart when they go to prison. They can't stand the solitude. They can't stand the loss of control. They can't stand being deprived of all the hundreds of little luxuries we enjoy every day. And compared to some of the guys who are in there for the long haul and don't have much to lose, they are nowhere near as tough as they thought they were.

On the outside, these people slap their women and children around and then justify it saying they were "asking for it" or they "deserved it". They always have an excuse.

Once behind bars, the "tough" guys rape and beat and bully other weaker prisoners. I found that the real threat is the quiet guy, the one who does his job and minds his own business. And when the hit comes down, he goes to work, gets the job done without a word being said, then goes home. These are the men who, when you piss them off, you never know it. These are the men who won't just beat you and talk shit about it. These men will break you down before you even know you've been in a fight. These are the men you leave alone. These are the men who'd rather kill you than fight you.

I have plenty of friends whose dads used to be the baddest motherfuckers this side of the Pecos and now they are disabled and can't even get around, because their bodies have been battered so that they are in constant pain, the kind of pain that wears you down year after year. Or they are old drunks, mad that they are too old or feeble to beat anyone up, so they sit around telling stories of the guys they *used* to beat up.

If you can talk your way out of a fight, you will gain respect, win more, and your opponent will more than likely become an ally. Here's a quote for you: "Any enemy worth having is worth having as a friend." Think about it. If he's tough enough to take you on, wouldn't you rather have him take on someone else on your behalf?

The Destroyer

Most people are born human. I had to learn it. Dad taught me terrible things.

I know that my dad has killed and murdered. He has spent time in military prison, and federal prison, and county jails across the country.

He dad tried to make me just like him: evil and insane. He used to tell me, as he sipped from a fifth of bourbon or Wild Irish Rose, "If I ever catch you drinking, I'll beat the shit out of you." Then in the same conversation, he would force the bottle to my lips and pour a drink down my eight-year-old throat and laugh because he knew it burned. Although I wouldn't complain, he knew, because I could not keep my eyes from tearing up. Sometimes I would loose my voice as the whiskey ate away at my vocal chords. But I had already learned that to complain was to invite disaster. There was no surer way to be beaten half to death than to show weakness. Simple, frail, humanity. That was the one thing above all others that he could not stand.

Most fathers teach their children life-lessons. They teach them how to make their way in this world. They teach values, morals, and a code of some sort. The only code I was taught was cruelty. Instead of learning how to work hard and earn a living, I was taught how to steal. He taught me how to use women, manipulate people, to frighten and intimidate men, how to kill, how to hate... everything. He taught me how to destroy. I was raised a racist, sexist, class-ist, Christian-ist.

The only thing my stepfather hated more than white people was God, in general, and Jesus specifically. He hated what he saw as the weakness in "turn the other cheek" and allowing Himself to be crucified. At any given moment he would rail against Jesus or some white person he saw on television just singing a song.

He used to take me to the grocery store with him. When no one was looking, he would pull up my shirt and shove down steak, fish, pork chops or some other meat he wanted for dinner. Why didn't he put it in his own pants, I used to wonder. Like so many other things, he taught me from as early as I can remember, I was never angered by it. It was all I knew. How can you complain about being beaten when your earliest memories are of being beaten? How can you even hope to be spoken to in a humane fashion when you and your mother and your sister have always been called names? Stealing? It's just the way it was done. And frankly, in my neighborhood, we weren't the only ones doing it. Seeing the other kids in the hood doing it, just confirmed the righteousness of it.

I am an animal. It's in my genes by now, but I fight it. I am 40 years old and I have been fighting my learned animal behavior for over twenty years. Some things I have managed to overcome with the help of God. Some things have taken root and can only be controlled by redirection. There are issues I deal with daily and some I fight against hourly. And this is after years of self-help books, self-help groups, several different psychotherapists and medication.

I was taught to kill. I learned how to kill the soul, the spirit and the body. I learned how to take away hope and cripple the will. I learned how to take and use and destroy myself, as well as others.

God has had mercy on me. He blessed me so that I was able to DECIDE to become something else. And somehow I have.

I have become a man over the years. You struggle... HARD. And fail and fall. And get up and fail again. And suddenly, you look up. And it's years later and you are something different. You are HUMAN.

I learned. I relearned. I learned how to give and share, and to show love and mercy. Yes, even forgiveness. I have had to struggle greatly to learn to forgive others, myself and most importantly, my stepfather.

I've had to battle anger, hatred, and selfishness for years. But in the Bible, God promises, "I will take away your heart of stone and give you a heart of flesh." And I held him to that promise.

I have hated myself from the core of my being to my fingertips. I am still learning to love myself and forgive myself, because I have made an art out of pain. True, I focused all that rage only on those who had wronged me, but those I hurt, I hurt bad. I did my best to destroy them. Like that young man on the train tracks, I tried to destroy them utterly.

I think in my life I have broken almost every law and in one way or another, all of the Ten Commandments. However close I came though, I never stilled a heartbeat. Nor have I ever raped or molested anyone. Small things to be thankful for, huh? Most folks would never even have to enter that realm of consideration. It's just that things in my life have been so bad that I've had to look deeeeeep in order to find some ray of light, of hope. And this is where I had to start. Ten years of family violence, abuse and neglect have left me with many, many scars. Some of them I'm not even aware of yet. The ones on the inside have been far more devastating than anything my body has suffered. We left my stepfather in 1978, and now, 27 years later, my sister and I are both still trying to unbind the shackles of mental, physical, and emotional degradation that warped our identities, our psyches, our souls, and our families. It is now decades later and I am still realizing the full extent of our damage.

www.ingramcontent.com/pod-product-compliance
Lightning Source LLC
Chambersburg PA
CBHW060105170426
43198CB00010B/781